Britain's Economic Growth

1920–1966

Britain's Economic Growth
1920–1966

A. J. YOUNGSON

Professor of Political Economy
in the University of Edinburgh

Ruskin House

GEORGE ALLEN & UNWIN LTD

MUSEUM STREET LONDON

FIRST PUBLISHED IN 1967
SECOND EDITION 1968
SECOND IMPRESSION 1970

Cloth bound edition ISBN 0 04 330098 7
Paper bound edition ISBN 0 04 330099 5

PRINTED IN GREAT BRITAIN
by Photolithography
BY JOHN DICKENS AND CO LTD
NORTHAMPTON

PREFACE

This book is a reconstruction and expansion of my *The British Economy, 1920-1957* (third impression, 1964). In particular, Chapter I of the earlier book has been revised and brought up to date, and the chapter dealing with events since 1945 has been similarly revised and enlarged. I have been able to take advantage of the considerable volume of work done on current British economic problems in the last few years, and I am especially indebted to Mr J. C. R. Dow's *The Management of the British Economy, 1945-60,* and to *The British Economy in 1975* edited by Dr W. Beckerman. I have also taken the opportunity to add a section of Comment and Analysis, in which I attempt to derive some lessons from our experience and even to pass some judgments upon it. It may be objected that we do not, or should not, study the past in order to draw 'lessons' or decide how to do better in future. This may be true for the Middle Ages or, say, the wars of Marlborough. But the chief justification for the study of recent economic history is precisely that it may help us to avoid the repetition of recognizable errors, and, in particular, to distinguish the wood of policy and circumstance from the trees of perpetual improvisation.

It is my hope that in its new form the book will continue to serve the needs of students who wish to understand something of the country's recent past, and also those of the general public which finds itself increasingly called upon to make up its mind about major issues of economic policy.

Edinburgh, October 1966   A. J. Y.

PREFACE TO THE SECOND EDITION

I have taken the opportunity of a reprint to bring some figures up to date.

March 1968   A. J. Y.

CONTENTS

CHAPTER I

World Economic Development Since 1920

ALMOST half a century separates us from the years just after the 1914–18 war, a period almost as long as from the French Revolution to the repeal of the Corn Laws. It is little wonder that the early 1920s seem to belong to a different age from ours. But the change, so far as it can be dated, occurred as late as 1945. On a broad view, 1920–45 was an extension of the nineteenth century. The world between the wars was dominated, as the nineteenth century had been, by the rivalries of European powers; and the war which broke out in 1939 was caused, like that which broke out in 1914, by the seemingly interminable struggle for political and economic power which went on between France, Germany, Great Britain and Russia. In or about 1945 the situation fundamentally altered. It was then that the greatest French poet of the time could write:

'Nous avons rendez-vous avec la fin d'un âge.'

The principal reason was the discovery of how to harness atomic power for military uses. This discovery promoted the rise to world supremacy of Russia and the United States, at the same time making their rivalry more intense and more dangerous. Meanwhile, countries like Britain and France sank enormously in power and importance; and the British empire, so powerful a political and economic unit even in 1939, collapsed in the face of British impoverishment and the rise of nationalism and anti-colonialism all over the world—a collapse encouraged, each for their own reasons and purposes, by the Russians and the Americans. Yet, in the dangerous and confused world thus created about 1945, there were forces making for compromise

9

and unification which had not existed, or had been ineffectual, before the war. Chief among these was the absolute necessity of avoiding the outbreak of yet another major war. This produced the movement towards European economic and political unification which was important by the 1960s. Also, the rival *blocs*, largely debarred from resort to military force, tried to win friends and influence people by offering material gifts and concessions—cheap loans, technical assistance, and so on. This coincided with the increasing need of the recipients, whose population growth became so rapid (partly as a result of the improved medical facilities which accompanied economic development) that without a rapid increase in output, there was a danger that standards of living would actually fall.

From a more narrowly economic point of view, the years since 1920 may be said to possess the following four principal features:

continued economic progress by the industrialized countries of Europe and North America;
a more rapid spread than before of modern techniques of organization and production into other countries;
alteration in the general trends of the development of world trade;
unprecedented growth of population.

These four aspects of world development are examined in the remainder of this chapter.

CONTINUED ECONOMIC PROGRESS BY THE INDUSTRIALIZED
COUNTRIES OF EUROPE AND NORTH AMERICA

Both the growth of production in 'old' economies and the spread of modern methods into 'new' economies have been associated with political nationalism. National rivalries within Europe had developed and grown acute in the years before 1914. The Versailles Peace Treaty solved few if any old problems and it created a number of new ones. It brought new countries into existence, gave Germany a number of new, legitimate grievances, and did not provide for France nor enable nor compel her to obtain for herself that rather cloistered political security which she sought. In a word, the Treaty of 1919 sought to deny what was manifestly the fact, that Germany was the strongest power in Europe. War debts and reparations made matters worse, putting extraordinary pressure on all countries' financial arrangements and distorting international trade. 'There was no planned economic co-operation to take care of the balance of payments difficulties created by these factors. If equilibrium in international payments was to be maintained, the flow of capital exports from the United States had to continue without any sudden breaks or else a process of deflation might be started in western Europe.'[1] Yet all the time the United States, now the real seat of economic and political power, for the most part stood aloof, contenting herself with lending money, demanding repayment of all debts incurred in the past, and maintaining her protective tariffs. In these conditions attempts to restore the old world of the gold standard *cum* private enterprise could not succeed; on the part of many nations such attempts were scarcely even sincere. France was reverting to her traditional policy of economic nationalism even before the close of the 1920s; and when the Federal Reserve authorities raised discount rates in 1928 and 1929 and so took the first steps which brought on the terrible depression of 1929-33, many countries were found ready to protect themselves from falling prices and unemployment abroad by means of tariffs, quotas and exchange control. Great Britain abandoned her struggle for the gold standard and gave up her traditional policy of free trade; Germany, with middle-class savings destroyed by currency collapse brought about by reparations payments and monetary mismanagement, and with 6m. to 7m. unemployed, turned to Hitler.

The economic nationalism of the 1930s was thus defensive. But it was also, in some cases, successful. In Great Britain unemployment was reduced and the national income rose quite rapidly; in Germany there was complete recovery, in the sense that unemployment disappeared and the national income rose by 25 per cent above its 1929 level; in Sweden unemployment was no worse in 1937-39 than in 1927-29, and the real national income was over 30 per cent higher. Other countries, however, notably France and the United States, made a much poorer

[1] A. Montgomery, loc. cit. p. 157.

showing. World trade failed to respond, and this was natural in view of the trend to increased self-sufficiency; but it was also a consequence of changes in the composition of national incomes, because public and private services—neither of which can as a rule be obtained from abroad—both grew in importance.

Meanwhile, the Soviet Union pursued a course of its own. The Soviet Government seems to have realized very early—probably it always realized—the vital political importance of productive capacity. Successive Five Year Plans beginning in 1928 drove Russia on in the struggle to achieve her declared primary economic task, the overtaking and surpassing of the most highly developed capitalist countries in production per head of population in the shortest possible time. In this task she has made great progress, for a really remarkable increase of the gross national product has been achieved in the last two or three decades. Discounting the element of exaggeration inherent in Soviet statistics, it would seem that industrial output in the USSR increased between 1928 and 1937 at between 14 and 17 per cent per annum and since 1948 has increased only a little less rapidly. It is not so easy to estimate the rate of growth of the Russian gross national product. 'The development of agriculture has on the whole, at least until recently, been very disappointing; housing has long been in a desperate position; and the service industries which play such a prominent part in the West have been relatively neglected. The rapid progress of manufacturing industry has, indeed, been gained partly at the price of retarded development elsewhere.'[1] Nevertheless, the conclusion seems inescapable that the Russian gross national product increased by between 6 and 7 per cent per annum between 1928 and 1937 and again between 1948 and 1965—about twice the 'normal' rate in capitalist countries.

The capitalist countries, however, have made a much better showing since 1945, especially the United States. During the whole period since 1945, indeed, there has been a long-sustained investment boom throughout the world, a boom which has benefited industrial nations and primary producers alike. Such a period of favourable trade, beginning immediately after the war

[1] A. Montgomery, 'Production and Ideology in the Soviet Union' in *The Scandinavian Economic History Review*, vol. IV, No. 2, p. 155.

and enduring without serious interruptions for many years, was not expected.

On the contrary, governments all over the world made plans to combat an anticipated tendency to underemployment after the war. This was only natural. In Britain between the wars unemployment had averaged almost 13 per cent; in the United States, clearly recognized before the end of the war as the most powerful of all capitalist economies, unemployment had been even heavier in the 1930s, and the gross national product in 1938 was smaller than in 1929. The view that capitalism was running down and that _tagnation was not only inevitable but was the immediate prospect gained a lot of adherents in the 1930s. Yet there was no scarcity of jobs in the post-war world as there had been between the wars; on the contrary, there was a scarcity of men and of capital. Why? It is never easy to account for long-run processes of economic growth, but in this case at least four factors played a part. (1) During the war, a lot of capital was run down, and consumers' purchases were restricted. The owners of capital, and consumers, acquired titles to goods, i.e. money, which they could not use at the time, but which they did use when the war ended and goods again became available. There was thus a reserve of stored up demand which boosted the immediate post-war economy. (2) A little later, fear of war caused stockpiling and rearmament. Again there was a boost to 'normal' demand for goods and service. (3) More important, numerous governments after the war accepted 'full employment' as an objective of policy in a way in which it had never been accepted before. It was even written into or implied in international charters and agreements. Equally important, the public in numerous countries expected governments to take steps to secure full employment—if necessary—such as would perhaps not have been tolerated in the 1930s. Thus redistributive taxation, fiscal policy, government expenditure greatly increased both in volume and in relative importance, all were used deliberately to maintain economic activity at a high level after the war; while a rapid fall in the value of money was accepted, at least for a decade, with remarkable complacency. All this was intimately connected with the great shifts in political and social power and opinion noticeable in so many countries since 1913. (4) Perhaps most important of all, there were innovations in which it seemed profitable to invest after the war—synthetic fabrics, jet engines, atomic power, mass enjoyments like television, holiday camps and week-end motoring. There was thus created the essential condition for a business upswing, 'the expectation that a secular trend favoured investment in specific fields and that investment activity in these fields was going to continue'.[1]

And this boom was general. In the 1920s there was prosperity in the United States, Sweden, possibly France; in the 1930s there was prosperity—of a kind—in Germany and the United Kingdom. But after the war, all countries participated. This was partly a result of the length and strength of the boom, itself a tribute, to some extent, to the skill and effectiveness of government guidance and intervention. It was also, partly, a result of its nature. Much post-war investment has been long period growth investment—ambitious plans to extend and modernize transport and to increase the production of power—schemes of electrification, of hydro-electric power, the building of atomic power stations, and throughout Europe the steady conversion of industry from coal to oil. Also, some post-war expenditure has arisen out of the attempt to produce world-wide economic progress, out of the encouragement given to weaker economies to modernize their methods and increase their productivity. In so far as the weaker economies have succeeded, their demand for imports has increased and they have become better fields for investment. Apprehensions that the development of 'new' economies would result in the etiolation of world trade, to the especial disadvantage of Great Britain, have sometimes been expressed; but experience suggests the contrary. Between the wars, for example, Germany, a highly industrialized country, was a better customer for British exports of metals, machinery and transport equipment than France, a country less highly industrialized. Similarly, British exports to Australia and to Canada are far greater today than in 1938, although these countries are far more industrialized than they were twenty years ago.

---

[1] W. Fellner, *Monetary Policies and Full Employment* (California, 1946), p. 77.

A MORE RAPID SPREAD THAN BEFORE OF MODERN TECHNIQUES OF ORGANIZATION AND PRODUCTION INTO OTHER COUNTRIES

Whereas in 1920 modern techniques of production were almost unknown outside western Europe, Russia, and the English-speaking world, these techniques are now in use, albeit sometimes on a very small scale, in almost every country. There has thus continued 'that fan-like spread of mechanized industrial techniques' from western Europe eastward and southward which was observable before 1920, accompanied now by greatly increased productivity in all fields of primary production. As a result, other parts of the world have grown relatively more important and Europe has grown relatively less important. One aspect of this can be seen in the declining importance of European exports in world trade:

Europe in World Trade, Exports as per cent of world totals
(current values)[1]

	Europe	United States	Rest of the world
1913	53	12	35
1928	46	15	39
1938	46	14	40
1950	38	17	45
1964	41	16	43

These changes are notable, and their significance for the future is very great. They do not compare, however, with the rapid rise to economic power of the United States (and corresponding decline of the United Kingdom) between 1870 and 1910, and their magnitude is often exaggerated. Industrialization in the newly developed economies has not yet gone very far. It is only in Latin America that manufacturing and construction have begun to make in the post-war period a larger contribution to total output than agriculture.

This is true in spite of the very great efforts which many countries have made to develop manufacturing industry and so reduce their dependence on primary production. The demand

[1] From Table A.64 in I. Svennilson, *Growth and Stagnation in the European Economy* (Geneva, 1954); and *World Economic Survey, 1967.*

for primary products is unstable in the short run, and there are some grounds for fearing that in the long run that demand will increase only slowly. Yet, up to the present time, primary producers have not done as badly as they are sometimes inclined to make out.

World demand for primary products was buoyant in the post-war years, founded upon the rising level of activity in the industrially advanced countries. Exports of primary products increased in volume by 35 per cent between 1948 and 1955. Some commodities, and therefore some countries, did better than others. Exports of petroleum more than doubled; agricultural and mineral raw materials increased by a quarter, food, oils and tobacco by rather less. And at the same time the terms of trade moved, on the whole, slightly in favour of the primary producers. All these factors combined to allow increases in domestic consumption in the primary producing countries as well as considerable additions to the stock of capital; and this increased investment, in turn, helped to bring about a major expansion of domestic production, part of it in the field of industrial production.[1] Between 1925 and 1960 the real national product increased at over 5 per cent per annum in several countries in Latin America, and, more recently, it has grown at over 4 per cent per annum in Ceylon, Iraq, Malaya and a number of other countries. Egypt, India and Pakistan have had rates of growth of between 2 and 3 per cent per annum. In several of these countries investment rose faster than both consumption and total output. The investment policy of governments was of varying but always considerable importance; the share of public capital formation in total gross investment varied from about 30 per cent in India to about 60 per cent in Burma and Ceylon. 'Agriculture, transport, communications, irrigation and power were among the sectors to which public investment was particularly directed. Expansion of output in the coal, steel and cement industries has also received emphasis in the public investment programmes of some of these countries.'[2]

---

[1] It should be remembered that agricultural output in 'underdeveloped' economies has often risen in recent years as a result of increased domestic demand for food as well as increased foreign demand for raw materials.

[2] *World Economic Survey*, 1956 (United Nations), p. 115.

Nevertheless, serious difficulties exist. Some countries, notably Egypt, India and Pakistan, producing for export mainly textile raw materials and textile manufactures, have experienced disappointing trading conditions in world markets. This has led to pressure on their balance of payments positions and consequential difficulty in the financing of development projects. A more common cause of trouble has been price instability. Comparing world prices of primary products as a whole with those of manufactured goods in 1948 and again in 1965, little change in the relationship is to be found. Over this period the average price of primary products as a whole remained about constant, while the prices of manufactured goods fell only slightly. But the prices of some primary products have moved far more widely than others. In particular, the prices of agricultural raw materials and minerals have oscillated much more widely than those of foodstuffs, reflecting the greater degree of variation in world demand for industrial raw materials. For countries exporting such raw materials, inventory fluctuations in the industrial countries have rendered export prices highly unstable. This has produced an erratic rate of internal development in several countries, and hence undesirable losses and social and political friction. This same problem gave a great deal of trouble between the wars, when attempts were made to meet it by means of cartel arrangements among producers designed to restrict supplies and raise or keep up prices. These plans were ill-conceived—the so-called Stevenson Rubber Scheme is the best known—and their inevitable collapse in the later 1920s caused distress in many poor countries and was a contributory factor in the making of the world depression which began in 1929. In the post-war world only one large scheme, the International Wheat Agreement, was tried. The countries chiefly affected were Canada and Great Britain. The Agreement was well thought out, and many observers considered it a success. Canadian farmers, however, were disposed to think that they had made a bad bargain, and the scheme has had few, if any, successors of consequence. This may yet prove one of the weaker links in the pattern of international economic co-operation which has been built up since 1945 and which is so strong—and so encouraging—a contrast between the 1950s and 1960s and the economic disintegration of the 1930s and the political divisions and rampant nationalism of all the inter-war years.

It is inevitable that comparisons should be drawn between the experiences of developed and of underdeveloped countries. But these comparisons are apt to be misleading, because different countries have succeeded in raising the volume of their production at very different rates. Some countries—for example Greece, Indonesia, the United Kingdom—have not done very well. Others, such as Canada, Ceylon, Puerto Rico, Sweden have grown at exceptionally high rates. This diversity of experience results in the surprising fact that rates of growth of total product have not, on average, been much greater in underdeveloped than in developed countries. Each group has had its fast and its slower growers.[1] But this statement loses much of its significance if two other considerations are taken into account.

(1) In almost all underdeveloped countries, population increases rapidly. Therefore *per capita* product increases more slowly than total product. This is not so true in the developed countries. Consequently, *per capita* product has grown in almost every developed country in these years by one to one and a half per cent per annum; but in quite a number of underdeveloped countries it has grown by far less (although in some it has grown by much more), and especially it has grown by less in India, Indonesia and Pakistan, with a combined population of almost 600m. people, or about one-fifth of the world total.

(2) Even if product *per capita* were to increase equally rapidly in the developed and in the underdeveloped countries, the differences in *per capita* income would continue to increase. This is best seen by means of an example. Suppose that *per capita* income in developed countries is of the order of $1,500 per annum, and in the underdeveloped is of the order of $500 per annum: a difference of $1,000. A rise of 5 per cent in each group would produce figures of $1,575 and $525: a difference of $1,050. Thus the difference in *per capita* income between developed and underdeveloped countries must have increased considerably over the past forty or fifty years.

[1] The reader should consult Table 7 in Professor Kuznets' *Post-War Economic Growth* (1964) for up-to-date statistical information.

ALTERATION IN THE GENERAL TRENDS
OF WORLD TRADE

Since 1913, a great change has taken place in the rate of growth of world trade and in its relation to the rate of growth of world production. In the nineteenth century, world trade expanded very rapidly, growing by almost 50 per cent per decade between 1850 and 1880, and by almost 40 per cent per decade between the late 1870s and 1911-13. This means that the proportion of world trade to total world output must have risen steeply; and we also know that the increased importance of international trade relative to national output must have been especially great for the underdeveloped countries. In other words, the underdeveloped countries were increasing their participation even faster than the developed countries in a rapidly expanding volume of world trade. But, as Kuznets has put it, 'These trends toward widening international economic flows of a peaceful type, in increasing proportion to rising domestic volumes, were suspended and indeed reversed between the First World War and the early 1950s.'[1] Between about 1910 and about 1960, the volume of world trade grew by only some 10 or 12 per cent per decade; and this means that the proportion of world foreign trade to world output must have declined.

These facts seem to have important implications. The growth of many underdeveloped countries prior to 1945 was primarily directed towards meeting expanding demands on international markets—demands for wheat, rubber, tin, and other foods and raw materials. This sort of development was apt to lead to 'a lopsided pattern of growth in which production of primary products for export was carried on with the aid of substantial investment of foreign capital, while the domestic economy remained far less developed, if not altogether primitive';[2] nevertheless, such development raised national output, and could and sometimes did serve as the basis for more extensive progress. Now, world demand for primary products expands less rapidly, almost certainly less rapidly than production within the developed countries. This is partly because population increase in the

[1] Kuznets, op. cit., p. 60.
[2] R. Nurkse, in *Economic Development for Latin America* (ed. H. S. Ellis, 1961), p. 238.

developed countries has slowed down; but to a greater extent it is because modern industry economizes in the use of raw materials, because new products are seldom 'raw-material intensive', and because modern technology invents synthetic substitutes for natural rubber, silk, jute, hides and skins, timber, and so on. As a result, primary producers—and most underdeveloped countries can be classed as primary producers—feel that they must find means of development apart from foreign trade. And this leads to their already-mentioned anxiety to develop home industries, even if only for the purposes of import substitution; a course to which they are often the more inclined for reasons of national emulation and national prestige.

UNPRECEDENTED GROWTH OF POPULATION

Reliable figures for the growth of population are still not available for several important countries. Nevertheless, it is clear that world population is growing at an unprecedented rate, and that most of this increase takes place in the underdeveloped countries. The following figures give an idea of the magnitudes involved.

Population in millions

	1850	1900	1950	1964
World Total	1,171	1,550	2,454	3,215
Africa	95	120	198	300
North America	26	81	168	285
South America	33	63	162	163
Asia	741	857	1,320	1,781
Europe and USSR	274	423	593	668
Oceania	2	6	13	18

But the persistence of increase, or such facts as that the birth rate in Trinidad in the 1940s was very nearly 40 per 1,000, are less important than two other facts. Firstly, the rate of growth is tending to increase in many 'new' economies. This is because in the last few decades the birth rate has stayed up while the death rate has fallen. And the death rate has fallen because social and medical services—accompaniments of economic progress—have been enormously improved, sometimes by internal and sometimes by international action in the poorer countries. Endemic diseases have been or are being wiped out, just as they were wiped out—although much more slowly—in Britain between the later eighteenth century and the middle of the nineteenth century. Secondly, such developments have already led to rates of population growth which are very high indeed.[1] When population in Britain was growing at its fastest, in the first half of the nineteenth century, it doubled in a little less than fifty years. But at the present day, in Ceylon, Egypt, the West Indies and several countries of Latin America, the population is increasing fast enough to double every thirty-five years. In a few countries—British Guiana and Puerto Rico, for example—those under fifteen years of age make up 60 per cent of the population! In such conditions, very high rates of growth of the national income are required in order to raise living standards; much investment is needed simply to prevent the stock of capital equipment per head of population from falling. There is very little sign, so far, that this problem is going to be solved. The rates of institutional change and of capital formation which would be required to double living standards in, say, South-East Asia in 80 or 100 years have seldom been approached anywhere and are not being approached today in the poorer countries outside communist control. But if a satisfactory rate of economic progress cannot be achieved by present policies, what will be the outcome? There are three possibilities. Either more help will have to be given by richer countries to poorer ones—this could mean commodity stabilization schemes and liberal immigration policies as well as more investment—while the poorer countries take more drastic steps than hitherto to modernize their own institutions and social attitudes; or steps will have to be taken directly to slow down the increase in population—both China and India have made a few hesitant attempts to do this; or the poorer countries will become military dictatorships or communist states, and their progress will be secured at a heavy price for everyone. Which of these outcomes we are to witness is the most important question in political economy today.

---

[1] A sample survey carried out in a Shanghai factory in the early 1950s showed that 17 per cent of the women were pregnant twice within a year, and 53 per cent once a year. In one Shanghai mill of 7,000 male and female workers, the women workers of the factory produced 7,000 children in seven years. These facts, given by a member of the Chinese Government, are quoted in the *Economist*, March 23, 1957, p. 986.

CHAPTER II

The Nineteen-Twenties

THE STRUGGLE FOR THE GOLD STANDARD

IN the spring of 1919 the retail price index stood at almost exactly double the figure at which it had stood when war broke out in 1914. Britain was still, formally at any rate, on the gold standard; and prices were still rising. If the British adherence to gold was to be more than a formality—if, that is to say, the various obstacles which had been put in the way of melting and exporting gold sovereigns were to be removed—there would have to be a very severe restriction of credit. 'To start peace with a trade depression seemed an appalling prospect.'[1] Accordingly, Britain announced the formal abandonment of the gold standard on March 31, 1919.

This policy gave the Government a free hand in solving its internal financial problems. The most pressing of these were the need to find the means to meet current expenditure, and the need to do something about the legacy of debt of every kind, short-term and long-term, left by the war. The first of these requirements was met, in 1919, not by increasing taxation but by borrowing; the second was met by manipulating the floating debt, which consisted of Ways and Means Advances from the Bank of England, Ways and Means Borrowing from Public Departments, and Treasury Bills. These last were 'the central feature of the money market'.[2] The monthly average of Bills outstanding never fell below £1,000m. in 1920 and 1921. The Government was naturally anxious to borrow as cheaply as possible, while the Treasury faced the formidable task of con-

---

[1] R. G. Hawtrey, *Currency and Credit* (2nd ed. London, Longmans, 1923), p. 407.

[2] A. T. K. Grant, *A Study of the Capital Market in Post-War Britain* (London, Macmillan, 1937), p. 80.

solidating the borrowings of the war years. Attempts were made to discourage competing demands for funds, and in other ways pressure was brought to bear on the market to take Treasury Bills. Even so, the rate for three-month Bills rose from $3\frac{1}{2}$ per cent in the summer of 1919 to $6\frac{1}{2}$ per cent in the spring of 1920.

This increase in the cost of borrowing reflected the growing demand for funds from industry and commerce. This demand was stimulated by the easy money conditions created by the abandonment of gold and the budget deficit, conditions which debt policy could not improve although it probably made them no worse. The basis of the boom, however, was the need to convert the economy back to peace-time purposes, while its character was determined by the combination of easy money, a facile post-war optimism, and the inevitable uncertainties encountered in a major economic reconstruction. For the post-war world was something new. Peace at last was to set men free—or so they hoped—to build and cultivate the plains and cities of their dreams. But they underestimated the difficulties. The chief of these, in the immediate post-war years, was the complete absence of reliable information about what could be sold and at what prices.

'Business men could only guess what prices would emerge for their products, and the profits to be obtained in different lines of activity. Past experience was no guide because of the gulf between war conditions and peace-time demands. Above all, it was impossible to see which profits and prices would be temporary, and which permanent. Demand was bound to be spasmodic in character, since temporary needs, arising out of artificial shortage, were superimposed upon the more normal currents of demand which might be expected to remain. The margin of error in determining the future of business ventures was enormously increased, and mere guesswork had to take the place of the tolerably accurate estimation possible under continuous peace conditions. The complete break in economic continuity destabilized enterprise.'[1]

The 1919-20 boom was of a hectic and disorderly character.

[1] A. T. K. Grant, op. cit., p. 57.

It fell upon an economy in which wage-earners already 'showed a disposition to insist on more pay and shorter hours (while) the well-to-do . . . indulged in an orgy of extravagance which naturally encouraged the wage-earners in the course they had chosen'.[1] There was a boom in the capital market, and over £380m. was raised for new issues in the course of 1920—a sum not exceeded in any of the remaining inter-war years. Inevitably, prices rose. Commodity prices, which had been falling since the end of the war, rose by 25 per cent in the course of the year. Only 1916 had seen a bigger percentage rise.

In the summer of 1920 the boom began to show signs of coming to an end. The volume of currency was approaching the limits set by a self-denying ordinance of the Treasury towards the end of 1919. In April 1920, Bank Rate had been raised to 7 per cent, and the Government had brought in a budget which provided for a surplus of about £230m. Credit expansion due to the needs of government was ending. Meanwhile, the illusory nature of some of the hopes entertained by purchasers of new issues began to become evident. To make matters worse, wage disputes led to strikes in the important coal industry and in the cotton trade. Unemployment increased from August, beginning in the consumer goods trades, and spread fairly rapidly. A year which had begun 'with feverish trade activity, and a continued rise in prices' ended with 'trade deadlock, short time, unemployment, a very heavy fall in the price of wholesale commodities, and a state of affairs in which the general public was buying as sparingly as possible, because retail prices had not yet reflected more than a fraction of the fall in wholesale values'.[2] There had been no financial crash or panic, but the boom was over. 1921 was to be 'one of the worst years of depression since the industrial revolution'.[3]

This boom, brief as it was, was important for several reasons. First of all, it led, in this as in other countries, to a substantial creation of new capital equipment. What was achieved in this direction was in fact remarkable. In the words of Bowley,

[1] *The Economist*, Commercial History and Review of 1919, p. 1.
[2] ibid., Commercial History and Review of 1920, p. 345.
[3] ibid., Commercial History and Review of 1921, p. 290.

'At the end of the boom period of 1919-20 the productive capacity of the world in nearly every respect was at least as great as might have been anticipated eight years before even if there had been no war.'[1]

This was all to the good, but a high price was paid. There was, first of all, the dislocation and depression of the ensuing slump. Not only that, but many firms became and remained seriously over-capitalized, while others acquired capital equipment which could make a return only if prices, or at least demand, remained at a reasonably high level. Secondly, some money put up by investors was used, not for capital creation, but for the purchase of existing concerns at fancy prices and the enrichment of so-called 'financiers' and speculators.[2] This discouraged investment for a number of years, and gave force to the growing volume of socialist criticism of capitalist-conducted enterprise; what the 'possibly unscrupulous city financier' did in the early 1920s had not been forgotten by Ernest Bevin, for instance, in 1929.[3] And lastly, the rise in prices which took place certainly went further that it would have done had the gold standard remained in operation, and the experience of a rapidly rising and then rapidly falling price level, not linked to gold, may have encouraged the widespread conviction of subsequent years that return to the gold standard was the course of order, prudence and wisdom.

The abandonment of gold in 1919 was not remarkable, for it was traditional policy to break the link with gold when in acute difficulties; but not to return almost at once appeared revolutionary. Neither the Government nor public opinion nor expert opinion, however, wished for daring innovations in finance. The

[1] A. L. Bowley, *Some Economic Consequences of the Great War* (London, Butterworth), p. 93.

[2] '. . . in the first year or two after the Great War there was small demand for the services of a careful, conservative firm like ourselves [Helbert Wagg & Co.]. The war-profiteers, and in particular the shipowners of Cardiff, that "city of dreadful knights", were busy unloading their factories and fleets upon a credulous public through mushroom issuing houses, long since sunk without trace. Values were monstrously inflated, but every offering was over subscribed. We had to sit with folded hands amid the rush and bustle of money-making all round us.' (L. E. Jones, *Georgian Afternoon* [London, Macmillan, 1958] p. 117.)

[3] See Bevin's evidence in *Committee on Finance and Industry*, *Minutes of Evidence* (HMSO, 1931), vol. I, p. 55.

influential Cunliffe Committee produced its Final Report eight months after the abandonment of the standard, and reiterated its opinion that

> 'the adoption of a currency not convertible at will into gold or other exportable coin is likely in practice to lead to over issue and so to destroy the measure of exchangeable value and cause a general rise in all prices and an adverse movement in the foreign exchanges.'[1]

The collapse in 1923 of the German mark—ultimately quoted at fifty billion marks to the pound—emphasized the dangers of currency mismanagement and enormously encouraged adherence to the gold standard as a refuge of stability and safety. Also, any private citizen throughout these early years could take a five pound note to the Bank of England and demand five golden sovereigns in exchange; and although he could not melt them down or export them, this tended to encourage a general belief that the gold standard would shortly be restored.

It might almost be said, therefore, that the Government had from the first a kind of moral obligation to work towards restoration of the gold standard; although it may be going a little too far to say that from the moment of its abandonment restoration became 'avowed policy . . . endorsed by nearly all persons of authority'.[2] Certainly there is no evidence that a deliberate policy of deflation was adopted in order to prepare the way for returning to the gold standard, at least prior to 1924. Bank Rate, put up after what seems to have been unnecessary delay in 1919, was not lowered until March 1921. From the end of April, money rates in Great Britain began to fall, and they fell even faster than those in New York. But long before this, in the middle of 1920, a trade recession was clearly developing, although most firms making goods for export were busy until almost the end of the year in working off export orders. 1921 began with the unemployment rate over 6 per cent and still rising. All thoughts of a deliberate policy of deflation were abandoned during the year in the face of the 'undoubtedly de-

[1] Loc. cit., para. 2.
[2] A. C. Pigou, *Aspects of British Economic History, 1918-1925* (London, Macmillan, 1947), p. 148.

plorable'[1] unemployment situation, and in the course of 1922 nearly all industries effected substantial reductions in wage rates, amounting in some cases to as much as 30 per cent of the rates prevailing in December 1921. In spite of this, nearly 1·5m. men were unemployed in January 1923.

For a time, the centre of interest in monetary policy shifted to the international sphere. The Genoa Conference, held in the spring of 1922, was a truly international conference—even Russia was invited—held in order to determine, if possible, the broad outlines of political and economic reconstruction in Europe. Politically, the Conference was a failure. In the economic sphere, however, resolutions were passed to centralize and co-ordinate the demand for gold with a view to stabilizing, as far as possible, the purchasing power of gold, and to economizing its use. These resolutions came to nothing in the sense that no binding obligations were entered into. But Montagu Norman, Governor of the Bank of England from 1920, testified later that throughout the 'twenties he had 'devoted the greater part' of his time, when not engaged in problems of policy at home, to the task of international economic reconstruction and co-opera-tion 'on the sort of lines originally sketched at Genoa'.[2] This work, however, could produce no early results. And attention shifted back to the gold standard and to Bank Rate when the depression in industry began very gradually to lift in the second half of 1922.

Money was cheap and unemployment heavy for almost the whole of that year. Bank Rate, which averaged 6·1 per cent in 1921, averaged only 3·7 per cent in 1922. The drastic reductions in wages already mentioned led to few stoppages in industry, and prices fell with unprecedented rapidity. Twenty per cent was knocked off the cost of living index between the middle of 1921 and the middle of 1922; nothing like this had been known since at least 1870, and nothing like it has been seen again. The dollar exchange, which had been pegged at $4·76 during the war by arrangement with J. P. Morgan, and since the war had fluctuated between $3·40 and $4, began to improve late in 1921, reached $4·40 by the summer of 1922, and in a

[1] *The Economist*, Commercial History and Review of 1921, p. 290.
[2] *Committee on Finance and Industry* (1931), Minutes of Evidence, vol. I, p. 211.

final spurt at the end of the year reached over $4·50. This recovery, in the view of the *Economist*, was

'due to a relative improvement in our foreign trade, to the fall in prices here and the rise in prices and expansion of credit in the United States, to a growing faith in the financial and economic position of Great Britain, and to lower purchases of raw materials from America by this country. Towards the close of the year the transfer of large balances, formerly held in this country, back again to London was responsible for some sharp upward movements.'[1]

For a short time, early in 1923, the pound stood above $4·68. Fluctuations in exchange rates are at any time notoriously difficult to account for with exactitude. This is particularly true of the early 1920s, when the balance of international trade was still seriously disturbed by the aftermath of war, when international payments in respect of War Debts or Reparations were constantly being demanded and often made, and when political or industrial disturbances were frequent and usually gave rise to speculative transfers of capital. The final upward movement of the dollar exchange in 1922–23 was probably partly due to expectations that Great Britain might shortly return to the gold standard. But the retention by the pound of a value above $4·40 from May 1922 to November 1923 must have been due to lower British prices vis à vis the United States and a healthy export position. Some of the advantage of 1922 was doubtless fortuitous and temporary; the low level of raw material imports from the United States, for example, was chiefly due to the running down of stocks consequent on slack trade; and British coal exports were abnormally high. Nevertheless, looking back, knowing what was to come, one is tempted to say that this was the moment for Britain to return to the gold standard, if she was to return to it. At least there was a real opportunity. The major objection, felt strongly by Norman, was that the problems of war debts and reparations were not yet settled. On the other hand, the great advantage of 1922–23 over 1925 was that at the earlier date wages and the whole cost/price structure were

[1] *The Economist*, Commercial History and Review of 1922, p. 322.

largely unsettled, and must have possessed a flexibility which they do not seem to have possessed in the later 1920s.

The opportunity, however, if it was one, was allowed to pass. The pound gradually fell away from the $4·70⅝ reached in March 1923, and ended the year around $4·30. Trade, on the other hand, showed a steady if gradual improvement, and the number of unemployed fell from 1·4m. in January to under 1·2m. in December. Wage reductions were few in number and prices steadied. In July Bank Rate was raised from 3 per cent to 4 per cent. This action was dictated not by consideration of the exchanges but by

'the suspicion that easy money here was being used to build up an unhealthy stock exchange speculative position both on domestic and foreign account, and the fall in securities which followed the movement rather suggested confirmation of the suspicion and justification of the movement.'[1]

This movement gave rise to a good deal of discussion about monetary policy and produced 'the forceful expression of opinion in several quarters'[2] that deflationary policies aimed at restoring the dollar exchange to pre-war par should be ruled out as long as unemployment continued at the current levels.

In January 1924 the first Labour Government came into office. This depressed the exchanges for several reasons, among them the Labour Party's announcement of the preceding year that the Party still stood for a capital levy. Sterling temporarily sank as low as $4·20—still a higher rate than anything prevailing before the autumn of 1921—but soon began to recover. Pressure for restoration of the gold standard increased. 'Opinion is hardening in favour of some action before very long,' wrote the *Economist*; 'enquiries from abroad are constantly being made as to the future of sterling.'[3] In July, for the first time, a deliberate policy aimed at pushing up the exchange rate was adopted. So far, hopes of improvement had rested chiefly on expectations—often somewhat wilfully held in spite of the evidence —that American prices must soon rise. But now, with money

[1] *The Economist*, February 16, 1924, p. 305.
[2] ibid., Commercial History and Review of 1923, p. 302.
[3] ibid., June 28, 1924.

rates falling in New York, Bank Rate was held steady at 4 per cent throughout the year while the joint-stock banks were persuaded to raise their rates to the Discount Market.

The pound began to appreciate rapidly. As from June, money could earn a higher, sometimes a much higher rate of return in London than in New York; the reverse had been true in the first half of 1924. Also, as expectations that Britain would soon go back to gold at the old rate came to be more and more widely held, speculators moved balances to London in the hopes of capital appreciation in terms of the dollar. This general expectation was reinforced by the fact that the Gold and Silver (Export Control, etc.) Act of 1920 was due to expire at the end of 1925, and many people thought that the Government would prefer to return before then, so as to avoid having to ask Parliament for authority to continue the embargo on the exporting of gold by the general public. It was no great surprise to British or foreign observers when Mr Churchill, in his Budget speech on April 28, 1925 (the Socialist Government having gone out of office in the preceding October) announced that the Government had decided to allow the 1920 Act to lapse and to return immediately to the gold standard.

Britain's return to the gold standard at the pre-war rate of $4·86 was not without critics, most notable among them those old enemies, Mr Lloyd George and Mr Keynes.[1] But there is no doubt that it caused, at the time, general satisfaction. To a world which was seeking to recreate that stability and prosperity which was attributed, rightly or wrongly, to what men called 'the nineteenth century', the gold standard was the heart of the matter, the ark of the covenant. Its restoration did not complete the task of reconstruction, but what remained to do would follow more easily, perhaps almost inevitably. Or so, at least, it was hoped.

Monetary policy after 1925 is inevitably simpler than before. The exchange was fixed, and had to be protected. There could no longer be vacillation or alternation between policies designed to facilitate Government financing, policies designed to maintain the external value of the pound, and policies designed to

[1] The controversy about monetary policy in the 1920s is dealt with in Chapter Seven.

improve the level of economic activity at home. Once more, just as prior to 1914, exchange considerations had a direct and dominant influence on monetary policy. A crude outline of the course of events after 1925 is given by the figures for Bank Rate. Raised from 4 per cent to 5 per cent in March 1925, it was reduced to 4 per cent on October 1st and quickly raised again to 5 per cent at the beginning of December. In April 1927 it came down to 4½ per cent, at which level it remained for the rest of 1927 and throughout 1928. The onset of the world depression caused increases, of course, in 1929. The net effect of returning to the gold standard seems therefore to have been to make rates higher than they had been before. Whereas from 1922 to 1924 inclusive Bank Rate averaged 3·76 per cent, from 1926 to 1928 inclusive it averaged 4·72 per cent. The difference is not startling, and neither average—certainly not the earlier one—is remarkably high considering that the country had just emerged from a long war during which the supply of capital for peacetime uses had not been adequately maintained.

In some ways the tighter money situation after 1925 was not a serious embarrassment. Between 1920 and 1926 there had been a substantial improvement in the structure of the national debt. The floating debt had been reduced by £500m. and the short-term unfunded debt by a similar amount. The position of the Treasury was thus very much easier than it had been in 1920, and there was no longer the same reason for anxiety whenever money rates moved upwards. With regard to the capital market, the surprising thing is that the somewhat higher money rates of the later 1920s did not reduce the volume of capital passing through the new issue market. Both in 1926 and 1927 more new capital was raised than in any previous year of the period save 1920. By the middle of 1927, indeed, a boom in speculative securities was well under way.

'During the year there were greyhound racing and film issues on a considerable scale. Gramophone shares were rocketing. Brazilian Traction doubled in price. The 10s 0d share of British Celanese rose in price from 5s 9d to 89s 3d. During the year the *Bankers' Magazine* index of variable dividend securities . . . , a conservative index, rose from 135·7 to 146·9. At the end of 1928 it stood at 158·8.'[1]

The public was 'on the feed'. The yield on ordinary shares fell rapidly from the middle of 1926 to the end of 1927, and the average rate on new issues of industrial debentures likewise fell. Enterprises of every kind took advantage of the favourable conditions to raise fresh capital, but the outstanding feature of the market was

> 'the repeated over-subscription of speculative issues, the attractions of whose deferred shares as gambling counters were more regarded by the public than their merits as an investment.'[2]

Why, in a period when the yield on consols was about 4½ per cent, the public should have been so anxious to find new uses for its money is not quite clear. The return to the gold standard, without doubt, gave investors more confidence and so stimulated their activity; it may also, on balance, have increased the average willingness of business to borrow. There is also the point that a prolonged period of fairly high long-term rates on safe borrowing may have made investors entertain altogether too optimistic expectations about what could and should be offered for risk capital. Had the yield on long-term Government securities been lower, money might have gone more freely into housebuilding and other relatively safe employments rather than into the purchase of the more risky—and dubious—kind of security which was appearing so frequently between 1926 and 1929. But this is itself a speculation.

The return to gold and the higher interest rates which went with it thus did not have obviously harmful consequences in at least two important directions. On the other hand, prices continued to fall. After having steadied in 1923-25, they pursued a gradual downward course to their lowest point in 1933. This probably acted as a mildly depressive influence upon business; and yet the fall was not sufficient to remove the competitive price disadvantage created for the old-established export industries selling in foreign markets by the combination of their own

[1] A. T. K. Grant, op. cit., p. 143.
[2] *The Economist*, November 10, 1928.

costs of production and the new fixed exchange rate. This disadvantage was made more serious when in 1928 Belgium and France also returned to the gold standard, but both of them at 'a very low level'.[1]

The difficulties involved in trying to work the post-war gold standard, however, were not solely, nor were they even chiefly those of choosing appropriate rates. The gold exchange standard of the post-war years differed from the pre-war gold standard in one very important respect. It economised in the use of gold by allowing countries to count claims on gold as equivalent to gold for monetary reserve purposes. But this depended on the main international reserve centres, such as London, possessing sufficient gold reserves or other liquid assets of their own to be able to meet any claims that might arise. Unfortunately, Britain did not have a large gold reserve in 1925 (about £150m.) and her liquid claims on foreign centres did not amount to much. The position, indeed, had been growing worse. The steps taken from the middle of 1924 to keep short-term money rates in London above those in New York had attracted liquid funds to London. Writing in 1926, T. E. Gregory concluded that

'on the face of it, in the last two years (in 1924 and 1925) we have borrowed, in the shape of increasing foreign balances in London and in other ways, a sum considerably over £100m. We have lent long £220m. and borrowed short £130m.'[2]

On top of this came further short-term borrowings—largely occasioned by a flight from the franc—at the same time that the coal strike and the General Strike of 1926 were completely upsetting the balance of payments. No gold reserve was built up against these liabilities. None could be. Any attempt would have required a considerable deflation at home, which would have further worsened the industrial position. All that the Bank of England could do was to prevent inflows of gold from having their full effect on the supply of money, and this it did. These inflows were small, and the gold reserves reached a maximum of only £172m. in the third quarter of 1928, having been

[1] Montagu Norman, *Committee on Finance and Industry, Minutes of Evidence* (1931), question 3362.
[2] T. E. Gregory, *The First Year of the Gold Standard* (London, 1926), p. 77.

£144m. in the first quarter of 1926. London's net liability on short-term account was meanwhile between £270m. and £300m. The Bank of England failed to build up a stock of new short-term assets to be held against the short-term liabilities which London was acquiring; it did succeed, however, in preventing the situation from growing worse.

The position even at the time of restoration was thus a difficult one, and it quickly became more difficult. From the start Great Britain did not have the liquid assets necessary to a great international banker, and she was never able to strengthen her position subsequently. There was no room for manoeuvre. The pound was always faced with potential dangers, but nothing could be done to reduce them without at least temporarily raising the level of unemployment at home and possibly causing a crisis in one or another of the economically weaker countries abroad. It has been argued that as far as prices were concerned the pound and the dollar had come into equilibrium by 1928. Norman, in 1930, seemed to take some such view.[1] But this could not, in itself, solve the fundamental problem of a chronic shortage of liquid reserves.

'For practical purposes there was only one remedy: that of going off the gold standard and starting all over again. The force of events was such that this remedy had unwillingly to be applied in September 1931.'[2]

OLD AND NEW INDUSTRIES

The task which faced British industry in the years between the wars was to adapt itself to novel economic conditions, both of demand and of supply. New products had become or were becoming important, techniques of production were altering, markets were changing, often radically, in size, nature and location. As a result, a great number of workpeople had to switch their jobs—this often required them to leave the district in which they lived and go elsewhere—while much capital became unremunerative and had to be written off, a process naturally disappoint-

[1] See *Committee on Finance and Industry, Minutes of Evidence*, question 3374.
[2] A. T. K. Grant, op. cit., p. 113.

ing to entrepreneurs and shareholders, and resisted by them accordingly. The numbers of people and the sums of money involved were large, and the task of adaptation was therefore a great one. From a practical point of view the problem was complex and formidable. The core of the trouble lay in two industries, coal and cotton; especially in coal. These industries were too big, or their costs were too high, for post-war demand. Expansion was possible only along other lines. What had to be done between 1920 and 1939 was to contract a few industries and to expand a large number of others, thus producing a more diversified industrial structure, one more in keeping with the new national and international patterns of costs and demand.

There is nothing unusual in an economy being faced with such a task. Adaptation proved unusually troublesome in this case, however, for three reasons. First of all, the industries to be contracted were long-established and had recently been expanded. For a hundred years before 1920 textiles—chiefly cotton—had been Britain's major export, and even in the years 1911–13 textiles were 40 per cent by value of Britain's visible exports. In the same years coal exports were almost 10 per cent of the total, having trebled in importance and increased far more in value in the preceding fifty years. These two 'traditional' industries, along with iron,

'ceasing to be the theatres of innovation in technique and organization which they had once been, and . . . ceasing to produce the increasing returns to human labour on which their great start in the world had depended . . . were [1900–13] growing exceptionally fast. In the decade before the First World War, coal mining, iron and steel, engineering and shipbuilding, and the textile industries in Lancashire and Yorkshire formed the dominant industries of the country. Their predominance seemed to increase as trade picked up after 1905 and the world entered a phase of boom.'[1]

Secondly, the conditions facing these 'traditional' industries in the early 1920s were quite abnormally unsettled, and their

[1] W. H. B. Court, *A Concise Economic History of Britain* (Cambridge University Press, 1954), p. 222.

prospects changed, at least in the short run, with bewildering rapidity. Then, when it became easier towards the end of that decade to discern the long run tendencies of costs and markets, and when the natural reluctance of those in the industries concerned to abandon old ways was beginning to be overcome, the economy was dragged down in the unprecedented slump of 1929-33, and reorganization became, for the time being, more difficult than ever. Thirdly, the new opportunities which were appearing in the 'twenties were very varied, and it was perhaps unusually difficult for investors and businessmen to choose between those which were and those which only seemed to be promising new lines of investment. Moreover, business men's problems were by no means at an end even if they succeeded in establishing themselves in one of the new lines destined to have a profitable future—motor cars, for example—because the rate of technical change was often very rapid and mistakes were easily made.

What is the justification for saying that the problems of the coal industry lay at the heart of Britain's industrial problem in the 1920s? Leaving aside questions of industrial relations, which are dealt with in another section, the answer is that there were more men in the coal industry who could not profitably be employed in it than there were in any other British industry at that time. From 1925 to 1929 unemployment in coal averaged over 16 per cent. Between 1924 and 1930 the manpower available to the industry fell from 1,259,000 to 1,069,000, a diminution of almost 200,000; yet unemployment in the industry in 1930 was over 180,000, or 20 per cent, 4 per cent higher than the unemployment rate at that time for the country as a whole. There were industries in which unemployment was more severe than it was in coal—steel and shipbuilding, for example; but the number of those who could not find employment in the industry in which they sought it was in every other case much smaller.

The severe and intractable difficulties of the coal industry in these years were due to many causes, but the most serious of them was the combination of high costs and restricted demand. Output in 1920 was 229m. tons, and in 1923 was not far short of the all-time record figure of 287m. tons achieved in 1913.

But the days of cheaply won coal in Britain were over. The industry was being driven to narrower seams and deeper seams. Its willingness, or ability, to introduce new techniques proved to be very limited, and as a result costs rose. To begin with, it was not clear that this mattered very much. In the boom of 1919-20 there was abundant demand for coal, and the industry, still under Government control, was profitable. The miners promptly came forward with their post-war programme: a six-hour day, nationalization, and a 30 per cent increase in wages. The Government, still in charge of the mining industry, did not accept this programme, whereupon the miners balloted six to one in favour of a strike. This threat led to the setting up of the Sankey Commission to investigate wages, hours of work and the nationalization proposal. The membership, conduct and reports of this Commission epitomize the troubles and conflicts of the industry in these years. There were on the Commission three coal-owners, three industrialists, three miners and three 'economists'—Chiozza Money (defeated as a Labour candidate in the 1918 election), Sidney Webb and R. H. Tawney. The chairman, Sankey, was a judge. Both 'sides' of industry were thus equally represented, and the stage was set for complete division of opinion and deadlock. The proceedings of the Commission, which did its work with great rapidity, included much baiting of royalty-owners and coal-owners, and many hours were spent less on the elucidation of facts and opinions than on the manufacture of socialist propaganda. Inevitably, the miners' 'representatives' reported that the men's demands should be met in full (they also proposed workers' control), and the coal-owners reported that they should be modified. Everyone recommended the nationalization of coal royalties; Sir John Sankey recommended 'that the principle of State ownership of the coal-mines be accepted', partly because of the 'present atmosphere of distrust and recrimination' between owners and men; while Sir Arthur Duckham, greatly to his credit, put forward practical and constructive proposals, based on some suggestions made by H.M. Chief Inspector of Mines, for a compromise arrangement between private ownership and Government control.

Nothing was done; not even the royalties were nationalized. The obvious excuse for inaction was division of opinion. But it was a poor excuse. The relations between owners and men were bad, the Commission had made them worse, and complete disappointment of all the miners' high hopes would make them worse still. If the nationalization proposals were vague or unworkable, there was the Duckham scheme. If there was not time for the Duckham scheme, at least the royalties could have been nationalized. True, nationalization of the royalties would have made very little practical difference to anyone; but it would have been a gesture of conciliation. That it was not made points to the real reason for doing nothing: to conciliate the miners might well be to promote the political influence of the Labour Party. 1919 witnessed 'a great shifting of political opinion towards the Labour Party'.[1] Lloyd George was manoeuvring for political position, but the price he paid was stultification of almost all hopes of co-operation and progress in the coal industry for twenty years.

The Coal Mines Act of 1919, which followed the Sankey Commission, introduced the seven hour day, and there were considerable wage increases, partly paid for by the Government. No one wanted a fight—yet. 1920, opening with 'feverish trade activity, and a continued rise in prices',[2] saw the Government grant a 20 per cent wage increase to the miners in April, partly to compensate for rising prices and partly as 'a stimulus to production'.[3] But production did not respond. Instead, new wage demands were presented in June, designed to carve up the large profits on export (the price differential at one time reached 78s 5d a ton; 36s 7d the domestic price, 115s 0d abroad). Argument ensued, and a very brief strike in October resulted in the passage of the Emergency Powers Act (used in the following year and again in 1926) and the granting of a new wage increase. This settlement was to last until March 31, 1921. Before then, however, seeing that the palmy days of exuberant demand were over, the Government hastened to decontrol the industry. At absurdly short notice the mines were handed back to their owners, who were left to cope with falling demand, increasing continental competition, German reparations pay-

[1] *The Economist*, Commercial History and Review of 1919, p. 2.
[2] ibid., Commercial History and Review of 1920, p. 345.
[3] ibid., p. 378.

ments in coal, and wage negotiations requiring to be begun at once with a frustrated and exasperated labour force. The miners' prime objectives were a national settlement (as opposed to a variety of district settlements) and a consolidated scale. They got neither. A threatened general strike did not take place, but the industry was struck from the day Government control ended —March 31st—to July 1st. In the very depressed industrial conditions of 1921 failure was certain, and it proved to be complete. The settlement was on a district-by-district basis, and substantial wage reductions, similar to those which had to be accepted in most other industries in 1921, were enforced. A Government subsidy of £10m. helped to cushion these wage reductions.

In 1922 the industry licked its wounds. Wages were now fixed upon the basis of what the industry could afford, and output was higher than in any year since the war. But no sooner was the industry beginning to settle down than fresh abnormal conditions appeared. In 1923 the French occupied the Ruhr. As a result, markets which had been closing to British coal from the summer of 1920 suddenly reopened. Coal exports rose from 64m. tons to 79m. tons and unemployment fell markedly. Industrial commentators sounded a strong note of cheery optimism; prosperity had come again. But a year later the favourable factors had once more disappeared.

By 1924 it may be said that the problems and weaknesses of the industry lay sufficiently exposed. The following figures summarize the position.

	1907	1912	1924
Employment	839,000	980,000	1,183,000
Production	267m. tons	261m. tons	266m. tons
Output per manshift	—	c. 19 cwts.	17·8 cwts.
Exports	64m. tons	64m. tons	62m. tons

The industry was raising about the same amount of coal as it often had raised before the war; but it had over 200,000 more men on the books than in 1912, and costs and prices were not behaving in such a way that the industry could afford a 6 per cent fall in the average physical product per man. In one respect, moreover, the full extent of the trouble was not revealed even in 1924, for from that time onwards the export position became worse. Whereas in the three years 1922-24 exports averaged 68m. tons, in the five years 1925 and 1927-30 they averaged just over 50m. tons. On the demand side, this was the crucial trouble of the industry. Foreign demand fell much more sharply than domestic demand. The most important single factor here was the loss of Russian markets; the next most important was new Polish competition in Scandinavia, due to the exclusion of Polish coal from Germany, the deficiency there being made good partly by the expansion of German coal output but still more of German lignite production. Restoration of the gold standard in 1925 increased the industry's difficulties in foreign markets. Home demand, meanwhile, failed to expand, although in several years it was not far short of pre-war levels. In so far as home demand was seriously disappointing, the cause was chiefly a combination of depression in the pig iron trade and fuel economy in the manufacture of steel.

To draw general conclusions about the coal industry in the 'twenties from its position in 1924 may seem to imply that the coal strike and the General Strike of 1925 were not of fundamental importance in the history of the industry. In a sense they were not, for an analysis of the problems of the industry is perfectly possible without reference to the events of 1925. The fundamental difficulty of the industry was that, given its costs, it was too big; alternatively, given its size, its costs were too high. Strikes did not affect that; and even from the point of view of industrial relations, from a 'psychological' point of view, these strikes only emphasized and increased tensions and antagonisms already marked and often outrageous before 1925.

The origins of the coal strike of 1926 were very similar to those of the disputes of 1919, 1920 and 1921. The wage agreement of 1921 was terminated in 1924, and a new agreement, more favourable to the miners, was negotiated. Based on the fortuitously favourable trading results of 1923, this agreement was out of date as soon as it was signed. In the middle of 1925 the coal-owners gave notice to terminate the agreement, and proposed substantial wage reductions. The miners refused, and the Government set up the Samuel Commission. This Commission turned down both nationalization and a Government subsidy, and recommended (1) nationalization of the coal royalties

(2) voluntary reorganization of the industry under private enterprise (3) various devices and 'fringe benefits' to improve relations between owners and men and (4) wage reductions, described as 'immediately essential'.

These recommendations were inferior to those made by Sir John Sankey and Sir Arthur Duckham six years before. To rely on voluntary reorganization would have been optimistic in 1919; in 1925 it was merely utopian. Wage reductions were certainly essential, but the Report as a whole was made nugatory by the Commissioners' insistence that

'before any sacrifices are asked from those engaged in the industry, it shall be definitely agreed between them that all practicable means for improving its organization and increasing its efficiency should be adopted, as speedily as the circumstances in each case allow.'

But the coal-owners and the miners were beyond being able to agree as to what were 'practicable means'. The miners still wanted nationalization, and they resisted wage reductions to the last.[1] Most of the coal-owners could think of no other way to reduce costs than by reducing wages, most of them were frankly contemptuous of 'reorganization', and as the Mining Association was run as a club to protect the inefficient and the unenterprising, it was going to be a long time before competition could put high-cost collieries out of business. Even Neville Chamberlain thought the coal-owners 'not a prepossessing crowd',[2] and their attitude was at least as uncompromising as that of the men; no doubt what had been said to many coal-owners and royalty-owners during the Sankey Commission brought forward what was worst, hardest and least progressive on the employers' side. Almost two months of negotiation brought no agreement, and on May 4th the General Strike began.[3] When it ended after nine

---

[1] 'Until . . . reorganization brings greater prosperity to the industry the miners should not be called upon to surrender any of their present inadequate wages and conditions'—i.e. until the industry is more profitable wages should not be reduced. The quotation is from a letter addressed to the Prime Minister from the Miners' Executive, sent on April 30, 1926.

[2] K. Feiling, *The Life of Neville Chamberlain* (London, Macmillan, 1946), p. 156.

[3] Why there was a general strike, and not merely a strike confined to the coal industry, is discussed below, pp. 70-73.

days the coal strike continued, and lasted almost until Christmas. The miners lost on every count. Wages were reduced, coal royalties were not nationalized, there was no reorganization of the industry, and hours were increased from 7 to 7½ or 8—a change condemned in advance by the Samuel Report and made possible only by Government repeal of some 1919 legislation in the course of the strike.

Bitterness in the industry increased; but at last men began to leave it. By 1930 the number of insured persons in the industry had fallen from the 1,259,000 of 1924 to 1,069,000, and output per manshift had risen from 17·8 cwts. to 21·6 cwts. The wage reductions were necessary and in a sense they proved effective. But other changes which should have accompanied them were not made. The numbers of coal-miners began to fall, but all the other long term problems of the industry remained, and the will to solve these problems was, after the strike, weaker than ever.

The history of the coal industry has been given in some detail partly because the industry was so important in itself, partly because its history exemplifies, although in a higher degree, the kind of troubles experienced by some other important industries in these years. The closest comparison is with cotton. Like the coal industry, the cotton industry enjoyed boom demand in the years immediately after the war. Overseas demand in 1919 was pronounced 'healthy' and long term prospects were thought to be encouraging: 'The prospects for a larger consumption of cotton fabrics in China in the years to come are distinctly bright.'[1] In the course of 1919 sixty-two cotton companies, with an original share capital of £2·67m., were sold for £15·31m., and many others were consolidated or recapitalized on the basis of their supposed current earning powers. Profits were incalculable, and there were plenty of 'financiers' ready to batten on public optimism and gullibility. In the spring of 1920 cotton prices 'reached a very dizzy height'.[2] British manufactured exports in 1920 were £479m. above the figure for 1919, and 20 per cent of this increase was contributed by cotton. But by the end of 1920 the market had collapsed and Lancashire was full of unemployed. The mills now had to meet much worse

[1] *The Economist*, Commercial History and Review of 1919, p. 436.
[2] ibid., Commercial History and Review of 1920, p. 399.

trading conditions with a financial structure far weaker than two years before, and it soon became clear that their marketing difficulties were not temporary. All over the world, in China, Japan, Brazil, Italy and above all in India, protected domestic industries had sprung up and were being expanded. They supplied their home markets and invaded foreign markets. Britain faced Japanese and Indian competition throughout the East, Italian competition in the Balkans and Middle East, United States competition in Latin America. To make matters worse, the falling incomes of agricultural producers in the 'twenties helped to turn their demand towards the cheaper, poorer-quality products upon which Japan, India and the domestic producers generally concentrated, and away from the higher-quality goods on which the British industry concentrated and where Britain's advantage still remained. Thus once more, as in the case of coal, the heart of the trouble on the demand side was the decline of exports, especially of piece goods; between 1924 and 1930, 75 per cent of the decline in the output of piece goods was due to diminished sales abroad.

The industry was accused of inefficiency. 'Chaotic industrial organization,' according to its critics, 'contributed to technical inferiority.'[1] To a large extent, statements of this kind merely reflect one of the prejudices of the times—a prejudice in favour of large-scale organization. Like the coal industry, the cotton industry was accused of 'almost fanatic individualism' and of harbouring 'an excessive number of small, weak firms'.[2] But the firms in cotton were small chiefly because high quality goods and short runs for special markets could best be done by small firms. Large scale production of standardized goods was suitable where there was cheap labour and available capital. British labour was not cheap, and the cotton industry was avoided by investors—the frozen assets of some banks which had foolishly taken a hand in the 'frenzied finance' of 1919-20, which had involved the cotton industry, were a well-known warning. If the industry could not compete in the cheap lines it had to hold on in the dear, and reduce its numbers. It held on, but there was no

[1] A. E. Kahn, *Great Britain in the World Economy* (London, Pitman, 1946), p. 98.
[2] ibid., p. 98.

fall in the numbers seeking employment in the industry until after 1930. Lancashire was loth to believe that the days of its old prosperity were gone, never to return.

Only two other industries deserve a mention in this abbreviated but melancholy story; iron and steel, and shipbuilding. The former began with high hopes of the post-war world. 'During the war, while the Ministry of Munitions exercised its control over the metallurgical industries, all concerned in the trade naturally looked forward to peace, as to a sort of golden age, when an era of unexampled activity and productiveness, exceeding all previous records, would be ushered in. These expectations have not (1920) been realized . . . although it may be said with some confidence that we are but suffering a post-ponement.'[1] Alas, never was confidence more misplaced. The 1920s saw a sharp decline in pig iron production, due partly to insufficiency of native ores and partly to the triumph of basic steel over cast iron, wrought iron and acid steels. Even more important for the industry as a whole was the burden of excess capacity resulting from wartime and optimistic post-war expansion. Steel capacity was estimated in 1927 at 12m. tons; only twice between 1920 and 1930 did output exceed 9m. tons. As a consequence, there was persistent financial weakness in the industry, and this in its turn precluded any large schemes of modernization. By dint of increasing concentration on the higher stages of fabrication the industry was able to struggle along; but the steel plants were obsolescent and the individual firms too small—for this was a case where economies of scale were very real—to be able to compete with the giant plants of America and the modernized German industry. Shipbuilding was similarly weighed down by a legacy of war-time expansion, worsened, in this case, by subsidized foreign competition and a particularly wild orgy of post-war speculation:

'. . . in one month alone thirty companies were floated with £4m. capital. The experienced shipowner sold, the ignorant man bought, and the banks financed the deals . . . in 1921, after the bubble had burst, ships . . . bought at £24 10s 0d a ton were sold for £5 10s 0d.'[2]

[1] *The Economist*, Commercial History and Review of 1919, p. 426.
[2] H. W. Macrosty, *Journal of the Royal Statistical Society*, 1927, pp. 71-2.

Unemployment in this industry was exceptionally heavy, averaging almost 30 per cent from 1924 to 1929. Far fewer men were involved, fortunately, than in coal and cotton, but the trouble was severe in the shipbuilding districts. Perhaps partly because of this, partly because severe employment fluctuations were nothing new in the shipyards, few men left the industry in the 'twenties.

But when we mention shipbuilding, there is a new element to bargain with: technological change. This was negligible in coal and cotton, and it was not important in primary steel production except in the field of fuel economy. But in shipbuilding there were numerous innovations in these years—changes in hull design, high pressure steam engines, geared turbines—while as early as 1920 it was said that 'the foreshadowed oil "boom" is . . . an accomplished fact'.[1] All these changes combined to make ship production still profitable even in the years when there was a glut of ships; and although Britain's share in world production fell markedly, Britain retained a large measure of technical leadership.

Technical change was particularly prominent in two important industries which, significantly, fared much better than most in the 1920s: the motor car industry and the electrical industry. The first British-designed car, a Lanchester, had appeared in 1895, and the first British company to produce cars, the Daimler Company, had been founded in 1896. By 1913, however, the total output of the industry was only 34,000 cars (Ford alone in that year made 199,000 Model T cars) and imports exceeded exports. Protected by the McKenna duties from 1915 onwards, the industry made a slow and awkward transition from wartime to peacetime production, and the slump of 1921 affected it very badly. Even after its recovery, by the mid-1920s, it remained to some extent what it had originally largely been, a scene for small-scale, specialist, sometimes rather amateur effort. Eighty-one makes of British cars in production in 1920 were no longer made in 1928. Yet production more than trebled in the course of the 1920s, exports exceeded imports for the first time in 1929, and the industry (including those engaged in cycle and aircraft manufacture) increased its labour force from 223,000 in

[1] *The Economist*, Commercial History and Review of 1919, p. 436.

1924 to 302,000 in 1930. Improvement of the product was continuous—better carburettors, more efficient combustion chambers, self-starters, windscreen wipers—and, just as important, the techniques of production were steadily improved so that costs fell and better cars were made cheaper. A twelve horsepower Austin in 1922 cost £450-£490; in 1928 the same car, but bigger, faster, more economical, more reliable, more comfortable and more refined, cost £325-£335. This was made possible by better engineering, larger outputs and flow production. Yet in 1929 the output of private cars in Britain was only 182,000, and the *Economist* could still complain.

'The idea of personal ownership as a luxury must be abandoned if the full benefits of motor transport development are to be reaped in this country.'[1]

Morris was leading the way in mass production, a deliberate attempt to match the achievements of Ford; but even making about one third of British output in the later 1920s, Morris Motors Ltd. still had a production of barely 60,000 cars per annum.

This scale of production, like the rate of growth, was far slower than in the United States. But the contribution which the car industry made to economic development was very substantial. The industry demanded not only such things as high speed machine tools, ferrous alloys, glass, magnetos and rubber tyres, but also roads and petrol. No very reliable computation can be made of the amounts spent on roads, bypasses and bridges in the 'twenties, but certainly a lot was done; the Watford bypass, the Edinburgh-Glasgow motor road, and the two great bridges on A.1 over the Tyne at Newcastle and the Tweed at Berwick were all built at that time. Oil—'this most speculative of industries'[2]—was a big new field of investment, with world consumption increasing, it was estimated, by about 10 per cent per annum. Petroleum refining employed fewer than 6,000 people in 1930, but the capital investment was very heavy and net output per head—£1,016—was higher in this industry than in any other in Britain.[3]

[1] *The Economist*, Commercial History and Review of 1928, p. 62.
[2] ibid.
[3] Jute came at the bottom of the list with a net output per head of £92.

The electrical industry was likewise a field of innovation and development. There were not only novelties like radio and complex equipment for cars, cycles and aircraft, there was also the development of the basic fields of electrification—generation, transmission and domestic and commercial utilization. The heavy section of the industry, producing generators, motors, switch and control gear, converters and transformers, grew at a moderate pace in the 'twenties, exporting nearly a quarter of its output. The light section, making wires, cables, batteries, telephones and a miscellany of other items intermediate between producer goods and consumer goods, grew somewhat faster but exported less, and the percentage of its output which was exported tended to fall through the decade. At the same time imports of this type of equipment rose. Thus Britain's competitive position was apparently stronger in the heavy 'producer goods' section of the industry, weaker in the light section. The overall rate of growth, however, was very encouraging: there were 157,000 people in electrical engineering in 1924, 192,000 in 1930.

The use in Great Britain of electricity in the 1920s, however, was conspicuously less than in many other countries. Per capita consumption in 1925 was two-thirds of the German figure, less than two-fifths of the American. It would not necessarily have been economical for Britain to consume as much electricity per head as these other countries. But it was notorious, even before 1917, that the organization of electrical generation and supply was antiquated, parochial and costly. Ill-devised legislation encouraged small-scale production and high operating costs, and restricted effective competition. Official 'encouragement' after the war to amalgamate too small concerns was totally ineffective.[1] In 1926 there was at last passed the Electricity (Supply) Act, setting up the Central Electricity Board to own and operate a national transmission system known as the grid.

'The Act of 1926 is a landmark in the history of electrical supply. After over twenty-five years of technical advance cramped by parochial legislation and local self-sufficiency, the importance of national electrical development was at last ap-

[1] A 'permissive' Act was passed in 1919. It made no difference.

preciated, and steps were taken to bring the organization into line with technical needs . . .'[1]

Compulsion was at a minimum, and some weaknesses remained due to reluctance to do any harm to vested interests. The original grid, virtually complete by 1933, cost £27m. The full impact of this legislation and expenditure could not be felt until after 1930, but there was some effect almost at once in reducing the absurd variety of voltages and frequencies which stood in the way of any attempt by manufacturers of electrical equipment to reduce their costs through standardization of output.

No other new industry provided as much additional employment in the course of the 1920s as did these two, automobiles cycles and aircraft, and electrical products and supply. There were many other novelties, and investors found great difficulty in deciding which horses to back; greyhound racing and film issues were fancied, gramophone shares were rocketing in 1927, and, to help solve the problem, there was a boom in investment trusts in the later 1920s. One of the newcomers, rayon, did well, and the labour force increased by fifty per cent, or 20,000, between 1924 and 1930. Gambling in the shares of British Celanese was conspicuous in 1927-28. The industry developed the home market with success, but its export position deteriorated rapidly as other countries, especially Japan, overtook its early lead. It is not to new industries, however, but to one of the very oldest, that we must look for the last great source of expansion in the 1920s; the building industry.

The number of men employed in the building industry at any particular time is to an unusual extent a matter of definition, but on any reasonable definition the number increased by at least 60,000 between 1924 and 1930. The closely related furniture industry expanded by 35,000, or 38 per cent, in the same period. There was a boom in building, almost uninterrupted from 1924 to 1939. This was not all housebuilding, for there was a lot of industrial construction going on in the years 1924-29 and 1932-37. But the building of dwelling houses was continuous. Over 1½m. new houses were built in the 1920s, of which about 1m. were built with some form of State subsidy. The number of families

[1] H. H. Ballin, *The Organization of Electrical Supply in Great Britain* (London, Electrical Press, 1946), p. 221.

was increasing, and standards were rising. Moreover, the rise of the new industries, mainly in the midlands and the south of England, along with the spread of homes and factories into the outskirts of the towns, made possible by petrol-driven road transport, created an unusually strong and buoyant demand for houseroom. Innumerable trades benefited; the manufacturers of paint, glass, carpets, window frames, concrete, the suppliers of stone, tiles and lead pipes, as well, of course, as the electrical industry itself and the makers of cars, lorries and motor buses. The building industry, indeed, was like a flywheel with a momentum which turned many smaller wheels in the economy. In the 1930s this flywheel was to spin still faster, and, in more favourable conditions, to help the population to realize the advantages of the investment undertaken and the technical progress achieved in the laborious 1920s.

EXPORTS, FOREIGN INVESTMENT AND THE
BALANCE OF PAYMENTS

Between 1920 and 1929 international economic relations passed through a period of intense, possibly unprecedented peacetime dislocation and disorder. This disorder, which profoundly affected Great Britain as a great trading nation, was the aftermath of war, and it can conveniently be analysed under three headings: tariffs; war debts and reparations; and price and exchange fluctuations and uncertainties. Of these three the last two are, of course, not completely separable.

The Treaty of Versailles created new nations, and these new nations, along with many old ones, created during the 1920s a more complex system of higher tariffs than had ever been seen before. There were two reasons for this development. First, there was the nationalistic ambition to promote industrial development for home markets, a development wanted largely for its own sake, although the non-availability of imports during the war had been a rational stimulus to this kind of policy. Secondly, there were strategic considerations which encouraged the building up of certain industries which it was plausible to suppose might be important in any future war. Thus there was widespread industrial growth in Australia, Brazil, Chile, India,

Japan and many other countries, much of which was begun during the war.

'The number of cotton spindles in Japan, China, India and Brazil in 1913 was about 10m.; by 1924 the number had risen to nearly 18m. Between 1913 and 1922 the number of cotton power looms in India and Japan rose from 120,000 to 200,000. The annual production of steel just before the war in Japan, China, India and Australia was 360,000 tons. In 1922 it was 858,000 tons.'[1]

These efforts were all protected by tariffs. The United States tariff was raised very high in 1922. Empire tariffs rose faster than foreign tariffs, although this still left the former lower than the latter. France became a specialist in the subtleties of protection by import duty; 'Take the French tariff and treaty system. It is a pure intellectual pleasure to watch them manipulate it. It is an extremely fine art.'[2] Even Great Britain was protecting some industries after 1915.

War debts and reparations presented a more serious obstacle to international trade. German reparations were fixed in 1921 at between £9,000m. and £10,000m., that is to say, more than four times the amount which British and American experts at Paris had thought that it might be feasible to collect.[3] This bill was to be met in thirty years. Up to the end of 1922 Germany had paid something like £250m. in reparations, but these payments were offset by sales of marks and of internal assets. After the currency collapse,[4] the Dawes Plan arranged for annual payments rising to £125m. per annum in 1928-29. These payments were punctually made, but Germany's creditors continued to have difficulty in realizing the benefit in tangible forms, while payment was an embarrassment to the German economy.

[1] F. C. Hirst, *The Consequences of the War to Great Britain* (Oxford University Press, 1934), p. 267.

[2] Sir Roland Nugent and Mr R. G. Glenday, *Evidence before the Committee on Finance and Industry* (1931), vol. I, p. 204.

[3] The story is told that it was Lord Cunliffe, then Governor of the Bank of England, who in 1919 had given Lloyd George the figure for German reparations. A prominent banker, 'staggered and sceptical, had asked Lord Cunliffe how he had arrived at such a total. "It came to me in church", was the Governor's reply.' Sir Lawrence Jones, *Georgian Afternoon*, p. 114.

[4] See below, pp. 52-53.

On the other hand, supplies of foreign currency were made available to Germany under the terms of the Dawes Plan, which also 'performed the indispensable task of limiting the pressure on the exchange market caused by the Government's liability to make reparation payments'.[1] The Young Plan of 1929 scaled the annual payments down to about £100m., and envisaged their ultimate termination in 1987-8. This scheme ceased to operate in 1931.

Meanwhile, other countries were trying to pay, or were supposed to be trying to pay their war debts. Great Britain, who was owed about twice as much as she herself owed the United States, wanted to collect only as much as she had to pay. This idea did not appeal to France. The United States insisted that her large war-time loans were commercial transactions, and demanded payment. She relented sufficiently, however, to adjust the debt to some extent to the debtor's capacity to pay. The result was that Britain contracted to pay rather more than four-fifths of what she owed America, France a little less than half and Italy just over a quarter. Everyone collected something from Germany. When the comedy was brought to an end in 1931, Britain had paid out £134m. more than she had received, but all the others had received more than they had paid, sometimes much more. (France benefited to the tune of £163m.) And the United States received back, all told, about £451m. of what she had lent.

These huge international payments inevitably distorted trading relations, and they disrupted the exchanges. The first currency to collapse was the Austrian mark, largely as a result of chronic trading difficulties and internal monetary mismanagement. This was in the summer of 1922. In the course of that same year Germany's efforts to make reparations payments, coupled with the internal monetary policy which she chose to pursue, caused the German mark to decline from 60 to the dollar to 9,000 to the dollar. Quarrels over reparations induced France and Belgium to occupy the Ruhr in January, 1923; and by the end of that month the mark was down to 49,000 to the dollar. During the spring and early summer of 1923 the printing presses in Germany really got going, and by the end of July

[1] D. H. Robertson, *Money*, Cam. Econ. Hndbks. (London, Nisbet, 1948), p.126.

over 1,000,000 marks were needed to purchase one dollar. A new currency was required, and the rentenmark appeared, with the exchanges now pegged at 4,200,000 marks to the dollar. The Dawes Plan helped to stabilize the situation in 1924, Austria having meanwhile been put on its feet via the Austrian Reconstruction Loan, largely subscribed in London. In 1923 Austria was 'the one shining proof as yet of the value of concerted European action',[1] but with the help of the League of Nations and more international loans both Hungary and Greece were later given similar necessary assistance. Stabilization, indeed, was building up from 1924 after the chaos of the immediate post-war years. Britain went back to gold in 1925, Belgium in 1926 and France and Italy in 1927. Except for the pound, all these currencies had a new dollar value, and further adjustments of internal prices and international trade were inevitable in every case.

The transition from war to peace thus took a great deal longer than most people anticipated. The post-war world contained only a little less conflict and uncertainty than had existed during the years 1914-18.

'In some countries the spirit of revolution was abroad, while in others the curious belief prevailed that the vast damage wrought by the war would somehow make it easier to maintain a higher standard of life than had ever existed in the past: so threats had to be bought off, and illusions fostered. For a time too it almost seemed as though half mankind sat in offices, drawing salaries at the public expense for spying on the other half, who were part idling and part unemployed. Further, the French had to pay for the wanton damage done by the Germans in time of war, and the Germans a few years later had to pay for the wanton damage done by the French in time of peace. The Russians had to fight the other Russians with one hand, and to inaugurate the millennium with the other. The British had to restore order in Ireland, and the Poles to create chaos in Eastern Europe—two processes whose features were less dissimilar than might be supposed. Everybody was in debt to everybody else: and above all everybody had run up an immense account with the great Sir

[1] *The Economist*, Commercial History and Review of 1923, p. 302.

Galahad of the West, whose bill did not seem to be any smaller because his heart was pure.'[1]

·This was the world in which Great Britain had to find export markets, or collapse.

It was only to be expected that the British balance of payments would be unsatisfactory in the immediate post-war years. Factory reconversion took some time, many European countries were too poor to buy much, there was currency instability and political instability, there were raw material shortages and strikes. By 1923, however, it was beyond doubt that Britain had worked back to a position in which she enjoyed a favourable trade balance, and she continued to do so in every year from 1924 to 1930 with the sole exception of 1926, when the coal strike cut exports severely. This favourable balance, which was available for foreign investment, was however much smaller than the surplus which Britain had generated just before the war. The best three years of the 1920s, 1927-29, averaged a surplus of £103m.; this compared very unfavourably with the £208m. averaged in 1911-13, and unfavourably even with the £145m. averaged in the quinquennium 1906-10. But the fact remains that there was a surplus.

Was this surplus sufficient, or did it at least appear to be sufficient at the time? The fact that it was much smaller than before the war, while the 'visible' deficit was much larger, naturally gave rise to some misgiving. But what caused most concern at the time was not so much the modest size of the surplus as the inability of the main export industries to find enough orders to enable them to work at anything like full capacity. British exports of coal, cotton and wool all made a worse showing in 1925 than in 1913, and a worse showing in 1929 than in 1925. Some trades, notably vehicles, chemicals and electrical equipment increased their exports. But these increases were an inadequate compensation for declines in other directions in each of three senses: (1) they did not enable the unemployed in the old lines to find employment elsewhere; (2) they did not reduce the deficit on visible trade; (3) they did not prevent Britain's share in world trade from declining—in 1929 the value of world

[1] D. H. Robertson, *Money*, pp. 109-10.

exports was 7·6 per cent higher and of United States exports 7 per cent higher than in 1925, but the value of British exports was lower by almost 10 per cent. To say that this situation is explained by Britain's deteriorating competitive position is merely tautological. A better explanation, also popular, is that British prices were too high. But this does not get us very far. Were they too high because of overvaluation of the pound, technical inferiority in industry or undue cost rigidities? No doubt each of these played a part. But what mattered more than any of them was that Britain was organized to make things in which her comparative advantage was of the past rather than those things in making which she could excel in the future.

The declining value of Britain's exports from 1924–29 has to be set against a rather more slowly declining value for her imports. Thus the deficit on visible trade increased, a little. But, due to differential price changes, the *volume* of Britain's exports fell quite considerably, while the *volume* of her imports rose to a similar extent. In other words, the barter terms of trade, as compared with 1913, moved strongly in Great Britain's favour. A given volume of exports now bought more imports. Britain used this advantage chiefly to purchase more food—food prices abroad had fallen particularly far—and more semi-manufactures and manufactured consumer goods. The decline of the staples reduced the need to import old-style raw materials. Britain could, of course, have held down the level of her imports and used her new terms-of-trade advantage to purchase more foreign securities, i.e. to increase her rate of investment abroad; but the proportion of the British national income which was saved in the 1920s seems to have been smaller than before the war, and this naturally made it less likely that the terms-of-trade advantage would be used in this way.

Obtaining more while giving less, Britain inevitably found some of her productive resources set free for other tasks. There was thus, in a sense, a great opportunity to raise the national income still further than the changes in the terms of trade and the increased productiveness in certain industries were raising it already. The tragedy was that the country was unable to use these liberated agents of production. Men stood unemployed, the coal they were ready to raise and the cotton cloth they were ready to produce unwanted either at home or abroad. Price reductions would not have helped sales much, and in the long run would merely have kept employees in industries doomed ultimately to decline. The capital equipment involved had to be written off, sooner or later. If more investible funds had been available, the process of making new kinds of capital equipment which would have given profitable employment in expanding lines of production would have been easier. But the economic difficulties made investible funds scarce, while monetary policy and banking policy did little to help, the former designed to suit international requirements and the gold standard, the latter too often tied up with the old industries and timid of the new.

Britain's ability to import did not depend solely, of course, upon her ability to export goods. There was, first, income from services, chiefly shipping and financial services. The shipping trade was severely competitive after the war, and British shippers had to compete with the susidized lines of some other countries. Net earnings from this source, although less relatively to national income than before the war, were nevertheless substantial in the 1920s. Financial and other services brought in a smaller revenue than shipping, and, unlike shipping, a smaller absolute amount than before the war. Secondly, there was the net income from overseas investment. Before the war this had been running at between £150m. and £200m. per year. But something between £850m. and £1,000m. of foreign investments—between a fifth and a quarter of the total—were lost as a result of the war, partly through sales and partly through the default of belligerents. For this and other reasons the income from foreign investments was rather disappointing in the early 1920s, and although by 1925 it had reached about £250m. this figure was never subsequently improved upon.

The net outcome of all these changes in visible trade and invisible earnings was, as we have seen, that instead of £200m. being available for overseas investment, as had been the case before the war, there was only an amount which fluctuated (after 1923) from £46m. to £123m., and averaged, for the good years 1927-29, just over £100m. On the other hand, the demand for investible funds to use abroad was very considerable. Pressing upon a limited supply of savings of this kind—in conjunction with a balance of payments position which, although favourable, was in any event not very strong—this drove up British interest rates in the 1920s, and non-Empire borrowers frequently found it cheaper to borrow in New York. Nevertheless, new overseas issues in the London capital market from 1921 to 1930 inclusive averaged £125m. per annum. Allowing for repayment of debt and foreign participation in the new loans, this probably represented a net movement of capital overseas of from £80m. to £90m. per annum. Money was found for loans to Austria, Hungary, Germany, Greece, Danzig, Belgium, Bulgaria and Poland. Governments and public bodies in the Empire obtained a great deal of capital. There were also large investments connected with the commodity markets. Rubber production secured a lot of money—far too much, £13·9m. in the single year 1925. In 1926 there were large borrowings by Brazilian coffee interests through the issue of bonds. And investment in oil production all over the world was continuous throughout the decade.

Britain thus made a considerable contribution—even if some of her efforts were misdirected—to the reconstruction of Europe and the further development of more distant territories. What was done was insufficient to increase the balance of interest and dividends due to Great Britain largely because primary producing regions overseas, where much British capital was already invested, were suffering from the effects of overproduction and falling prices, their situation often made worse by the failure of ill-conceived schemes to restrict output and maintain prices. The best known of these schemes was the Stevenson rubber restriction scheme, which lasted with British Government backing from 1922 to 1928; but similar efforts were made in respect of copper, tin, zinc, coffee, diamonds, tea and other commodities, with unfortunate results in almost every instance. The attempt to operate such schemes and their ultimate collapse added to trade uncertainty and dislocation. And whatever made trade more difficult and overseas territories like Australia and Malaya and Rhodesia less able to purchase British goods and embark on schemes of capital development made it more difficult for Great Britain to gain the elbow room needed to effect the necessary transformation of her economic structure.

THE EXTENSION OF GOVERNMENT ACTIVITY

It sometimes seems to be thought that positive economic legislation, like socialist government, is an invention of the years after 1914. The nineteenth century is depicted as an era of laisser faire, and laisser faire is interpreted as meaning uncontrolled and unlimited private enterprise. There is some truth in this view, but not much. The first worthwhile Factory Act was passed in 1833; the last of a series of important Bank Charter Acts in 1844; the first general Coal Mines Act in 1850. All this legislation was amplified, extended or made more effective in the second half of the nineteenth century. There were dozens of Acts. In the twentieth century a new phase of legislative activity began, bringing Old Age Pensions in 1908, Labour Exchanges in 1909 and National Insurance against Sickness and Unemployment in 1911. All these later measures required financial help from the Government, and the money was obtained, for these and other purposes, by progressive taxation of a kind until then unknown in this country.

Four years of war radically altered the country's economic organization. In all important respects the economy came to be controlled by decisions taken by the Government or in its name. By 1918 there was a Railway Executive; the Ministry of Shipping; and the Canal Control Committee. This provided complete control of transport. The Ministries of Food and Agriculture determined the utilization of land, fixed prices, bought and sold agricultural produce. Coal mining was under a Coal Controller, who virtually ran the industry. Iron and Steel was under the Ministry of Munitions, which superintended about 2m. employees in the industry, and itself owned about 285 factories. The State conducted about 90 per cent of the country's import trade, by value. Even more remarkable were the international controlling agencies: the Wheat Executive, the International Sugar Committee and, most important of all, the Allied Maritime Transport Council, chief organ of allied economic co-operation. This whole system was at its zenith in the autumn of 1918; by mid-1921 it had vanished, and almost its only working legacy was the Railways Act of 1921, which amalgamated the railways of the country into four large groups. The general attitude was expressed by the *Economist* in 1918 when it remarked that the nation should cease to 'pay people for putting difficulties in the way of private enterprise'.[1]

By 1921, therefore, the much spoken-of nationalization of coal and the railways having been by then rejected, the Government was pretty well back where it had been in 1913 in its relation to the economic order. There were some changes. The Gold and Silver (Export Control Etc.) Act of 1921 put an embargo on free movements of bullion and kept Britain 'off gold'. Taxation was much higher than it had been before the war, especially direct taxation. The income tax, which had stood at 1s 2d in 1913-14, was 6s 0d in 1920-21. Import duties were also higher. Temporary duties imposed during the war in order to conserve foreign exchange and save shipping space were continued afterwards, and added to by the Safeguarding of Industries Act of 1921. This was supposed to protect industries vital to the national interest; these included motor cars, clocks, watches, films, optical instruments, glass, wireless valves and magnetos. Empire products received preferential treatment. In 1923 the Conservative Party fought the General Election on the issue of solving unemployment by protection, and was defeated. There was a fleeting remission of the duties in 1924, but in 1925 they were reimposed and extended. In that year gloves, cutlery and gas mantles received protection, and the list was further lengthened in 1927 and 1928. The total volume of protection was, by any standard, small, but the tariff system was becoming increasingly protective and decreasingly revenue-producing in character, and industries like the car industry and artificial silk were not unappreciative of the benefits they were receiving.

Another sphere in which pre-war Government activity was extended was in the provision of unemployment benefits. The National Insurance Act of 1911 had covered only those in engineering, building and shipbuilding. During the war munitions workers were included, and after it, in 1920, the scheme was greatly enlarged so as to include almost all workers earning less than £250 a year except domestic servants and agricultural labourers; over 11m. workpeople in all. Benefits could be drawn for only fifteen weeks in any one year, and contributions by

---

[1] *The Economist*, December 5, 1918, p. 243.

employers and employed were supposed to give the scheme a self-financing insurance character. Unfortunately, heavy unemployment from the start first threatened and then wrecked the scheme's solvency. A series of Acts was passed in 1921 and 1922 which extended the period during which benefits could be drawn, altered the rates of benefit, added dependants' benefit, and increased the contributions. The net result was that the unemployed were enabled to draw benefits greater than the contributions would support, the gratuitous or 'uncovenanted' benefit ('the dole') being financed by borrowing from the Treasury. It was also laid down, for the first time, that payment was to be made only to those 'genuinely seeking work'. This legislation, consolidated in the Unemployment Insurance Act of 1922, was the basis of all action in this field throughout the 1920s. Benefits were altered from time to time, but the only important further change was the making of uncovenanted benefit a matter of statutory right. Similar although less remarkable developments took place as regards national health insurance and widows' and old age contributory pensions.

Other kinds of action taken by the Government had little if any precedent before the war. There was, for example, the British Sugar (Subsidy) Act of 1925, guaranteeing diminishing but generous subsidies for ten years to the infant and sickly beet sugar industry. This was supposed to create employment and help agriculture. There were also some experimental subsidies in the early 1920s going to airlines. The first daily London to Paris service had begun in 1919, and by 1924 there were four subsidized services to the Continent; but they were struggling in the face of subsidized foreign competition. In 1924 Imperial Airways Ltd. was formed, with Government approval, to absorb the four companies and was subsidized. It was still being subsidized ten years later, although probably less than most of its competitors, and as early as 1929 had to its credit a regular service from Croydon to Karachi. The aircraft industry, among others, also benefited from the work done or organized by the Department of Scientific and Industrial Research, created by the Government in 1915 and kept going with Government money. Help in founding Industrial Research Associations was given to several industries, including engineering, glass making and food manufacture, while the Department 'itself undertook certain research work which was considered of national importance . . . Under this heading came the direct work of the Department's research stations, in fuel utilization, food storage, fundamental physical problems and building materials and methods.'[1] There was also help for exporters, given through the working of the Export Credits Guarantee Department set up in 1928. The Department gave credit to exporters, usually for periods of less than a year, enabling them to offer longer credit terms to customers abroad than their own resources would have permitted. Other countries operated similar schemes. Another kind of Government action which was new was of a negative sort; the intermittent discouragements to, and embargoes on, foreign investment.

Had Government action been limited to the measures so far described, the situation would not have been remarkably altered from before the war. What was new or almost new in principle —subsidization, for example—was not done—not yet—on a large scale; where old activities were extended they were not extended—yet—out of recognition. But the 1920s also saw the introduction of other Government measures, measures which involved the acceptance of novel and important principles affecting the Government's rôle in economic affairs, and some of which were of first class importance, in practice, at the time.

The least important, in its immediate effects, was the Coal Mines Act of 1930. This was the Labour Government's attempt to do something for the coal industry and the miners. The Act was divided into two parts, each path-breaking in character. Part One introduced district production quotas, set by the owners, to be divided among the collieries by district boards, which were also to fix minimum district prices. This amounted to a Government-sponsored cartel for the elimination of competition, the justification being that it would enable owners to maintain wages when hours were reduced from eight to seven and a half, as provided for in the Act. Part Two set up a Coal Mines Reorganization Commission which was to prepare and promote schemes of amalgamation, the idea being that the

[1] R. S. Sayers, 'The Springs of Technical Progress in Britain, 1919-39,' in *Economic Journal*, June 1950, p. 280.

creation of larger units of production would eliminate high-cost production and even, perhaps, ultimately make the cartel arrangements unnecessary. The coal-owners, those rugged individualists and high priests of private enterprise, accepted the arrangements to eliminate competition with alacrity, but fought the Reorganization Commission from the start and condemned it to futility. Not much was achieved. The restrictionism of the 1930s was foreshadowed. But what mattered most was that a British Government had given authority to an industry to arrange about output and prices, and was trying to take a hand in changing its internal structure.

Secondly, the Government increased its participation in economic affairs by making greatly extended use of the device of the public corporation. Public corporations were far from new in the 1920s. The Post Office was a public corporation, and it dated back to the reign of Charles II; a notable example created not long before the war, and eminently successful, was the Port of London Harbour Authority. But these were almost the only ones existing at the end of the war. The next ten years saw the appearance of several more. One of the most important of these has already been mentioned; the Central Electricity Board, set up by an Act of 1926 to undertake and develop the wholesale transmission of electricity. The Board consisted of seven expert members appointed by the Minister of Transport. It was soon spending very large sums of money in the vital tasks of reducing the costs and increasing the supply of electricity both to domestic consumers and to industry. The Central Electricity Board was objected to both by vested interests and by those who believed that the supplying of goods and services should be left in private hands; but it was in a position to play and it did play an important and constructive part in the modernization of British industry. There was, on the other hand, very little objection to the establishment, in the same year, of the British Broadcasting Corporation. This public corporation, governed by a Board of five persons nominated by the Prime Minister, took over from the British Broadcasting Company which had operated since 1922. It was, of course, a monopoly. Its economic significance was small but its social importance was very great, and its success further weakened the case in principle against Government-sponsored bodies ultimately if indirectly responsible to Parliament.

Thirdly, the Government began to make itself responsible, in a way and to a degree quite without precedent, for the provision of new houses. Victorian Britain had relied on private enterprise to build houses, which had often meant, in practice, reliance on the speculative builder. House building was neither subsidized nor controlled. The war changed all that. By an Act of 1919, passed almost casually, arousing neither opposition nor enthusiasm, the Government began the policy of prodding local authorities and of subsidizing either them or the actual builders of houses.

This legislation was not controversial at the time, largely because of the acknowledged importance and magnitude of the problem. House building and most house maintenance had been at a stand during the war; it was estimated in 1919 that at least 800,000 new houses were 'needed'; and there had been talk of 'homes fit for heroes to live in'. Even those who resisted all kinds of 'socialism', 'collectivism' or 'control' in respect of industry did not find it difficult to acquiesce in the subsidization of house building. It could and can be regarded as a policy of subsidy in aid of wages; but in 1919 'the immediate need for action . . . swept aside all discussion of principle',[1] while the sense of common citizenship which the war had fostered greatly weakened the customary acceptance of wide income differences and the old fondness for encouraging people to 'stand on their own feet'.

There was a series of Acts from 1919 onwards designed to encourage house building. There were two Acts in 1919, and one in 1923 and another in 1924. The first of these Acts guaranteed local authorities against loss on approved municipal schemes. This proved expensive, partly because building costs rose so high during the boom. The 1923 'Chamberlain Act' provided a subsidy of £6 a year for twenty years for suitable houses; this was raised to £9 a year for forty years under the 1924 'Wheatley Act'. This Act was much the most effective in causing houses to be built; under its provision over ½m. houses

[1] C. L. Mowat, *Britain between the Wars 1918-1940* (London, Methuen, 1955), p. 43.

were built before the scheme came to an end in 1933. In all, over 1½m. houses were built in Britain between 1919 and 1930. This was a gross addition of about 20 per cent to the country's stock of houses—a very large building operation in a short space of time. About a third of these houses were built by local authorities with State assistance, about a third by private enterprise with State assistance, and about a third by private enterprise without State assistance. The houses were needed chiefly to keep up with the internal movement of the population and to raise standards. The Housing Acts were needed partly because of the continuation, by an Act of 1920, of the control of rents of working-class houses begun in 1915. As long as rents were controlled, the incentive to build was diminished. An attempt at decontrol by the Conservatives in 1923 was abortive, and rent control remained to work its full and sometimes baneful effects right through to the 1950s.

From this legislation many important consequences flowed. The Acts themselves

'carried the Government into the business of housing . . . The building of houses with the aid of Government subsidies was one of the largest enterprises—certainly the largest collective enterprise—of the years between the wars. It meant that the new Ministry of Health was in large part a Ministry of Housing, and as such one of the most important departments of State. It helped to cover the outskirts of towns with municipal housing estates and to embellish the villages with the ubiquitous "council houses" of the inter-war years. . . .'[1]

Also, the volume of investment in house building, providing employment and stimulating investment in related trades such as furniture making, carpet manufacture and many others, was an important factor in sustaining the national income; while better living conditions at controlled rents brought, to some people at least, an improvement in their living standards which figures of wages and prices do not adequately reflect.

WAGES, TRADE UNIONS AND INDUSTRIAL RELATIONS

There are two strands in the development of trade unions and

[1] C. L. Mowat, op. cit., p. 45.

industrial relations in the 1920s, just as there were in the 1830s. Then, there was Owen and the Grand National on the one hand, the gradual and far less noticeable development of craft unions on the other; in the 1920s, likewise, there was on the one hand the ILP and the General Strike, on the other the growth of industrial and general labour unions and of the authority of the TUC and the General Council of the TUC. No doubt the comparison is an imperfect one: in particular, there was no separation of the TUC and the big unions from the General Strike as there was of many skilled unions from the Grand National. It remains true, however, that the development of trade unions in the 1920s is not to be understood simply by reference to the General Strike. That the General Strike was the most conspicuous event of the 1920s in the whole field of industrial relations does not mean that it was also the most important influence, far less the most constructive influence. It is perhaps unfortunate that the British trade union movement should exhibit this recurrent weakness for episodes warlike and romantic but essentially futile. Organizations like the Grand National and events like the General Strike no doubt originate at least in part in the influence within trade unionism of the fighting, romantic Celt; it is not without significance that the conference of trade union executives who were negotiating before the General Strike began whiled away 'the long hours of waiting'—so we are told —'with singing: Welsh and Scottish songs . . . and inevitably, "Lead, Kindly Light".'[1] A fondness among historians for dwelling on such exciting events must not blind us to the importance of more sober practical achievements.

The background to labour problems in the 1920s is one of rising real incomes. From 1921 to 1929 the national income rose; income per head of population, at 1900 prices, was almost 25 per cent higher in 1929 than in 1921. The share of wages in the national income changed but little. Between 1924 and 1929 money wage rates and money earnings fell slightly but the cost of living fell considerably further; as a result, employees' average real income from wages, measured by 1924 prices, rose by about 10 per cent. If unemployment is allowed for, the rise in the standard of living of wage earners is of

[1] C. L. Mowat, op. cit., p. 303.

course less than this, but remains in the neighbourhood of 8 to 10 per cent.

If national income, income per head, real wages and wage earners' incomes allowing for unemployment were all rising, why were labour relations so disturbed in this decade? Waiving the question whether rising living standards should be expected to eliminate labour troubles, there are three points to be made which limit the significance, in this connection, of rising real incomes:

(1) Although real incomes were rising throughout the 1920s, they began their ascent in 1921 from a level lower than that which had obtained in 1913. Indeed, the average of the years 1912-14 was not surpassed by three consecutive years until 1924-26, and it was only in 1927 that a conspicuous improvement on the immediately pre-war years was recorded. Thus living standards, although rising, were no better or very very little better than pre-war living standards until towards the end of the 1920s.

(2) The course of money wages was exceedingly irregular down to 1923. Wage increases 'without parallel'[1] in 1920 were followed by 'drastic reductions'[2] in 1921. If the level of money earnings is taken as one hundred in 1913, the level was 244 in 1920 and 147 in 1922. Thus about two thirds of the wartime and post-war increase in money earnings had disappeared by the end of 1922. These changes were of course connected with changes in a similar sense in wholesale and retail prices. In 1923 prices and wages both steadied, but after the restoration of the gold standard in 1925 a fresh price fall began. Thus the wage earner experienced demoralizingly rapid changes in money income before 1923, and his increase in real income in the later 1920s came about through lower prices and not, as would probably have been more popular, through higher money wages.

(3) Real wages in some trades fell considerably, and men in these trades therefore became much worse off relatively to

---

[1] *The Economist*, Commercial History and Review of 1920, p. 352.
[2] ibid., Commercial History and Review of 1921, p. 289.

others than they had previously been. There were big losses in a few trades. Coal, once again, is the outstanding example. Male earnings in industry as a whole fell between 1924 and 1931 by about two shillings a week; in coal they fell by nearly eight shillings. In the numerically important industries of textiles and engineering and metal using in general the fall was about three shillings. In some less prominent industries wages actually rose; in paper and printing, for example, and in the manufacture of coke and cement. They also rose in local government. As a result of these changes, some occupations gained and others lost in financial status. The coal-miners were the aristocrats of the labour market, in terms of wages, in 1906; in 1924 they came almost at the bottom of the scale, only textiles, general engineering and local government standing lower. By 1931 this revolution in status had been completed; they who had come first came last. The trades which ranked highest in 1931 had been fourth, fifth and sixth, in a list of ten, in 1906. The large, well-organized industries were the sufferers. In them, real wages in many cases fell, and the high standing of the occupation disappeared. Employees in these industries—even those who were lucky enough to be employed—had not one grievance but two.[1]

Wage earners were on the whole better organized to fight money wage reductions in the 1920s than they had been before the war. It is true that by 1914 'well-developed methods for negotiation and the settlement of disputes had been established in many of the chief industries, including coal mining, iron and steel, engineering, cotton, and boot and shoe making',[2] and that trade boards had been set up in several industries where wages were judged to be unduly low. But in several important trades 'conflict over trade union recognition was still raging and no effective joint machinery was in operation'.[3] There were already, before 1914, signs of strain in the coal industry, and on the

[1] The statements in this paragraph are largely based on Table XI, p. 51, of A. L. Bowley's *Wages and Income in the United Kingdom since 1860* (Cambridge University Press, 1937).

[2] J. H. Richardson, *Industrial Relations in Great Britain* (Geneva, 1938), p. 91.

[3] ibid., op. cit., p. 92.

railways, where the companies refused to negotiate with officials of the unions.

The war strengthened the trade unions' hand. Recognition of unions and organized collective bargaining became the rule, and there was a great increase of nation-wide negotiations and agreements. Total membership of unions, which had been 4·1m. in 1913, was 8·3m. in 1920. With the reconversion of industry, post-war difficulties, unemployment and a decline in the total labour force, union membership fell rather rapidly from this peak, but settled around 5·5m. from 1922 to 1925. After the General Strike it fell further, and from 1927 to 1931 stood around 4·8m. Strength of organization varied from trade to trade, but the big unions dominated the movement in a way unknown before the war. The National Union of Railwaymen had been formed in 1913. In 1920 there came the Amalgamated Engineering Union, in 1921 Ernest Bevin's Transport and General Workers' Union, and in 1924 the General Municipal Workers' Union. Nearly one half of all trade unionists at the end of the 1920s were in mining, textile work, the metal trades, and on the railways. It is notable that of these four trades the first two were depressed and the last two were, at best, marking time.

But the war not only made trade unionists more numerous and the country more accustomed to collective bargaining; it also greatly enhanced the status and extended the influence of the whole trade union movement. Trade union leaders had been frequently consulted by the Government during the war on many questions of economic and social importance. Partly as a result, the trade unions emerged from the war with a greatly increased claim to be consulted in future on economic matters and on questions of social policy; and the public was inclined to acknowledge the justice of this claim. The trade union movement further strengthened its position in the economic and political organization of the country by setting up, in 1920, the General Council of the TUC as a permanent executive committee representative of all affiliated unions and authorized to act and speak in the general interest of these unions; and by arranging closer and more effective co-operation with the Labour Party. With its enhanced status, more centralized organization and closer political affiliation it was only natural that the movement should begin to express a definite and recognizable point of view in national affairs. A concise statement was contained in the memorandum submitted on behalf of the trade union members to the joint committee of the National Industrial Conference in March 1919:

'The extent to which workers are challenging the whole system of industrial organization is very much greater today than ever before, and unrest proceeds not only from more immediate and special grievances but also, to an increasing extent, from a desire to substitute a democratic system of public ownership and production for use with an increasing element of control by the organized workers themselves for the existing capitalist organization of industry.'

This National Industrial Conference was summoned by the Minister of Labour in 1919 to review the whole subject of conditions of employment. It included representatives of the employers, the trade unions and the Government. Among its recommendations were the establishment of a forty-eight-hour week in industry as a whole; the establishment of minimum time rates; increased Government investment in housing and industry; contracyclical investment by Government; and larger-scale social services. It also recognized that employers' associations and trade unions were the proper organizations for industrial negotiation, and put forward a scheme for a National Industrial Council to advise the Government. Nothing came of this last. It was an idea based, no doubt, upon experience of the moderately successful Joint Industrial Councils sponsored by the Whitley Committee in 1917. These Councils, intended to facilitate regular consultation between employers and employees on virtually all questions of mutual interest, had done something to improve industrial relations during the war: but they disappointed the fairly large section of worker and intellectual left wing opinion which entertained at the end of the war lively if remarkably ill-formulated hopes of worker control; they suffered sometimes from apathy, sometimes from abuse by shop stewards trying to undermine the authority of management or, alternatively, from abuse by managers trying to by-pass the trade unions; and they inevitably lost ground in the ups and downs of trade and prices after the war.

Post war conditions were obviously such as to put a severe strain on industrial relations and on any method of negotiation. Undoubtedly far too much was hoped of the return to peace, and divergences of interest which could be and were ignored while the war was to be won reasserted their importance after 1918. The situation was made a good deal worse by the wider conflict which was then arising due to the growth of socialist opinion. In the General Election of 1922 more Labour than Liberal candidates were elected. The election sent to Westminster the 'Clydeside brigade', many of whom 'had earned their passport into politics as agitators among the Clyde workers during the war, and they had no intention of resting on their laurels'.[1] Attitudes to Bolshevik Russia, an inspiration to some and a terror to others, further divided opinion. The conduct of the Sankey Commission in 1919 (the men had 'successfully kept "private enterprise" on its trial before the Commission', G. D. H. Cole boasted afterwards; and clearly would have hanged it if they could) seemed to many employers to show that they had everything to fear and not much to hope from socialism.

Nevertheless, the course of industrial relations was smoother than might have been expected down to 1925. The coal industry gave trouble, of course, and there was a lock-out in the engineering industry in 1922. But after 1920 the number of disputes was not excessive. Relations were perhaps not very good, but the cautious and compromising policies of MacDonald, head of the Labour Party and Prime Minister in 1924, helped to preserve a moderate, progress-by-evolution, wait-and-see attitude. Baldwin, also, was a man of peace—not the last in Tory politics between the wars. Baldwin was humane, an individualist who did not believe in systems but who did believe in compromise and the vitality of compromise. Live and let live was his principle; and he was Prime Minister from the end of 1924 to 1929. Yet in this period there took place both the General Strike, which some felt at the time to be as serious as the war itself had been and, in the coal industry, one of the longest and most bitterly contested strikes in British history.

[1] C. L. Mowat, op. cit., p. 147.

The precise causes of the General Strike of 1926, that is to say what factional alliances and political schemes and personal conflicts and ambitions lay behind it, may never be fully known. But its general origins and character are clear enough. The trouble began as the fourth wages dispute in the coal industry since 1918. The history of these disputes has already been outlined.[1] The industry was deficient in enterprise and grossly overmanned. It had to reorganize and contract. It had become, unfortunately, a battlefield for conflicting politico-economic ideologies, and each abortive struggle made constructive proposals less easy to come by and harder to accept.

The trouble in 1925-26 was that the coal-owners proposed to preserve—or rather to recreate—profitable operation by reducing wages. The miners and their leaders rejected the idea of wage reductions and manoeuvred for some form of nationalization, i.e. dispossession of the owners. In these circumstances compromise proposals, of the kind made by the Samuel Report and accepted by Baldwin, were bound to be anathema to both sides. No reasonable proposal could be formulated which did not involve some wage reductions and some measure of compulsory reorganization. But the men rejected wage reductions and the owners refused compulsory reorganization. Thus the acceptance of any reasonable proposal meant defeat to both parties. After six years of fiddling with the problem there remained only a choice between very strong measures and disaster. Whether even very strong measures—Government control in at least some areas and specific proposals about wages and redundancy—could have prevented a strike must be doubtful; in any case, very strong measures of a constructive kind were never in prospect.

The coal strike became a national or general strike in realization of the plans originally proposed by the Triple Alliance. This was an agreement of pre-war origin between miners, railwaymen and transport workers for mutual support, including the possibility of sympathetic strikes. The agreement failed to operate in 1921, to the accompaniment of much recrimination; but in 1926 things were better organized. The Industrial Committee of the TUC decided in 1926 to support the miners in

[1] See above pp. 38-42.

their dispute with the coal-owners. The miners' struggle, it was felt, was the common struggle. Even to that ordinary, strong, intelligent, sane, ignorant Englishman, Ernest Bevin, with his wonderful capacity to learn and to make things work, the case so appeared: if it came to a fight, he said, all would have to 'become one union' (shades of the Grand National!) and the miners would 'have to throw in their lot and cause into the cause of the general movement'.[1]

The general strike began on May 3rd, and lasted until May 12th. Those called on to do so came out on strike almost to a man. There was little violence, although the Government prepared for the worst and the public resisted and improvised. The leaders showed little enthusiasm for the struggle, once it had begun, for it was soon realized that it was a struggle between the trade unions and the Government. It was true enough, as *The Times* said, that it was ridiculous to suggest 'that any considerable number of men are animated by revolutionary motives';[2] but the fact remained that no Government could stand by idle and view the whole matter as simply an enlarged industrial dispute. Baldwin was right when he said, 'The General Strike is a challenge to Parliament and is the road to anarchy and ruin.' If the strikers had won, the Government would have had to sanction arrangements which it had refused to make itself—which in fact it opposed; and the Government was democratically elected. Thus a strike carried out in support of resistance to inevitable wage reductions in an overmanned and badly run industry was soon seen to raise the gravest constitutional issues. Were the trade unions to follow the Government or was the Government to follow the trade unions? When the moderate and perceptive men who led the strike saw that this issue was involved, victory no longer appealed to them and the strike was brought to an end. The coal strike was continued, and although men were drifting back to work throughout the summer new wage agreements in each district were not concluded until almost the end of the year. Hours were increased and wages were reduced.

These events brought little credit to anyone. Birkenhead voiced a widespread feeling, and one not without some justifica-

[1] Speech delivered on April 29, 1926, quoted in Mowat, op. cit., p. 301.
[2] *The Times*, May 11, 1926.

tion, when he wrote that 'it would be possible to say without exaggeration that the miners' leaders were the stupidest men in England if we had not had frequent occasion to meet the owners'.[1] Baldwin increased his prestige in the country, and Bevin gained stature within the trade union movement. But the most important result of all was that the illusion that almost 1¼m. men could get a good living in the coal industry in the 1920s was dead.

In 1927 the Government passed the Trade Disputes and Trade Union Act, which illegalized sympathetic strikes and intimidation, and provided that trade unionists as such need not automatically contribute to the funds of the Labour Party (as had previously been done) but should contribute only if they expressly stated their wish to do so. This legislation was of little benefit to anyone, although it gave the trade union movement and the Labour Party a good political grievance which they used to advantage. More sensible efforts were made in other ways to improve relations within industry and to find better methods of settling differences. The Turner-Melchett discussions began in 1927 and continued in Conferences in 1928 and 1929. The initiative for these discussions came from the employers; the trade union movement was on the defensive; and there is no doubt that the talks increased confidence and the willingness to negotiate. There remained, certainly, with a million men unemployed and money wages barely steady, an underlying tendency to suspicion and recrimination, a casting about for a scapegoat. But something had been achieved by 1927. The more far-sighted employers no longer saw trade unions as organizations designed to usurp the authority of management. They recognized that the encouragement of responsible trade unionism—and there was plenty of it in the 1920s —was the best defence against disruptive elements such as communists and, in some cases, shop stewards. The invitation to discussion issued by Lord Melchett in 1927

'expressed the view that the movement towards industrial co-operation had recently received a great accession of

[1] Quoted in W. H. Steed, *The Real Stanley Baldwin* (London, Nisbet, 1930), p. 89.

strength, that common interests of employers and workers were more powerful than the apparently divergent interests which seemed to separate them, and that full and frank cooperation would contribute to the restoration of industrial prosperity and the corresponding improvement in the standard of living of the population.'[1]

[1] J. H. Richardson, op. cit., p. 218.

CHAPTER III

The Economic Crisis, 1929-1932

SCARCELY anyone thought, in the later 1920s, that they were living through the closing years of the upswing of a trade cycle. Great Britain, admittedly, enjoyed a recognizable boom in the new issue capital market in 1928, and ordinary share prices rose rapidly. But the unemployment situation was very little better in 1927 and 1928 than before 1926; the balance of payments on current account was more favourable, but not by much; the country's share of world trade had fallen, between 1924 and 1927, quite considerably; and prices were still falling gradually, as they had done almost without interruption since 1922. Times were dull, and the outlook was never particularly promising. In the United States, on the other hand, an upswing which was soon to come to an end was not recognized because the good times which the country was enjoying were confidently expected to last for ever. From 1923 to the autumn of 1929 large groups of people and most kinds of economic activity—agriculture was the most conspicuous exception—enjoyed 'an era of prosperity approaching that of wartime'.[1] Its continuance was confidently forecast. 'Our situation is fortunate,' reported an expert economic committee early in 1929, 'our momentum is remarkable.'[2] The chief reason for the failure to grasp the impermanent, cyclical nature of the long American boom of the 1920s was that prices were fairly stable. If prices were not rising, so the argument went, there could be no cyclical upswing and no inherent weakness leading to collapse.

But the economic world of the 1920s was not built on very solid foundations, and when the collapse began it began in the

[1] H. U. Faulkner, *American Economic History* (New York, 1943), p. 608.
[2] Conference on Unemployment, *Recent Economic Changes in the United States* (New York, 1929), p. xx.

United States. No brief explanation of a cyclical downturn is a good one, but it is perhaps justifiable to say that there were two main reasons for the onset of depression in the United States. There was, first, the saturation of the market for those products the selling of which had been the backbone of the boom: automobiles and related goods; electricity and electrical equipment; houses and other buildings. There was a wide range of these goods, they all reached a very large market, many of them were continually improved and reduced in price, and so saturation point took some time to reach. These considerations explain the length and strength of the boom. But, even so, it was unreasonable to expect it to last for ever. Secondly, there was the monetary policy of the Federal Reserve System authorities. This policy was one of price stabilization. It was pursued with success in the sense that neither the wholesale price index nor the cost of living index moved more than 8 per cent between 1922 and 1928; the wholesale price index, indeed, was at the same level in 1928 as it had been in 1922, the cost of living index being then only 3 per cent higher. The trouble about this policy was that it to some extent engendered and to a large extent concealed inflationary pressures and effects. Productivity per head in manufacturing industry was increasing; but the benefit was not passed on to the public in lower prices, or to workers in the form of higher wages. Hence

'there was an increase in the proportion of total income going to profits (including those left in the business) and a corresponding decrease in the relative proportion going to wages and salaries—this in spite of a very considerable increase in real wages, reckoned in terms of commodity buying power.'[1]

This way of distributing the national product had two bad consequences: it did nothing to help sustain purchasing power needed to take up the goods produced; and it made the successful businesses increasingly self-financing, which meant that their activities were less and less susceptible to control by the monetary authorities.

For several years all went well. But the policy of the Federal Reserve authorities became increasingly difficult to maintain,

[1] J. M. Clark, *Strategic Factors in Business Cycles* (New York, 1934), p. 106.

chiefly because powerful international forces were at work tending to lower the level of commodity prices. Money pumped into the system with a view to keeping up these prices did not always produce the intended effect; instead, it was sometimes used to purchase bonds and shares. This became increasingly dangerous when, after 1927, investment in producers' durable equipment and in private non-residential construction began to fall off. Both revived in 1928, but downturn was unmistakeable in the summer of 1929. The industrial boom was over. But the stock exchange boom went on. 'Deluded by the insane propaganda inculcating the belief that prosperity was permanent,'[1] thousands of investors maintained an orgy of idiotic speculation until at last, on October 29, 1929,

> 'huge blocks of stock were thrown upon the market for what they would bring . . . Again and again the specialist in a stock would find himself surrounded by brokers fighting to sell—and nobody at all even thinking of buying . . . the scene on the floor was chaotic . . . and when the closing gong brought the day's madness to an end the gigantic record of 16,410,030 shares had been set; . . . the average prices of fifty leading stocks, as compiled by the *New York Times*, had fallen nearly forty points.'[2]

The termination of the American boom would not have mattered so much if the rest of the world had been in a healthy economic condition. But it was not. The world economy suffered from two great weaknesses, both a result of the war, one general, the other largely manufactured by America, Germany and France combined. And the collapse of America, by then established as the most powerful economic unit and the greatest lender in the world, exposed these weaknesses and turned them into crippling deficiencies.

The general weakness was the persistent imbalance between the supply of and demand for foodstuffs and raw materials. The world was cursed with plenty. During the war, European demand on an exceptional scale for foodstuffs and raw materials had induced an expansion of supply overseas, and the post-war

[1] H. U. Faulkner, op. cit., p. 643.
[2] F. L. Allen, quoted in Faulkner, op. cit., p. 644.

boom encouraged still further investment. Moreover, agricultural techniques were greatly and rather suddenly improved all over the world. Not only the tractor and the combine harvester, but also

'the scientific work of the plant-breeder, the parasitologist and the soil chemist, and the better organization of transport and marketing have brought new areas into cultivation, increased the yields, and cheapened the costs of production. The peasant farms of eastern Europe, working under small-scale enterprise, with little machinery, less scientific research, and costly commercial credit and transport organization, face [1932] a greatly increased and more formidable competition.'[1]

Thus some primary producing areas gained at the expense of others; but there was pressure on agricultural prices everywhere. Agriculturalists usually tried to maintain their incomes by increasing production, thereby driving prices down still further; other primary producers entered into restriction schemes to maintain prices, but when these price-control schemes broke down in the later 1920s, successive accumulations of stocks were dumped on already demoralized markets. To make matters worse, Russia suddenly re-emerged as a great wheat exporter in 1930.

The second great weakness in the economy of the world was the structure of international indebtedness. Britain, the great pre-war lender to overseas territories, was impoverished, and her foreign lending in the 1920s was smaller in volume, more variable in amount, and to a larger extent short-term than before the war. France, Britain's only rival in the nineteenth century as an exporter of capital, was affected immediately after the war by a flight of capital which led to the holding of large short-term balances ('funk money') abroad; after the stabilization of the franc in 1926-27 this money began to be repatriated. These movements of French funds added an element of instability and uncertainty to financial arrangements. But most important of all was the emergence of Germany as the world's greatest borrower and of America as the world's greatest lender. These two trans-

[1] League of Nations, *World Economic Survey* 1931-2 (London, Allen & Unwin, 1932), p. 86.

formations were not unconnected with one another. The war had not greatly impoverished Germany, and the runaway inflation of 1922-23 had even helped in the renovation of her industrial equipment. But reparations pressed heavily upon her, and the general insistence that they be paid was strengthened by America's insistence that war debts be paid. Germany found the money to pay France and other countries by borrowing from America; in 1927 and 1928 she increased her indebtedness by over $2,000m., almost equal to the whole of Great Britain's foreign lending from 1924 to 1930 inclusive. No other country borrowed nearly as much—Australia was Germany's nearest rival—but there were other cases where borrowing was on a scale large enough in relation to the productive powers of the economy concerned to give rise to difficulty in servicing the debt. This difficulty was not made any less by America's high tariff policy and by the inability or reluctance shown by most debtors to reduce their price levels. The world was thus treated to the spectacle of 'a network of public debts entailing an annual flow of funds from poorer countries to richer ones—an arrangement calculated to work smoothly so long, but only so long, as the richer countries would lend money back to the poorer ones'.[1] This they were, at first, willing to do. Capital flowed out, especially from America, on a scale large enough to finance new investments and to enable borrowers to pay the interest charges on previous borrowings as well. Money incomes in the borrowing countries were maintained, and America was able to retain, and even to expand, her export surplus on commodity trade. But towards the end of 1928 American willingness to lend overseas suddenly fell away, chiefly due to the preoccupation of American investors with the stock exchange boom. At the same time, the repatriation of French balances reduced liquidity. As a result, debtors all over the world strove to cut down their imports and increase their exports. Inevitably, many raw material prices—notably those of wool, cotton and petroleum—began to sag rather sharply. Then the American boom broke in October.

An admirable brief analysis of this tangle of causes and events was made by a Swedish economist writing within a few years of the downturn:

[1] D. H. Robertson, *Money*, p. 185.

'A period of industrial depression set in almost simultaneously with an agricultural crisis due to quite different causes, at a time when the powers of resistance and the stability of the economic situation were, for various reasons, reduced and were much smaller than during the decades immediately preceding the war.'[1]

To begin with, Great Britain was not seriously affected. Bank Rate was raised from $5\frac{1}{2}$ per cent to $6\frac{1}{2}$ per cent late in September 1929 in order to retain funds in London and help ration the long queue of borrowers who could no longer be satisfied in New York; when the New York stock exchange boom collapsed, gold flowed to London for safety, and Bank Rate was reduced. But gradually Great Britain, like every other country in the world, was affected by the accelerating downward movemer.● of prices. During 1930 the wholesale price index in Britain fell by 18 per cent, the cost-of-living index by 8 per cent. The purchasing power of raw-material producing countries was meanwhile enormously diminished, and British exporters suffered accordingly, the quantum of world trade falling by about 7 per cent between 1929 and 1930. Profits fell, new industrial issues on the London Stock Exchange fell in volume by almost one third, and the British unemployment rate rose from over 10 per cent to almost 16 per cent.

1931 was much worse. It was dominated by the spread and ultimate culmination of the greatest international financial crisis ever known. Falling prices, including falling share prices, began to put an impossible strain on the banks. First the Credit-Anstalt, in Austria, had to have international assistance (including a substantial loan from the Bank of England in June), had to reorganize, and to negotiate a partial stand-still agreement with its foreign creditors. This produced widespread loss of confidence in European finance, reduced international banking liquidity, and led one country after another, unable to realize assets held abroad, to 'freeze', in turn, its own foreign indebtedness. Germany, having close financial connections with Austria, was naturally the next victim. The Hoover moratorium on all inter-governmental debts arising out of the war, including repa-

[1] B. Ohlin, *Now or Never*, vol. VII, No. 77, p. 128.

rations, probably prevented a general disaster in central Europe, but by the time that the moratorium was agreed in July the Reichsbank was in so weak a position that it, too, needed international assistance. This was given, the Bank of England again participating. Unfortunately, the German public now began to lose confidence, and there was an internal flight from the mark which led to bank 'holidays' and acute financial trouble in the middle of July.

It was now London's turn. London had lent liberally—perhaps too liberally—in the financial reconstruction of central Europe in the 1920s. Inevitably, Britain was a large sufferer from the freezing of assets in European countries in 1931; nevertheless, other countries, finding themselves in an unexpectedly illiquid position, continued to come to London as the chief European provider of credit and liquid funds. French balances were still being repatriated, and financial conditions were still deteriorating in the countries bordering on Austria and Germany. London began to lose gold at an alarming rate. From July 15th to the end of the month the Bank of England's gold losses averaged nearly £2·5m. per day. (In the worst months of 1929, during the American boom, gold had rarely been lost at any rate over £250,000 per day.) Bank Rate was raised, but the drain continued; and on August 1st the Bank of England announced that a credit of £50m. had been arranged with the Bank of France and the Federal Reserve Bank of New York.

A Labour Government had the misfortune to be in power at this time, with Mr Snowden as Chancellor of the Exchequer. Elected in May 1929, it was soon facing appalling difficulties. Unemployment, which the Party had rashly undertaken to conquer, rose from 1·5m. at the beginning of 1930 to 2·5m. by December.[1] The boasted schemes of public works spoken of during the Election came to little. Instead, there was the Unemployment Insurance Act of 1930. This Act, 'based upon wilful optimism',[2] marked the extreme limit of relaxation of restrictions on the drawing of benefit. During the 'twenties unemployment benefits had been extended to all insured persons irrespec-

---

[1] Assisted by the provisions of the new Unemployment Insurance Act described below.

[2] R. C. Davison, *British Unemployment Policy* (London, Longmans, 1938), p. 8.

tive of whether or not they had paid into the fund sufficient contributions to make them eligible members of a solvent scheme. Naturally, the fund ran into debt. But no Government was anxious to introduce restrictions, because the only alternative to benefit was the Poor Law—and no Government was anxious to risk the consequences of turning half a million unemployed into legal paupers. Therefore benefit as a *right* continued, and 'British workers acquired the habit of possessing this legal right to a fixed sum during unemployment. They came to regard the local employment exchange as a bank where, subject to the rules, they always had a balance, and this sense of rights entered into the very grain of British social life.'[1] By 1930 the Insurance Fund was over £100m. in debt. The 1930 Act made it still easier to draw benefit and slightly improved the rates; there was now nothing, not even a 'genuinely seeking work' clause, 'to check the accumulation of spurious claims from people who were not genuinely in the labour market or who, for other reasons, had no moral title to benefit'.[2] Practically anyone who could show that he or she had worked in an insured trade at some time and was now not working could draw benefit; and very large numbers did.

Naturally, the Treasury had to increase its subvention of the already insolvent Insurance Fund; and there appeared a substantial Government deficit (about £40m.), a novel and shocking departure from the orthodoxy, established by Sir Robert Peel nearly a hundred years before, that in peacetime the budget must balance. The Treasury was unwilling to let this pass, and announced that 'continued State borrowing on the present vast scale without provision for repayment by the Unemployment Insurance Fund will quickly call to question the stability of the British financial system'.

Suspicion of Great Britain as a safe repository of money grew. On July 14th the Report of the Macmillan Committee on Finance and Industry was published, and this Report, although in general sensible and reassuring, drew attention to the large volume of London's short-term liabilities. This feature of Britain's position was not new, but was an inheritance from the

[1] R. C. Davison, op. cit., p. 5.
[2] ibid., p. 9.

stabilization policy of 1925, and its aftermath; on the other hand, Britain remained unable to increase her short-term assets, and increased international illiquidity and uncertainty made this position unusually precarious. There was also the Royal Commission on Unemployment Insurance, critical of the 'unsound' finance of the Unemployment Insurance Fund. And lastly, there was the Committee on National Expenditure, the so-called May Committee. This Committee reported on July 31st. It forecast a Government deficit of £120m. at the end of the financial year in April; and recommended increased taxation and reduced expenditure, especially in the field of unemployment payments.

It is easy to condemn the May Report as a document of the most rigid and even culpably unimaginative financial orthodoxy. Orthodox it certainly was; it could have been written by Mr Gladstone. But so long as the overriding aim of policy was to stay on the gold standard ('to defend the pound') it is not easy to see what else could have been proposed. Apart from the fact—and it was a fact—that foreign opinion demanded the balancing of the budget and that if it was not balanced the drain of gold was sure to continue, there was the need to slow down the already existing drain and to reverse, if possible, the adverse balance of payments on current account. Had there been no adverse balance of payments on current account, borrowing by the Government could have been the basis for new employment-creating expenditure; but in the circumstances borrowing would have made matters worse by keeping up money incomes and hence the demand for imports. There were in fact only three possible courses. Abandonment of the gold standard, which almost everyone agreed would be a disaster; international action to halt the world-wide fall in prices, of which there was no prospect; orthodox policies of retrenchment, which were what the May Committee proposed.

The May Report was drawn up by bankers and accountants; it was not their business to suggest a new economic strategy, and they probably could not have done so had they tried. They may have erred, as is naturally the way of bankers and accountants, on the side of caution. But they knew the rules and they did the sums. That was all they did; yet the result was a political document of the first importance. It suggested that the limits of financial prudence had been overstepped and that fairly drastic measures were required if bankruptcy was to be avoided. It suggested what those measures should be, and they were not of a kind to be readily accepted by any Government, least of all, perhaps, by a Socialist Government.

For three weeks MacDonald and his colleagues endeavoured to agree on adequate economies, but the necessary reductions in unemployment expenditure were extremely distasteful to several members of the Cabinet. While the Cabinet argued the gold drain continued. The Treasury was negotiating for a further international loan to protect the pound, but it was clear that no help would be forthcoming until at least some of the May Committee's recommendations for economy had definitely been adopted. On August 23rd it was disclosed that the foreign credits made available at the beginning of the month were almost exhausted. And on the following day the Labour Government resigned, being succeeded by the first 'National' Government.

The pressure on London at once diminished, but the position of the pound was still a very weak one. On August 28th the British Government obtained credits in Paris and New York amounting to £80m., and on September 10th Snowden introduced a revised Budget, designed to balance the national accounts. But the international situation was still degenerating, and fresh pressure was building up on sterling. On September 15th the Admiralty announced that the promulgation of pay cuts in the Navy had led to orderly but, from the point of view of naval discipline, improper demonstrations on board a few ships at Invergordon. Picturesquely described as a mutiny, this news caused a minor financial panic, British Government stocks were heavily sold, and over £30m. of gold was lost in three days. Now the late August credits of £80m. were, in their turn, almost exhausted. There was nothing for it. On September 21st Britain went off gold.

'His Majesty's Government have decided, after consultation with the Bank of England, that it has become necessary to suspend for the time being the operation of Sub-section (2) of Section 1 of the Gold Standard Act of 1925, which required the Bank to sell gold at a fixed price . . . During the last few days the withdrawals of foreign balances have accelerated so sharply that His Majesty's Government have felt bound to take [this] decision . . . His Majesty's Government have no reason to believe that the present difficulties are due to any substantial extent to the export of capital by British nationals. Undoubtedly the bulk of the withdrawals have been for foreign account . . . His Majesty's Government have arrived at this decision with the greatest reluctance. But during the last few days the international financial markets have become demoralized, and have been liquidating their sterling assets regardless of their intrinsic worth. In the circumstances there was no alternative but to protect the financial position of this country by the only means at our disposal.'

Thus the much vaunted and hard fought for gold standard lasted this time, as far as Britain was concerned, only six years. The reserves were inadequate. They had been inadequate in 1925, and it had not proved possible to build them up. There was no internal drain or panic, and there is no evidence that Britain had lent too much abroad or lent too much on long term. Falling prices in a world ridden with uneconomic indebtedness, a good deal of it of French and American manufacture, created a situation which required some financial centre of enormous strength to maintain liquidity and confidence. London was not that centre, although London remained as long as possible the only market in which money could be deposited or from which it could be withdrawn with perfect freedom.

The immediate consequences of abandonment were not serious. The dollar rate fell from the old par value of $4·86 to about $3·80. When it was realized later in the year that Britain might soon impose a tariff on imports, goods were rushed into the country by foreign exporters and the rate fell to $3·30 and even a little lower; but in a short time sterling recovered, the repayment of foreign credits restoring confidence in sterling while the persistent weakness of the American economy sapped confidence in the dollar. Moreover, the behaviour of British wholesale prices was better than had been expected. Instead of rising all the way to meet the depreciation of the pound, wholesale prices at the end of 1931 were only about 8 per cent above the level at which they had stood just before Britain left the gold standard. (The cost-of-living index continued to fall until 1933.) Stock prices, of course, fell all over the world, and interest rates were put up. The American financial situation deteriorated, not so much because American financial institutions held funds in London as because numerous countries decided to back their currency with gold rather than dollars; hence pressure on the dollar and a movement of gold out of the US. This further weakened confidence, and hoarding of currency in the US by American nationals became widespread. Other countries, such as Greece and the Netherlands, were embarrassed by the fall in value of their sterling reserves. Scandinavian countries, and most Empire countries, followed Britain off gold. Many countries, whatever their financial policy, sought to obviate the commercial consequences of Britain's abandonment of gold by introducing new 'anti-dumping' tariffs.

That the immediate consequences were not serious must not, however, obscure the fact that Britain's abandonment of the gold standard was a turning-point in modern economic history. Britain had tried to restore nineteenth century financial stability so as to facilitate the international movement of goods and transfer of capital; and she had failed. Her failure had consequences of the greatest importance, both direct and indirect, which took years to work themselves out. As far as Britain herself was concerned, the direct consequences were almost wholly favourable; the indirect and remote consequences, on the other hand, most conspicuously the set-back to international economic co-operation in general and the resultant rise of nationalism, autarky, suspicion and hatred in Europe, were in most ways, without doubt, disastrous; they are beyond the scope of a merely economic study.

The 'National' Government which came to power in the late summer of 1931 had one avowed economic policy; to balance the budget and save the gold standard. It balanced the budget more or less, but, as far as the other limb of its policy was concerned, in vain. It then proceeded to adopt that policy which the electorate had rejected in 1906 and 1923 and about which Mac-Donald, during the 1931 campaign, declared that he retained 'an open mind'; the policy of protection. Many people regarded the adoption of this policy as the imposition of a Conservative Party nostrum upon an electorate deluded, as the *Economist* said, by fear and patriotism into voting for what it thought was a 'National' but what turned out to be merely a Conservative Government. But this judgment underestimates the universality of the drive towards protection in those crisis years and to some extent misunderstands the nature of the protective policy itself. The dominant factor in international economic relations was the evaporation—if that is the right word—of international liquidity. Whether caused by falling prices, non-renewal of foreign loans, the freezing of assets or Britain's abandonment of the gold standard, this loss of liquidity put terrific pressure on all countries—especially debtor countries—to export. But these exports were most unwelcome to the receiving countries, for they tended to intensify unemployment and to drain away the recipients' reserves of foreign exchange. The result was a general resort to tariffs and, in extreme cases, to quotas. The American tariff had been raised in 1930. In 1931 special customs duties were imposed by Canada, South Africa and Italy, and in 1932 France greatly increased her use of the strangulating device of the quota, as did Germany. All these protective measures invited and often produced retaliation in kind.

Britain joined the *sauve qui peut* with the passage of the Import Duties Bill early in 1932. This imposed a general duty of 10 per cent on most imports, but exempted Empire goods and those named in a free list, which included most foodstuffs and raw materials. The bill also set up an Import Duties Advisory Committee to give advice on the imposition of additional protection. The first recommendation of this committee was that duties of $33\frac{1}{3}$ per cent should be placed on most kinds of steel for a limited period, renewal being conditional upon a reorganization of the industry. It also recommended, in April, a raising of the general level of duties on manufactured goods to 20 per cent, on luxury goods to 24 or 30 per cent, and on a few items (including some chemicals) to $33\frac{1}{3}$ per cent. These recommendations were at once adopted.

Thus equipped, Britain took part in the Imperial Economic Conference which opened in Ottawa in July. Britain's motives in seeking an assured expansion of imperial trade were partly political, partly sentimental, but they were also partly economic. Britain now had a tariff, and could offer extended preferences in return for appropriate concessions by Empire countries. But Empire countries were reluctant to expose their 'infant industries' to the winds of British competition, while Britain could not offer a great deal to countries like Canada and Australia and New Zealand unless she was prepared to impose considerable duties on foreign foodstuffs. After hard bargaining, which did nothing to sweeten Imperial relations, the results were meagre, and most of what was achieved was achieved not by lowering tariffs within the Empire but by raising them to those outside. Thus the general level of Empire (including British) tariffs was raised a little further. Fresh duties and quotas were introduced relating to foreign foodstuffs coming into the United Kingdom, and duties were imposed on the import of a number of foreign raw materials. Some trade was diverted, the German manufacturer and the Danish and Argentinian farmer being the most conspicuous sufferers. Germany retaliated.

These manoeuvres, which attracted much political attention, were not nearly so important as two other steps taken by the Government in 1932. The first of these was the setting up, in April, of the Exchange Equalization Account. This was Britain's essay in the art of exchange control, of which the foremost exponent was Germany. Germany, however, was engaged simply in the rationing of foreign exchange. The British scheme was at once more ambitious, more liberal and more constructive: the aim was, in the words of the then Chancellor of the Exchequer, Mr Neville Chamberlain,

'to smooth out the variations in exchange caused by three sets of phenomena—firstly the seasonal fluctuations; secondly, the operations of speculators, which increase those seasonal fluctuations, and other fluctuations, too; and, thirdly, [the] special flight of capital from other countries for the sake of finding a safer place to stop in for a time . . . '[1]

[1] Parliamentary Debates, May 1933, 1038.

The requirements were a fund with an ample supply of gold and sterling, administered by officials enabled to act swiftly, and authorised to act widely and secretly.

The Exchange Equalization Account began life with capital assets of £17m. and borrowing powers for up to £150m. In May 1933 the borrowing powers were increased by £200m. and in April 1937 by a further £200m., making a total fund of £567m.

The account was operated by officials of the Bank of England under the general direction of the Treasury. The aim was to offset any buying or selling of sterling unconnected with ordinary commercial transactions. Thus, if there was a 'flight from the pound' and abnormal amounts of sterling were offered for sale, it was the duty of the fund to sell foreign currencies or gold and buy sterling; conversely, if there was a flight from some foreign currency into sterling causing an abnormal demand for sterling, it was the duty of the account to sell sterling. By these means—always provided that the account had adequate resources to dominate the market—Britain could fix whatever was considered to be the desirable rates of gold to sterling, and hence of sterling to any foreign currency linked to gold. Also— and this was no less important—movements of gold into and out of the country could be prevented from having their normal effects in the way of enlarging or contracting the credit base through the normal operations of the banking system: the gold flowed into or out of the account, and the account thus insulated the domestic credit structure from hostile, transitory or irrelevant external influences.

To begin with, those operating the Exchange Equalization Account had a hard job. As a seller of sterling the account was in a strong position, but it did not have much gold or much of a supply of currencies with a fixed gold equivalent with which to purchase sterling when it was offered for sale by other people. The problems raised by the payments due to America on War Debt late in 1932 subjected sterling to considerable pressure. The account tried to support sterling but did not have the resources necessary, and the dollar exchange fell to $3·17 before a recovery set in. This was a critical period for the Exchange Equalization Account which was being subjected to a barrage of hostile criticism from foreigners, especially Americans, usually ill-informed and not always disinterested. Early in 1933, however, the situation completely altered. Hitler came to power in Germany, and this was followed by the terrible collapse of the American banking system. Holland, Belgium and even Switzerland fell into serious difficulties. Almost overnight Britain became, in the eyes of the holders of capital, the safest repository for funds in the world. The account was required to take up such large amounts of foreign exchange and gold that its borrowing powers had to be extended in May, and from that time onwards it possessed the resources to operate with effect both as a buyer and a seller of sterling.

The second important step taken by the Government in 1932 was also monetary; this was the conversion of the 5 per cent War Loan, 1929-47, to a $3\frac{1}{2}$ per cent basis, and the consequent lowering of all interest rates. This was an obvious step to take, but its importance can hardly be over-estimated.

The amount of 5 per cent War Loan outstanding early in 1932 was £2,085m., or 27 per cent of the total national debt. War Loan had entered the 'conversion zone' in the summer of 1929, and it followed that the price of War Loan was stable at or near par. This stability in the price of War Loan tied the whole structure of long-term gilt-edged interest rates to a basis of 5 per cent. In other words, no significant reduction in the long-term gilt-edged rate was possible so long as 5 per cent War Loan remained outstanding. A conversion operation could have been undertaken, of course, at any time after the summer of 1929. But it is not difficult to understand why the authorities chose to act in the summer of 1932. Confidence in sterling and in the British economy in general was growing both at home and abroad in the first six months of 1932, and the price of consols was rising. Sufficient gold had been accumulated by February, 1932, to repay the credits given in 1931 to defend the pound, and therefore Bank Rate could be and was lowered. Lastly, the National Government was endeavouring to reduce its own expenditure and other people's incomes. The conversion of War Loan from a 5 per cent to a $3\frac{1}{2}$ per cent basis, if successful, would save the Government £31m. per annum. Moreover, unemployment benefit and the salaries of certain public employees had already been cut; to be fair, reductions should also be made in the incomes of holders of the National Debt, as the Macmillan Report had pointed out.

With these considerations in mind, the Chancellor announced in June that 5 per cent War Loan could be converted to a 3½ per cent stock, repayable in or after 1952 at the option of the Government. When the offer expired at the beginning of December, 92 per cent of the stock (some £2,000m.) had been converted, and only £164m. had to be repaid in cash. This was the biggest and also one of the most successful conversion operations in the history of the National Debt. It is important, however, not to exaggerate the rôle of the Government by suggesting that it 'forced down' interest rates. The so-called 'cheap money policy' was, at least to begin with, a matter of taking advantage of and facilitating the independent tendency of interest rates at this time to fall. From 1919 to 1931 inclusive the yield on 2½ per cent consols averaged 4·6 per cent, and the annual average yield had never fallen below 4·3 per cent. But between the end of December 1931 and the beginning of July 1932 the yield on consols fell from 4·54 per cent to 3·52 per cent. Why was this? Partly, perhaps, because some people realized that with the abandonment of gold and the setting up of the Exchange Equalization Account the Government was moving into a position in which a conversion operation would be possible. But the prime reason was a fortunate conjuncture of modest profit expectations in business with a firm faith in the future of the economy in general. Business had done badly in 1931, and the outlook in 1932 was sombre. On the other hand, the business man and the investor were cheered, a little, by devaluation and tariffs, although their optimism did not lead them the length of bidding up share prices or undertaking fresh investment on any but a modest scale. The holders of British Government stock, for their part, both at home and abroad, were convinced by the spring of 1932 that the economy was being soundly managed, that it was being managed as well as, if not better than, any other, and that if there was no great prospect of immediate improvement neither was there any likelihood that worse might yet befall. Consequently, when the conversion offer came along investors found little motive to exchange Government stock either for equities or cash; there was neither enough to hope for nor enough to fear. Patriotism, certainly, played a part. But by June 1932,

> ' "continuing" in the newly-offered 3½ per cent War Loan had become not so much an act of patriotic sacrifice as an obvious and sensible step for the investor to take . . . Put bluntly, the question resolved itself into this: was this new War Loan, giving a return of £3 10s 0d per cent per annum for more than twenty years, the best investment of its kind available? There could be little doubt by the end of June 1932 that the answer was in the affirmative . . . Given the sharp reduction brought about by the general trade depression in the yield of most other securities, after adjustment for the greater uncertainty attending expectations as to their future earnings, most investors had very little option but to convert.'[1]

Thus the Government cannot be said to have 'forced down' interest rates; it followed them down. It took steps, of course, to help make the conversion offer a success—most notably, it caused the Bankers' Deposits at the Bank of England to rise, and as a consequence the total of bank deposits during 1932 increased by £200m., or no less than 14 per cent. Yet industrial production and wholesale prices were, and remained, steady. The increase in the money supply caused no uneasiness because it was designed to fit in with policies of retrenchment—essentially conservative policies. The one sure way to alarm investors both at home and abroad would have been to support an ambitious and unwelcome conversion operation with a large-scale expansion of money. All policy had to guard against the supreme fear that the managed pound might repeat the awful history of the German mark ten years before.

By the end of 1932, therefore, radical changes had been made in Britain's economic organization. The link with gold and therefore with world price levels had been severed. This made possible the pursuit of an independent, autonomous monetary policy. Cheap money, the logical and natural consequence of going off the gold standard, had been adopted. This policy was

---

[1] E. Nevin, *The Mechanism of Cheap Money* (Cardiff University of Wales Press, 1955), pp. 99-100.

facilitated by the ingenious equilibrating device of the Exchange Equalization Account. Moreover, a general tariff had been adopted. All this was quite new. Coming after a ten-year struggle to re-establish the international gold standard, ten years of dear money, and eighty-five years of free trade, these changes were revolutionary. In mid-1931 the old order, or as near an imitation of it as could be had, stood intact; eighteen months later it had been replaced.

The speed and skill with which adjustments were made were greatly to the credit of bankers, civil servants and politicians. Their task was perhaps made easier by the fact that the old policies had been resolutely pursued and had clearly failed. The success of the new measures was perhaps to some extent due to the fact that the crisis struck Great Britain fairly early. When Hitler came to power in January 1933 the German economy was in a state of almost complete collapse. When Roosevelt took office in March 1933 the American economy was likewise in a desperate plight. In neither case had remedial measures of any importance been begun. As for France, she seemed to be unscathed until 1934, and continued in much the old way under ever-increasing difficulties until 1936. The United Kingdom, by contrast, got off to an early start. Of course, the British measures did little to improve the world situation or even Great Britain's own situation up to the end of 1932. Industrial production in Great Britain was at its lowest ebb in the third quarter of 1932. In the United Kingdom, Germany, France, Sweden and the United States real national income reached the lowest point in 1932.

CHAPTER IV

The Nineteen-Thirties

CHEAP MONEY AND THE PRICE LEVEL

THE monetary history of the 1930s can almost be summed up in a single sentence used by the *Economist* to describe the events of 1937: 'Money continued to be cheap, and the authorities wished it to remain so.'

The primary causes of the continuation of cheap money were that there took place no upsets to investors' confidence, such as it was, in sterling or the future, and that the Government did nothing to cancel or offset the increase in the money supply made in 1932 in order to facilitate the conversion operation. This increase in the money supply thus turned out to be a permanent addition to the stock of money in the economy, and during the 1930s as a whole there was no contraction in the volume of bank credit. Bank Rate, which was reduced to 2 per cent in June 1932, remained at this level continuously until 1939. Naturally, this did not completely stabilize the cost of borrowing. The average rate on 2½ per cent consols from 1933 to 1938 inclusive was only 3·15 per cent as compared with an average of 4·26 per cent for the years 1920-29; but there was a persistent rise in the rate after 1934. This was probably in part due to an upward revision of expectations regarding the marginal efficiency of capital. But it was also partly due to a gradual decline in the supply of Treasury Bills, a decline which caused, in the summer of 1938, a shortage of liquid assets and a consequent contraction of bank credit.

The decline in the supply of Treasury Bills, which inevitably militated against the cheap money policy, came about for two reasons. First, the Government issued further funding loans during the 'thirties which made possible a reduction to the extent of about £200m. in the volume of outstanding Treasury

Bills, as well as a reduction in the volume of short term securities quoted on the Stock Exchange. Secondly, the Exchange Equalization Account was not able completely to prevent foreign capital movements from influencing domestic credit conditions. The net inflow of funds between March 1932 and March 1938 was about £400m.[1] The majority of foreign investors probably wished to hold cash or gilt-edged securities, preferably of a short-term character. But what was issued against the inflow of foreign funds was, predominantly, a supply of long-term securities. Accordingly, foreign investors held idle balances or bid for Treasury Bills: the net effect was a fall in the clearing banks' share of Treasury Bills and a rise in the long-term gilt edged rate from about 3 per cent in 1935 to $3\frac{3}{4}$ per cent in 1939.

This very moderate rise in interest rates in the later 1930s was not of major importance. Money remained comparatively cheap. On the other hand, the rise in interest rates and the causes of that rise justify the comment that

'the pre-war cheap money policy was pursued with none of the single-mindedness and theoretical conviction which characterized its post-war successor. The attitude of the authorities, one suspects, was primarily one of benevolent neutrality; conversion apart, low interest rates could do no harm and might possibly do some good. Mr Chamberlain's elevation of it in 1936 to a fundamental "branch of policy" probably attached to cheap money rather more significance than it possessed in the minds of those actually concerned with the practical administration of monetary control.'[2]

In a decade of cheap money and steady but gradual recovery from depression it was natural to look for a fairly stable price level. Prices in Great Britain did, however, show a tendency to move gradually upwards, rising from the inter-war minimum to which they had descended in 1933 to a level 11 per cent higher by 1938. This level, however, was about the same as that which had prevailed in 1930. The rise in prices was caused by

[1] F. W. Paish, *The post-war finanical problem and other essays* (London, Macmillan, 1950), p. 216.
[2] E. Nevin, *The Mechanism of Cheap Money*, p. 158.

the gradual recovery of trade, of wage rates and of earnings. Wholesale prices throughout the world behaved in a similar fashion. The movement was a fairly steady one except in the first quarter of 1937, when a 'breakneck rise in the prices of many commodities'[1] took place, based on rearmament demand and encouraged by a transient wave of speculative optimism.

OLD AND NEW INDUSTRIES

The industrial changes of the 1930s were of the same kind as those which took place in the 1920s; that is to say, a gradual contraction of several traditionally important industries and a gradual or not so gradual expansion of a number of newer, smaller industries; a growth in the amount of employment provided by trade and services; and continuous technical improvement, which, along with the redistribution of labour, helped in the course of the 'thirties to raise productivity per head in manufacturing industry by no less than 20 per cent.

But although the 'twenties and the 'thirties were very similar from the point of view of the character of industrial change, the conditions in which change took place were very different in the two decades. The 1920s were characterized by the slow growth of international trade, by the recovery of the foreign exchanges, on the basis of the gold standard, from the demoralization of the post-war years, and by the maintenance within Britain of high interest rates. In the 1930s, on the other hand, international trade was difficult and restricted.[2] The volume of world exports, having risen from 65 in 1921 (1913 = 100) to 120 in 1929, fell back to 89 in 1932 and 1933, climbed slowly to 114 in 1937, and then declined again to 103 in 1938. The average volume of world exports for the years 1931-38 was much the same as for 1921-29; but whereas the volume of trade in primary products was larger in the 1930s than in the 1920s, the volume of trade in manufactured articles was smaller; measured by value, of course, both types of trade were much reduced in the 'thirties,

[1] The *Economist*, Commercial History and Review of 1937, p. 301.
[2] The statements which follow are based on figures to be found in *Industrialization and Foreign Trade* (League of Nations, 1945) and I. Svennilson, *Growth and Stagnation in the European Economy* (Geneva, 1954).

considerably below the 1911-13 level. Great Britain, in the 1920s still the greatest exporter of manufactured articles in the world, was obviously profoundly affected by this stagnation (to put it no worse) of international trade.

And in the second place, the 1930s differed from the 1920s in that money was cheap instead of dear. How much difference this made to industry is hard to say. According to one careful investigator, 'statistics suggest ... a fall of 25 per cent in the cost of debenture borrowing and a fall of 24 per cent in the cost of borrowing on preference shares'[1] between 1932 and 1936; raising money through ordinary shares also became noticeably cheaper. The volume of industrial issues (for home production, trade and transport) rose from £70·9m. for 1931-32 to £244·1m. for 1935-36. This last figure was rather higher than the peak figure for any pair of years in the later 1920s—£240·4m. for 1927-28—and, making some allowance for the fall which had taken place in the prices of capital goods, it seems likely that industrial investment in real terms was about 10 per cent higher in 1935-36 than in 1927-28. This was the result of increased confidence, better prospects and cheap money. It is not a startling result—1937-38 saw less new issuing for industry than 1929-30—but it constituted and contributed to recovery, and cheap money played a part. It should also be remembered that industry, like the Government, was able to convert fixed-interest debts to lower interest levels. This was done on a substantial scale, especially from 1933 to 1935, and conversion produced, in effect, a perceptible rise in the net earnings of businesses.

Conditions both at home and abroad were therefore different in important respects in the 1930s from what they had been in the 1920s; and other differences, to be described later in this chapter, might also be mentioned—the fall in foreign lending, more active Government policy, the extension of protection. The problem remained the same: how to contract in some lines and how to expand in others. But although unchanged in substance, this problem presented itself with some important changes of emphasis and detail.

In the first place, the coal industry, although still in a bad way

[1] E. Nevin, op. cit., p. 217.

and giving plenty of trouble, was no longer the major economic
liability which it had sometimes seemed to be in the 1920s. For
one thing, it was much smaller. The number of insured persons
in the industry had fallen during the 'twenties from about 1¼m.
to not much over 1m., and by 1937 was below 900,000. Unemployment, it is true, was heavier, just over 21 per cent from
1934 to 1938 compared with less than 19 per cent from 1927
to 1929. Thanks to the fall in the number of those seeking
work in the industry, however, this did not mean an increase
in the average number of coal-miners unemployed; moreover, the level of unemployment in the industry fell in every
year from 1932 to 1937, and in 1937 and 1938 was lower than in
any year since 1924 (with the exception of the wholly abnormal
year, 1926). The selling price of coal was rising after 1932,
while costs of production fell, at least until 1935.

With over 20 per cent of its labour force unemployed,
the situation of the industry was unsatisfactory enough in all
conscience; yet the overall position was clearly better than ten
years before. There were three main causes for the improvement. First, individuals had moved out of the industry; in
Glamorgan and Monmouthshire the industrial labour force was
actually smaller in 1937 than in 1927. Second, mechanization,
which had lagged in the 'twenties, made rapid progress after
1930. In 1928 26 per cent of the industry's total output was cut
mechanically, and 12 per cent conveyed by mechanical con-
veyors; by 1936 the percentages were 55 and 48 respectively.
Largely as a result of this, output per manshift rose by over
10 per cent between these two dates. Consequently, quarterly
earnings of miners were higher in the mid-'thirties than in
the late 'twenties (and the cost of living was lower) while
the profitability of the industry rose steadily from 1933.

The third reason for the improvement in the fortunes of the
industry was the working of Government-sponsored schemes of
regulation and control. During its brief tenure of office, the
Labour Government had found time to pass a few pieces of
legislation not directly connected with the economic collapse and
destined to play an important part in the developments of the
'thirties; among these was the Coal Mines Act of 1930. This
Act contained two important parts. The first, based largely upon

a voluntary scheme operated for a couple of years in England in the late 'twenties, provided for the control of output. A Central Council determined an upper limit to output and allocated tonnages among the individual districts. This was supposed to 'prevent unnecessary competition . . . improve the financial position of the industry . . . [and] give the industry time to introduce schemes of voluntary reorganization which would secure greater efficiency and thereby increase competitive power'.[1] The organizing of district schemes was compulsory, but the coal-owners in each district were free to frame and work them as they chose. Provision was made within all the schemes for the fixing of minimum prices, and there were penalties for non-observance of the main provisions. The second part of the Act created a Coal Mines Reorganization Commission 'to promote and assist by the preparation of schemes and otherwise, the amalgamation of undertakings'. Whether mere amalgamation could have done much to produce economies of scale is doubtful, and it is more than doubtful whether this line of policy could have done much to eliminate uneconomic producers. But the work of the Commission was condemned to futility from the start by the requirements that whatever be done had to be 'in the national interest' and that no amalgamation might be carried out if financially injurious to any of the undertakings concerned. The Commission struggled on for a few years in the face of intense hostility from the industry and produced a workable scheme of partial amalgamation which was thrown out on the legal technicality that partial amalgamation was not complete amalgamation and that complete amalgamation and nothing less was the Commission's business. In 1936 the Government introduced a reasonable Bill for compulsory amalgamation. The Mining Association and the Federation of British Industries succeeded in having this Bill materially altered, and the final Act in 1938 had no time in which to be effective. Thus nothing was done to enforce efficiency or eliminate high-cost producers. Only the royalties, at last, were nationalized.

Part One of the 1930 Act, however, was certainly effective. Quotas were allocated and prices set. What difference did this

[1] J. H. Jones, G. Cartwright and P. H. Guénhault, *The Coal Mining Industry* (London, Pitman, 1939), p. 64.

make to the development and prosperity of the industry? The allocations made by the Central Council habitually exceeded the actual outputs of the various districts; but this is consistent with the output of some mines or of some kinds of coal being restricted, and there is evidence, especially for the earlier years, that there was some local curtailment of output from time to time. As regards price control there is more definite evidence. Coal prices were extraordinarily stable from 1930 to 1933, falling by only 3 per cent while the general price level fell by about 15 per cent; and after 1933 they rose. There can be no doubt that this peculiar behaviour of coal prices was a result of the working of the 1930 Act. But, as critics of the Act have pointed out, production fell catastrophically: from 262m. tons in 1929 it fell to 210m. tons in 1933 (the lowest figure since 1898, excepting the strike years 1921 and 1926); gradually recovering thereafter to 245m. tons in 1937. Was the fall in output a consequence of the maintenance of prices? Prices may have had some influence, but beyond question the major factor in the demand for coal in these years was the level of industrial production. In Great Britain, this was 17 per cent lower in 1933 than in 1929. Inevitably, the demand for coal fell; price reductions could have done little, if anything, to maintain it. To argue about the price elasticity of demand in these circumstances is like attending to nice adjustments in the rigging while the ship is filling with water.

The success of the control schemes in maintaining prices was reflected in the maintenance of wages; even during the depression, wages were maintained in every district except South Wales. On the other hand, one thing which the control schemes could not do was to secure Britain's position in foreign markets. Coal exports after 1929 fell more drastically than production, and they did not recover. This was due, at least in part, to the British industry's inability to reduce its costs; and in this connection it is worth noticing that output per manshift, which rose in Britain by less than 10 per cent between 1930 and 1937, rose in the other major coal producing countries in Europe by amounts varying between 20 per cent and 45 per cent. The failure of the export trade was particularly serious for South Wales, and only a little less serious for Scotland and the North-Eastern area.

In Lancashire also unemployment was a serious problem, for the difficulties faced by the cotton industry were exacerbated by the depression. During the 'twenties the industry had exported between 70 per cent and 80 per cent of total production by value. The development of the Japanese industry, and of native industries in India, China and other countries was eroding the market for British cotton goods during the 'twenties, and after 1929 this competition was intensified. Japan was a low-cost producer, and when she abandoned the gold standard in December 1931, she enjoyed an extraordinary if temporary advantage in the depreciation of the yen. 'The populations of many tropical territories found their simple standard of life supported or even improved during these lean years by their ability to buy cheap Japanese goods.'[1] Many countries, however, raised their tariffs against British and Japanese textiles alike. India, who in 1932 took 28 per cent of Japan's cotton exports, applied a quota by an agreement reached early in 1934. The British Government sought to restrict imports of Japanese goods into many colonial dependencies by the use of tariffs and quotas. But the sale of British textiles continued to fall, especially in the Far East; a small increase in sales to West Africa was a paltry compensation. Part of the trouble was that Britain's comparative advantage lay in producing the finer counts of cotton; Lancashire could no longer compete in the coarser grades, and during the depression demand for the finer counts fell away particularly sharply.

Not all the industry's troubles, however, originated abroad. There was still the burden of heavy overcapitalization caused by foolish speculation and extravagant financial incompetence during the post-war boom; some of the banks were involved, and they used their resources—naturally enough, but perhaps to an extent which, from that general point of view which no one of them could take alone, was excessive—to prevent liquidation and consequent writing down of their assets. As a result, the industry had no money to invest in such luxuries as ring spindles and automatic looms, and it had too much capacity, which caused short-time working and therefore a continuation of excessively high unit costs and general financial weakness. Some progress

[1] H. V. Hodson, *Slump and Recovery*, 1929-37 (Oxford University Press, 1938), p. 349.

in reducing capacity was made by the Lancashire Cotton Corporation in the early 1930s, backed by the Bank of England through the Bankers' Industrial Development Company. Then in 1936 the Government essayed the rescue of the industry, imposing a spindles reconstruction levy to buy up and scrap some of the excess capacity. The Board set up to administer the scheme was given powers not only to collect the levy but also to borrow up to £2m. Some scrapping was achieved, but of course the costs of the more efficient firms with no surplus capacity were necessarily raised. For a couple of years, nevertheless, in 1936 and 1937, the industry was almost prosperous. Costs had been got down and some capital written off, world revival halted the trend to cheaper cottons, the North American market even expanded a little, while the volume of home consumption rose above the level of the 'twenties. Unemployment in the industry, which had been 28·5 per cent in 1932, was only 11·5 per cent in 1937 (the insured work force was down by almost 100,000). But in 1938 domestic demand declined, while foreign sales of piece goods in the first half of the year were the lowest since 1848. Accordingly, a more thorough-going attempt at reconstruction was envisaged in the Act of 1939, which gave the industry wide powers to reorganize itself, chiefly by fixing prices with only a minimum of Government supervision. But, as with the 1938 Coal Act, it was too late. The sands had run out.

Another major industry in trouble during these years was the shipbuilding industry. Unemployment in 1932 was actually 62 per cent; only one other industry of any consequence had an unemployment rate of over 50 per cent, and that was marine engineering; the national average in 1932 was 22 per cent. In common with all other shipbuilding industries, the British industry was embarrassed by the plenty of tonnage resulting from war-time building and building in the post-war boom, and by the decline in international trade. But during the 'twenties and the 'thirties the British industry lost ground to the shipbuilding industries of other countries. Shipbuilding in other countries in 1926-29 was 30 per cent above the level of 1909-13, and by 1938 it was double the pre-war level; British output on the other hand, fell to 79 per cent of its pre-war level in 1926-29, and to 61 per cent in 1937. What the foreigner gained

Britain lost. Still building half the world's tonnage in 1926-29, Britain built only one third in 1937-38.

There are two reasons or possible reasons for this loss of an old supremacy. First, foreign shipping, and thence foreign ship-building, was extensively subsidized; all over the world both were increasingly regarded as adjuncts of national defence, and dependence on Britain or any other foreign supplier was looked on with more and more disfavour. But there was also evidence that British shipbuilding costs were higher than costs abroad. The *Economist* pointed out that Scandinavian countries, using well paid labour and 'with little or no advantages by way of subsidies or legal preferences, maintain their competitive position with more success than we do'.[1] Certainly, British costs rose rapidly—by as much as 50 per cent, according to one official estimate, between 1929 and 1938; and at the end of 1938 tonnage to the value of £6·5m. was building for British shippers abroad, whereas in British yards only £3·5m. was building for foreign customers. British shipbuilders blamed the high prices charged by suppliers, notably the steel industry. Against this, it was alleged that 'Dutch shipyards [can] build ships entirely of British material for less than the cost in British yards'.[1]

The intensity of depression in the industry caused a voluntary attempt at the reduction of capacity. This took the form of a new company, National Shipbuilders' Security, formed in 1930 by shipping interests, supported by the banks (chiefly through the Bankers' Industrial Development Corporation) and obtaining additional finance *via* a levy of 1 per cent on all ship sales or contracts by company members. By 1935 berths with a total capacity of about 1m. tons, or two-fifths of the industry's total capacity, had been bought and closed down or scrapped. In 1934 the Government had made available up to £9·5m. for loans in aid of shipbuilding (this helped to restart work on the 'Queen Mary', whose gaunt unfinished hull was a melancholy reminder of joblessness and wasted resources on Clydeside from January 1932 until April 1934) and in 1935 granted a subsidy to tramp shipping. In spite of all this, and in spite of the departure of 30,000 men from the industry between 1930 and 1935, unemployment in 1937 was 24 per cent—more than double the

[1] *The Economist*, January 21, 1939, p. 128.

national average. Naval building was substantial from 1937 onwards, but at the beginning of 1939 both the shipping and the shipbuilding industries were deemed to be 'threatened with serious calamity'.[1] It seems impossible to conclude that the industry was efficient. It was curiously slow to adopt the diesel engine and to get into the business of tanker construction; on the labour front there were constant disputes about job demarcation, and restrictive practices seem to have been far from uncommon.[2] Spokesmen for the industry blamed excess capacity, rearmament, the high cost of supplies and discrimination abroad. Undoubtedly, hard times made the going difficult, and industrial relations were bad, partly as a result. But the industry had itself to blame for at least a part of its troubles.

The steel industry was one of the shipbuilding industry's most important suppliers. Unlike shipbuilding, steel was protected. The Import Duties Advisory Committee, set up by the Government to advise on the structure of the tariff, recommended duties of 33⅓ per cent for a short period from the spring of 1932, their renewal being dependent on reorganization of the industry. The Committee aimed at some kind of co-operation between firms resulting in changes in prices and capacity such as would make the industry profitable, and would produce, in the long-run, economically efficient working. Divested of high-sounding phrases, jargon and technicalities, the Committee's proposals were 'aimed at national and international Kartells free from monopoly evils, plus some degree of national planning'.[3]

The industry was not slow in recovering from the worst of depression in 1931. The tariff plus the depreciation of the pound gave British producers an immediate advantage in the home market; imports fell, and British output rose. The rise was not of very remarkable dimensions, but at least the British industry was doing better than its continental rivals. The Continent responded by engineering the first genuine European Steel Cartel, set up in June 1933, and in 1934 imports from the Cartel rose

[1] *The Economist*, January 21, 1939, p. 127.

[2] Perhaps the most convincing evidence came later, during the war. Then, few ships' captains who had their vessels repaired or refitted in British and American yards had anything good to say about the British industry.

[3] D. L. Burn, *The Economic History of Steelmaking, 1867-1939* (Cambridge University Press, 1940), p. 449.

very considerably. This importation 'in large measure ... reflected a demand satisfied adequately and often best by Thomas steel, which was still not made in Britain'.[1] The home industry, however, resenting these inroads upon what it thought should be its own preserve, tried to negotiate with the Cartel, and failed. Turning to the Government for more protection as a bargaining weapon, the steelmakers' wish was granted: the $33\frac{1}{3}$ per cent tariff was raised to 50 per cent, what the industry had asked for in 1931. At once the British Iron and Steel Federation was able to complete an agreement with the Cartel; the Cartel obtained a preference in the British market, and in return accepted a limitation upon its exports to Britain.

But no sooner had the industry largely succeeded in shutting out foreign competition, than home demand began to outrun supply. This was partly due to rearmament, partly to the general increase in activity which culminated in 1937. Ingot production, higher in 1936 than the previous peak (in 1917) rose again in 1937. Steel in excess of the agreed quota was bought from the Cartel, and there were even imports from Canada, India and Russia. Prices rose, for the first time since 1929. The rise, however, was moderate. The industry, in accepting protection in 1932, had become more or less bound not to raise prices. This implied condition can have caused it no great suffering—costs of production for a given output were falling in the 'thirties, raw material costs had fallen, fuller capacity working reduced costs still further. But price stability became impossible in 1937. The industry took to submitting proposed price changes to the IDAC, a policy which that Committee 'approved, and welcomed what it described in a soothing if not very intelligible phrase as a decision not to leave prices to "the uncertain play of supply and demand".'[2] The price control policy was on the basis of costs-plus-profit, and it did not take the IDAC long to find out that 'the returns showed a wide range of costs'; but in its sympathy for the industry it readily allowed that prices could not be based 'solely on the working of the newest and most efficient plants'.[3] The search for price stability also involved the

[1] D. L. Burn, op. cit., p. 449.
[2] ibid., op. cit., p. 471.
[3] ibid., op. cit., p. 472.

Federation in the difficulties of trying to control raw material prices. In 1938, however, production fell. And in 1939 there came the war.

There is no question that the industry in these years was, to put it no more strongly, moderately prosperous. Employment rose by 10,000 between 1930 and 1935, unemployment fell, capacity was considerably enlarged by rebuilding and additional building.[1] Yet the fact remains that the industry was, by and large, a high-cost industry—even the 33½ per cent tariff could not prevent profitable sales of foreign steel in Birmingham. What was worse, the industry showed little signs of reducing the discrepancy between its costs and those of its rivals. Labour and fuel were used more efficiently in 1937 than in 1929, but lip service only was paid to the ideal of economy through more concentrated production; little was done to achieve it. There was still a dearth of modern blast furnaces in 1937, and the new coke batteries were often not large enough to realize all the possible economies of scale. Much the same outcome, according to the leading authority on these matters, would have been realized if the industry had been protected unconditionally. The supervision of the IDAC made pathetically little difference. In one way, indeed, the half-hearted urge to wider 'planning' made matters worse. When in 1935 Richard Thomas wanted to build a new strip mill in Lincolnshire, they were persuaded by the Government, under pressure from the trade unions and public opinion and Mr Bevin, not to leave South Wales. They set up at Ebbw Vale—probably a higher cost location—and may have done more damage to the communities of Swansea and Llanelly by operating in Ebbw Vale than they would have done operating in Lincolnshire. A year later there was trouble over the failure of a scheme to erect a new Thomas steelworks at Jarrow. The resulting agitation 'played a big part in leading both the industry and the Government to provide for supervising, coordinating and planning further expansion';[2] social as well as industrial considerations were to be borne in mind. The result, not surprisingly, was more timidity and more muddle. 'The

[1] By the end of 1938 steel furnace capacity was 14·5m. tons. Two thirds of the furnace capacity existing in the summer of 1936 had been replaced.

[2] D. L. Burn, op. cit., p. 462.

steelmakers who patched old and ill-sited plants, in the established tradition, discovered they were humanitarians. They could point to the homes which their workers had bought. Who would take the responsibility of destroying the savings of a lifetime?'[1]

But the acid test of all this policy lay in export markets, and there the answer was plain. Britain's share of world exports of steel fell from 21 per cent to 17 per cent between 1929 and 1938. And this understates the decline, for all her rivals sustained losses by the closing of Britain's home market, while Britain had a privileged position in Empire markets. Britain's continental rivals gained a lot of ground in 'neutral' markets, especially in South America. The conclusion is irresistible; the steel industry, like the coal industry, had wasted the 1930s.

It is thus more than doubtful whether the steel industry in these years served the home market as well as the home market served the steel industry. Shipbuilding, of course, did not achieve much (on the other hand, its complaints about the high cost of raw materials were clearly not unjustified). But the automobile industry did. Here, too, there were complaints about steel prices —'Lord Nuffield is becoming a confirmed free trader' said the *Economist* in 1935—but there was less anxiety, for motor vehicles were still mostly for sale at home. Their production was increasing rapidly. Counting private cars and commercial vehicles together, 237,000 were produced in 1930, 404,000 in 1935, 508,000 in 1937. Employment (for motor vehicles, cycles and aircraft) rose from 245,000 to 410,000 between 1930 and 1938. Like steel, the industry was heavily protected, and, unlike steel, had been so protected since 1915. Again like steel, protection was consistent with exportation, and the volume of exports rose through the 'thirties at about the same rate as production. The industry secured a considerably larger share in world exports of vehicles in the 'thirties than it had had in the 'twenties; after the USA, indeed, Britain in the 'thirties was much the largest exporter. But its successes abroad were owing to a large degree to tariff preferences; about 85 per cent of total exports in 1937 went to Empire countries. The industry did not do much, nor did it try to do much, in European markets, which it left chiefly to French and German producers.

[1] D. L. Burn, op. cit., p. 465.

The structure of the industry came in for a lot of criticism. It was dominated by six large concerns—Austin, Ford, Morris, Standard, Vauxhall and what subsequently became the Rootes Group. In 1937 these six producers accounted for 86 per cent of new home market registrations, and they were responsible for almost the whole of the export trade. Between them, in 1937, they made about 330,000 cars. Had each manufacturer made only one model, they could have realized full economies of scale; but each manufacturer made at least half a dozen, some of them in very small quantities. This 'full range' policy, therefore, tended to keep prices up. In fact, given the oligopolistic character of the industry and the natural choosiness of its customers at home (fostered by advertising), expensive product differentiation was the inevitable outcome. This remains true even although the industry was to some extent an 'assembly' industry, buying components from other producers. In the end, after 1945, the preservation of some variety and individuality paid off in exports to the United States. But too much of it hampered the industry's development in the 1930s.

Peculiarities of the British vehicle taxation system had also to be reckoned with. The only thing which can be said for that system is that it made the British coinage seem relatively simple. A complicated formula favoured small engines, especially those with a narrow bore and a long stroke. This cramped designers, and discouraged the manufacture of large cars for the home market. Small cars, however, had no great sale abroad—the two-car family was still a rarity, even in America, and the small cars of the 'thirties had too little power for rough going. Thus the Government protected the industry with one hand, but with the other imposed what was in effect an export tax. Quantity production was more difficult than ever. It is scarcely surprising that the industry paid little attention to markets overseas or to building up an after-sales service in foreign countries. There were attempts in the late 'twenties to produce a car 'which would be big enough to compete with the Americans, at least for part of the export demand, whilst being small enough for a reasonable proportion of its output to be sold at home'.[1] Unfortunately, no

[1] P. W. S. Andrews and E. Brunner, *The Life of Lord Nuffield* (Oxford, Blackwell, 1955) p. 204.

sooner were such cars on the market than the depression caused buyers overseas to think more favourably of the small car. This helped to sustain exports in the depression, but demand altered again in a few years. Moreover, in 1936 the Air Ministry started the 'shadow factory' scheme, under which new factories were to be built by the Government and operated by firms in the motor industry to manufacture parts for aircraft engines. Rearmament also produced widespread orders for tank and aircraft parts of all kinds. Thus the energies of the industry began to be diverted from car manufacture, and interest in the export trade fell away. But despite its difficulties and with all its faults, this was one of the great expanding industries of the 1930s.

The electrical industries were also very important, and they too were expanding, Employment in them rose from 192,000 in 1930 to 248,000 in 1935. Expansion took place in every branch of the trade, especially in the manufacture of lamps, radios, gramophones and heavy electrical equipment. The growth of demand which was the condition of this expansion was caused by the modernization and electrification of industry (including parts of the railway system) and by the building of new homes and the desire of consumers to have in their homes not only electric light but also electric fires, refrigerators, wireless sets and so on. But behind these two branches of demand there lay the work of the Central Electricity Board and the Grid. The Grid, linking up the more efficient producers of electricity and spreading the load, was completed only in 1933. It cost £27m., and in its building manufacturers gained valuable experience in the design and construction of high voltage apparatus. It promoted the concentration of production in a reduced number of modern and conveniently situated power stations. Brought into existence in order to bring down the cost of current and widen demand, the operation of the Grid and the efforts of the Central Electricity Board produced results which exceeded all expectations. In 1935 the Board realized a trading surplus of over £1m.—a fact which must have given supporters of the Grid considerable satisfaction, remembering that 92 per cent of the Board's second issue of stock had been left on the hands of the underwriters! Between 1930 and

1936 the grid scheme produced a saving of between £12m. and £20m. on the construction of new generating plant, rendered unnecessary by the new ability to spread the load. In addition, concentration of production in the most efficient generating stations was saving nearly a million pounds a year by the later 1930s. There is no doubt that this was an impressive object lesson in the economies and expansive powers available through Government-sponsored centralization and control.

Given these striking organizational improvements at home, it is not surprising to find that production was chiefly and, as compared with the 'twenties, increasingly for the home market. Significantly, however, British exporters gained ground in international trade after 1930. Of course, they were helped by devaluation to begin with, and by imperial preferences continuously. Nevertheless, the fact that in 1937 and 1938 British exports of electrical equipment of all kinds were nearer their 1929 peak (by value) than either American or German exports does seem to indicate improvement in the industry's competitive power. Competition in this industry was, of course, considerably diluted by both national and international agreements, associations, conventions and combinations.

Several other industries contributed to progress and the continuing diversification of industry in those years. The heterogeneous group called chemicals was the largest; this group includes explosives, paints, oils, drugs, dyestuffs and fertilizers. Employment in the group, stable between 1924 and 1930, rose by some 40,000 or about 18 per cent between 1930 and 1938. Output, as in all the expanding industries in the 1930s, rose considerably faster than employment. This expansion must certainly have been assisted, perhaps very materially assisted, by the tariff. The dyestuffs section of the industry had been heavily protected since 1915, and in 1931 the whole industry received the benefit of protective duties up to $33\frac{1}{3}$ per cent; particular commodities were singled out from time to time during the 'thirties for additional protection. The aim of government seems to have been, indeed, a large measure of self-sufficiency in chemical production for strategic reasons. Year after year 'steady progress was made in filling the gaps in materials which are essential if this country is to be free from the necessity of imports',[1] and as the national income continued to rise the chemical industry prospered on the business of meeting additional demand as well as substituting for imports. The output of heavy chemicals, dyestuffs, drugs and petroleum increased especially rapidly. The oil and petroleum sections of the industry were of course linked to the use of petrol and diesel engines on the one hand and on the other to the enormous increase of oil drilling and crude oil production all over the world. World production and consumption of oil exceeded all previous records in 1937, being about 30 per cent above the levels of 1934, and the profits of the oil companies were the best since 1929. Growth of output in these years was especially rapid in Venezuela and Bahrain. In 1937—again for strategic reasons—drilling was being carried out 'even in Scotland'.[2] The growth of the aircraft industry was similarly connected with strategic considerations. There were 12,000 people in the industry in 1924, 21,000 in 1930, 35,000 in 1935; and only after that did the rearmament programmes begin to affect the industry. At about the same time, new vistas were opened for the commercial use of aircraft when, in July 1938, the upper component of the Short-Mayo composite aircraft became the first heavier-than-air machine to fly the North Atlantic with a commercial load. In the summer of 1939 Imperial Airways started a mail service and Pan-American a passenger service. Both concerns used flying boats. The manufacture of rayon, mostly for the home market, also increased in these years. It was greatly affected by technical progress, so that an increase in employment between 1930 and 1935 of only 18 per cent (12,000 people) caused output to double. Prices fell, quality and variety were improved, and a mass market for quasi-luxury textiles rapidly became established.

These major and minor manufacturing industries were the most important of their kind in terms of increased production. But one other industry, not manufacturing, was at least as important as any of them: this was housebuilding. The volume of housebuilding carried out in the 1930s was unprecedented and prodigious. Over 3m. houses were built in Britain in this

---

[1] *The Economist*, Commercial History and Review of 1938, p. 14.
[2] ibid., Commercial History and Review of 1937, p. 11.

decade, an addition to the total stock of dwelling houses of approximately 29 per cent. Building was concentrated largely in the London area and the home counties, and in the Midlands. But although concentrated geographically, it was well spread out through time. Every year up to 1936-37 saw more houses built (with the sole exception of 1932-33, when output stood still), and the decline from 1936-37 to 1938-39 was a small one. At the peak, in 1936-37, almost 400,000 houses were built, almost twice as many as the average in the years 1930-33—and these years saw more activity than was usual in the 1920s.

Government measures had much to do with the volume and timing of this activity. The 1924 Wheatley Act remained in force until 1933, and there was also the 1930 Housing Act, giving financial assistance to slum clearance projects; both Socialist measures, and both 'pre-slump'. Government assistance under these Acts helped to build between a quarter and a third of the houses constructed from 1930 through 1932, and the existence of the Acts probably does something to explain the sustained rate of building in these years. From 1933 to 1935, however, Government-assisted building shrank rapidly to little more than 10 per cent of the total—a much enlarged total, almost 50 per cent greater than in the first three years of the decade. This decline in Government-assisted building was in spite of instructions issued to local authorities in 1933 to prepare and make an immediate beginning with programmes of slum clearance; the reason is simple; time was needed to carry out these instructions. In 1935 there came another Act, under which local authorities were 'to inspect and make reports and submit proposals as to abatement of overcrowding which was defined and made a penal offence; urban authorities were to secure redevelopment of congested areas and use their powers with regard to reconditioning'.[1] Under the stimulus of this Act and the 1933 instructions, the volume of state-assisted building picked up again, and was about a fifth of the total in the later 1930s.

Thus of the 3m. houses built in the 1930s, only $\frac{3}{4}$m. were built with State assistance; the remaining $2\frac{1}{4}$m. were built un-

[1] L. R. Connor, 'Urban Housing in England and Wales' in *Journal of the Royal Statistical Society* (1936) xcix, 7.

aided by private enterprise. The Government's concern was to raise housing standards and abolish the slums. Government efforts were therefore directed, on the whole, to re-housing the poorest members of the community; their motive was humanitarian. But the efforts of private enterprise were governed by the laws of supply and demand. Why did the working of these laws produce so great an outburst of building when, from the point of view of the general level of activity, it was badly needed, but partly for that very reason was scarcely to be expected?

In the first place there was a shortage of houses in the sense that there were fewer houses than families—almost a million fewer—and that, as a result, 'appallingly high rents [were] taken for sub-tenancies in many parts of the country'.[1] The consequence was overcrowding—far worse in Scotland than in England and Wales—and the growth of slums. This imbalance between the stock of houses and the demand for accommodation was partly due to the cessation of building during the first war, to the spread of different (not in all respects better) ideas as to what constituted reasonable accommodation, to the growth of industrial employment in southern England and the Midlands ('The Midlands and South, to which large numbers of young adults have migrated, have benefited from an almost continuous boom in building and house equipment'[2]), to the development of motor transport and hence of suburban living, and to an exceptional increase in the number of families.[3]

All these considerations act on the side of demand. On the side of supply there is only one[4] important consideration; but it is so important that it is clearly the main element in explaining the great growth of building in these years. This is the general fall in interest rates—the so-called 'cheap money policy'. The number of building plans approved rose suddenly in the autumn of 1931—just a few months after the War Loan had been largely

[1] *The Economist*, December 24, 1932.
[2] PEP *Report on the Location of Industry* (London, 1939), p. 16.
[3] It has to be remembered that the addition to the population in the period 1891 to 1911 was greater than in any twenty years before or since. Hence an exceptional number of people were married and looking for houses in the 1920s and 1930s.
[4] It is true that there was a decline in building costs; but as Nevin (op. cit., p. 274) points out, it strains credulity to suppose that a 3 per cent fall in the prices of building materials and a 5 per cent fall in builders' wage rates had much to do with a 70 per cent increase in private housebuilding between 1931 and 1933.

H

converted. The consequent reduction of interest rates made house-property a particularly attractive form of investment, and there was a sudden increase in the willingness of investors to own houses to rent. They calculated, no doubt, that rents were sticky, and a house almost as good an investment as a fixed interest security. They were not mistaken. Although interest rates fell continuously until 1936, the level of house rents remained almost unaltered. Indeed, between 1931 and 1939 'income from rented dwelling houses was actually rising slightly at a time when income from gilt-edged securities was falling heavily . . . an "investment" demand [for houses] arose because of the rise in the relative attractiveness of housing as a lucrative outlet for accumulated funds . . . something over a third of the demand for newly constructed houses in the 1930s originated from this aspect of dwelling houses as a form of fixed interest investment'.[1]

The importance of this increased willingness to 'supply' houses has been a little disguised by the comparative rigidity of building societies' mortgage rates in the 'thirties. But although mortgage rates declined only slightly, repayment periods were considerably lengthened, and the percentage of the price commonly advanced on mortgage rose from perhaps 70-80 per cent to as much as 90-95 per cent. The building societies found themselves competing with banks and insurance companies to lend money to would-be purchasers. These purchasers had a little more money to spend on buying a house in the 'thirties, because of the fall in the cost of living. But it was mostly cheap money which created a broad if not a primrose path to house-ownership, and made effective the latent demand.

The consequences, for the most part unlovely to look at and often deplorable, were economically massive and pervasive. Investment in new dwelling houses exceeded the 1926-29 average in every year of the 'thirties except 1932 and 1933; in 1936 and 1937 it was more than 50 per cent higher. Factory and other building did not pick up until 1935; thereafter, under the influence of rearmament, it grew away at a great pace, being twice the 1926-29 average in 1937 and treble that average in 1939. Putting the two together, building investment was sur-

[1] Nevin, op. cit., p. 279.

prisingly well sustained from 1930 through 1933 and thereafter rose to very high levels in the later 1930s.[1] Inevitably, employment in building rose rapidly; 260,000 more men were employed in 1938 than in 1930 and the industry became more important than coal mining or agriculture. More rapid house-building also created a small boom in furniture making, and no doubt had something to do with the rapid expansion which took place in electrical wiring and contracting, artificial stone and concrete, brick and tile making, paint, varnish, red and white leads and many other trades. The consequences of rearmament can have been hardly less widely spread; trades which rearmament benefited, and which certainly expanded rapidly, included constructional engineering, aircraft manufacture, and the making of scientific and photographic instruments and apparatus.

AGRICULTURE

The amount of Government legislation and Government-sponsored 'planning' for agriculture in the 1930s is at first sight surprising. Bills were passed in 1931, 1932, 1933, 1936 and 1937. No other industry received anything like this amount of attention. In 1934, indeed, the *Economist* commented that the Ministry of Agriculture's schemes appeared to be the Government's 'only plan of action for assisting the country out of depression'.[2]

This judgment, however, was not justified. There was cheap money, whether conceived as an anti-depression measure or not; and there was protection for industry. And it was because

[1] Net investment in building and contracting was peculiarly important in the slump years, because, although it continued at much the same level as in the 1920s, investment in other capital goods (including stocks) during the slump was a substantial *minus* quantity. The figures in constant £'s are:

	Net Investment in building and contracting	Net Investment in other capital goods (including stocks)
1924-29	£64m.	£52m.
1930-32	£65m.	£-27m.
1933-38	£85m.	£81m.

(Source: E. H. Phelps Brown and B. Weber, 'Accumulation, Productivity and Distribution in the British Economy, 1870-1938,' in *Economic Journal*, June 1953, Table III).

[2] *The Economist*, Commercial History and Review of 1933, p. 3.

there was protection for industry that something had to be done for agriculture. A general agricultural tariff was not the answer, because some products, such as milk, faced no foreign competition, while others, such as butter and wheat, were imported from Empire countries with which a bargain ('you take our manufactures and we'll take your foodstuffs') had been struck at Ottawa. The Government therefore resorted to a mixture of quotas, tariffs, industry-organized marketing schemes to keep up prices, and straight subsidies.

Legislation began with the Agricultural Marketing Act of 1931, a product of the same Socialist Ministry and the same school of thought which gave birth to the Coal Mines Act of 1930. According to the 1931 Act, producers were to prepare marketing schemes which, if approved by the Government and by a majority of the farmers concerned, were to become legally enforcible. The only scheme which came into operation under this Act related to hops. It was a small, monopolistic, price-raising scheme which limited production and put money into the pockets of those who grew hops during the 'datum period'.

The Agricultural Marketing Act of 1933 repeated the 1931 legislation and added provisions for the restriction of imports.[1] Under this Act three schemes were established: for potatoes, pigs and milk. Of these, the potato scheme was the most successful. Imports were controlled by licencing, growers were controlled by a moderately flexible system of quotas and fines, and the supply put on the market each season was controlled by altering the minimum size of potato to be marketed. As a result, annual price fluctuations, until then severe and irregular, were greatly reduced, and the average level of prices was not, as in the case of hops, advanced. The obvious disadvantage of the scheme was the familiar one with quota schemes—rigidity in the share of the market held by different producers. The pigs scheme, with no fewer than three Boards, the Pigs Board, the Bacon Board and the Bacon Development Board, was much more complicated and worked much worse. Briefly, the aim was to reorganize the industry so as to stabilize prices and increase British production at the expense (mainly) of the Danish ex-

[1] Special powers to restrict imports had had to be obtained by the Hop Marketing Board.

porter. When the scheme began, in 1933, about 50 per cent of pork and 85 per cent of bacon and ham were imported. Foreign countries were persuaded to reduce their exports to Britain in 1932; there was further persuasion and restriction in 1933; and after that there were quotas. The Pigs Board and the Bacon Board struggled to agree on mutually profitable prices, but considerable difficulties arose because regard had to be had both to the price of feeding stuffs and the probable selling price of bacon. To make matters worse, the Bacon Board had no control over the pork market, and so pig producers co-operated with the Board only so far as they felt that it suited them; while the Pigs Board overestimated the capacity of the industry and failed to supply the curers with the stipulated quantity of pigs (which they needed to keep their factories in operation). In 1937 the scheme actually broke down. A new one, involving Government subsidies, was introduced in 1938. The scheme did some good, as seasonal and cyclical fluctuations in prices were reduced. But when Danish bacon became harder to obtain because of the quotas, its price rose to the levels which the higher cost British producer had to ask for his inferior product.

'Indeed, our treatment of imports of bacon entailed the paradoxical consequence that in 1934 we paid a little more money (£30m. against £29·9m.) for considerably less bacon (7·6m. as against 9·1m. cwt.) than we did in 1933. Thus the restrictions have not worked disadvantageously to the Danish industry, and actually the Danes would prefer the quota policy to be maintained ... it would be difficult to justify raising prices for the benefit of overseas producers and at the expense of home consumers as a permanent principle of domestic agricultural policy.'[1]

Far more important, and no less open to criticism, were the operations of the Milk Marketing Boards. In the 1930s milk was twice as important, in terms of value, as any other farm product; in value it was over a quarter of total agricultural output. Moreover, there seemed to be room for a great expansion of milk consumption.

[1] Viscount Astor and B. Seebohm Rowntree, *British Agriculture* (London, Longman, 1938), p. 219.

Milk production was carried on all over Britain, but broadly speaking there were two systems of production, one located in the eastern counties and the other in the west. In the east, the cows were fed concentrates, and they produced a fairly level, all-the-year-round supply for the nearby liquid milk, urban markets. In the west, production was seasonal but low-cost, and the milk was marketed chiefly for conversion into cheese, butter and other milk products. During the 1920s milk prices were fixed as a result of bargaining between the National Farmers' Union and the National Federation of Dairymen's Associations. Harmony between NFU and NFDA and between east and west prevailed so long as the liquid price and the manufacturing price for milk were not too widely separated. But between 1929 and 1931 the manufacturing milk price fell by over 50 per cent while the liquid price rose slightly. Farmers in the west, faced with a collapse of their market, began to invade eastern liquid markets. Had this gone on, the liquid price would have fallen, many high-cost eastern producers would have been forced out of business, and supply would have become highly seasonal. Instead, the producers banded together to form Milk Marketing Boards, the first for England and Wales, then four others outside England and Wales.

By the end of the 1930s the scheme for England and Wales had an annual turnover of more than £43m. and this Board had thus become 'one of the greatest financial concerns in the country'.[1] It fixed statutory minimum prices for liquid milk; and in order more or less to equalize profits all over the country and keep the peace between east and west, it divided England and Wales into eleven regions and paid to each producer within each region a uniform ('pool') price, regardless of the price at which he actually sold his milk, this uniform price being determined for each region by total revenue, raised or lowered by contributions from or to the 'inter-regional compensation fund'. This fund existed to ensure 'that those regions which have a very large proportion of the low-priced manufacturing milk should have a pool price not differing too widely from that of the region with the highest proportion of liquid sales'.[2]

[1] Astor and Rowntree, op. cit., p. 276.
[2] ibid., p. 277.

This milk scheme had three serious defects. (1) It increased the receipts of milk producers in the west, and caused an increasing number of farmers to take up dairying. 'The market was flooded with milk from farmers who had not previously sold milk but had kept it to feed to calves and to turn into butter. This . . . not only embarrassed the milk market but seriously affected the rearing industry. It occasioned a scarcity of dairy cows and a consequent rise in their price.'[1] (2) With milk production rising all over the country, the Boards persisted in keeping up the price of milk in the liquid market and selling what the public would not buy at this price to the manufacturers for what it would fetch. Thus the farmer-controlled Boards did nothing to increase liquid consumption; they looked after their members' interests without reference to the general interest. (3) The Scottish Board dumped its surplus on to the high-priced English liquid market. So an arrangement was made, 'on the historical analogy of the Danegeld',[2] according to which the English Board paid the Scottish Board about £100,000 per annum to keep out of the English market. The Aberdeen Board then began to dump its surplus milk in the London market, and Scottish cream was sent south in ever larger quantities.

These measures were not the only ones designed to help farmers in these years. There was the sugar beet subsidy, begun as far back as 1924; there was the Wheat Act of 1931, guaranteeing wheat prices by means of an excise on flour (made mostly from imported wheat); there was the 1937 act guaranteeing prices for oats and barley; subsidies for cattle began in 1934, preceded by import restrictions, and fertilizers were subsidized in 1937. All this amounted to an extraordinary patchwork of policy. Assistance was doled out first to one branch of farming and then to another, often causing a wasteful redistribution of farmers' efforts and resources and sometimes penalizing branches of farming not receiving assistance. There was no strategy, only a series of unco-ordinated measures, mostly directed to propping up the status quo. In a sense, these measures were not unsuccessful. Food prices, falling in the rest of the world, did not rise. The volume of gross agricultural

---

[1] Astor and Rowntree, op. cit., p. 280.
[2] ibid., p. 284.

output at home rose by about 20 per cent between 1930-31 and 1936-37, and wages rose slightly. On the other hand, the volume of employment continued to decline at much the same rate as in the 1920s. Imports of foreign foodstuffs fell heavily, but imports of empire foodstuffs rose; the net effect was a small rise as compared with the 'twenties. The consumer paid more for food than he would have done in a free market; sometimes he had to substitute inferior British beef or British bacon for a better foreign product. Little justification appeared for the complacent belief, typically English, that so long as production was made profitable, efficiency could be left to look after itself. And to those who knew the industry there did not seem much better justification for the strategic argument, either. Keeping down food imports caused unemployment of sailors and ships, and discouraged shipbuilding. Little was done to build up the fertility of the soil—instead, beef and bacon production was encouraged, and this required more imported feeding stuffs. Indeed, if half the annual subsidies paid to farmers between 1934 and 1938 had been given to the Admiralty instead, four aircraft carriers could have been built with the money, and Britain could have entered the war in 1939 with five modern carriers instead of one; always supposing that a sufficient number of admirals could have been found willing to spend the money in this way.[1]

EXPORTS, FOREIGN INVESTMENT AND THE BALANCE OF PAYMENTS

The World Economic Conference of 1933, arranged by the League of Nations with a view to restoring an international economic regime by concerted measures, foundered largely on President Roosevelt's unexpected insistence that for each country improvement must begin at home. The manner in which this opinion was made known was abrupt and unfortunate, but

[1] The chances would not have been good: 'The fleet aircraft carrier was the only class of naval vessel in which no new ships at all were laid down between the spring of 1939 and that of 1942.' (M. M. Postan, *British War Production* (London, HMSO and Longmans, 1952), pp. 63-4.)

it must be acknowledged that the sort of independence which he suddenly showed himself resolved to preserve for the United States was much the same as that currently exploited by the British Government itself. The failure of the conference, however, was another severe shock to international confidence, and it was followed by what the *Economist* described in 1934 as 'the intensification of economic nationalism'.[1] In 1938 the same journal was still contemplating the same policy, 'the all but universal scramble for self sufficiency'.[2] Prospering through international trade was not easy.

Britain was losing markets although not yet actually losing money in international trade and transactions in the 1930s. She was losing markets partly because countries like Australia and Brazil and China were developing their own industries and excluding foreign goods—especially old-style British goods—by means of tariffs; partly because she proved unable to compete with more enterprising and efficient rivals like Belgium and the United States; partly because some of the primary producing countries who had been large purchasers of British goods were particularly badly hit by the depression of 1929-33 and its aftermath. Britain's share of world exports fell from about 11 per cent in the later 1920s to about 10 per cent in the later 1930s. Moreover, the volume of world trade throughout the 1930s was seldom much above the average level of the 1920s and was often below it.

Broadly speaking, Britain's position changed because while the staple exports declined in importance, exports of the rising industries did not grow fast enough to replace them. Thus betwen 1929 and 1937 the volume of exports of iron and steel and manufactures thereof, of cotton and of coal fell by about one-third; vehicles, chemicals and rayon grew; but they were far less important than the older lines, and in any case they grew more slowly than the older lines declined—not surprisingly, in a world where trade as a whole stagnated. The direction of exports did not alter a great deal, but those changes which took place were significant. Between 1928 and 1938 exports to the United States fell, as a percentage of the total, from 6

---

[1] *The Economist*, Commercial History and Review of 1933, p. 3.
[2] ibid., Commercial History and Review of 1937, p. 3.

per cent to 4 per cent; those to Latin America fell from 10 per cent to 8 per cent; while those to Empire countries rose from 34 per cent to 38 per cent. These changes were largely due, of course, to the Ottawa agreements. The retreat from dollar markets did not seem important at the time, but it was later to have serious consequences.[1]

As regards imports, the picture was rather different. Britain's share of world imports rose from 15·5 per cent in the later 'twenties to almost 17·5 per cent in the later 'thirties. This rise was also a rise in the actual *volume* of British imports. The rise in food imports, large in the 'twenties, was only slight in the 'thirties. But the importation of raw materials and of semi-manufactured goods for use in industry was large. Non-ferrous metals, oil and petroleum, rubber, pulp and rags and esparto grass—all these came in to feed the rising electrical, chemical, paper and other industries. In the boom of 1937, iron and steel machinery were wanted. All the time, house-building and construction required imports of timber on an exceptional scale. These imports were processed and the results sold chiefly in the home market. There is thus some sense in describing the 'thirties as a 'self-sufficiency boom'. As to the sources of imports, the Ottawa agreements had a very marked effect in diverting British demand from foreign to Empire sources. The share of the Empire in total British imports rose from 17 per cent to 26 per cent between 1928 and 1938.

Now these two changes, a fall in the volume of merchandise exports and a rise in the volume of merchandise imports, could not have come about and equilibrium have been preserved unless (1) Britain's net earnings from 'invisible' trade (freights, interest and dividends etc.) increased or (2) Britain reduced her rate of capital accumulation overseas or (3) the prices of Britain's imports fell relatively to the prices of her exports; or, of course, there took place some combination of these three changes. What did not happen was (1); net earnings from invisible trade fell almost as severely as earnings from mer-

---

[1] A bi-lateral trade agreement was concluded with the United States in 1938. This was the nineteenth in a series sponsored by Cordell Hull and begun in 1934. The agreement did not operate for long enough to make any difference before the war broke out in 1939.

chandise exports.[1] What did happen was a combination of (2) and (3).

The barter terms of trade had moved sharply in Britain's favour after the 1914-18 war, and they moved sharply in her favour again after the onset of the 1929-33 depression. Figures cannot be exact in this connection, but we may say that if the barter terms of trade are taken as 100 in 1913, they were about 120 from 1921-29 and about 133 from 1931-38. The precise causes of these two sharp upward movements cannot easily be stated. The underlying cause in each case, however, was the same; a downward and rightward shift of the supply functions of a great variety of primary producing industries—wheat, fruit, rubber, tin, bauxite, oil—coupled with a fall in inter-continental transport costs. Supply increased and costs fell; therefore prices fell, and they fell a long way. And the causes of this were productive investment and technological progress in ship-building and in primary production, stimulated first by wartime demand, then (although this did not affect shipbuilding very much) by the rapid growth of manufacturing production in the world during the 1920s. When incomes in manufacturing countries fell after 1929, primary producers maintained pro-duction in the usual way and scrambled for markets, thus causing price reductions even greater and more enduring than in the case of manufactured goods.

Britain took advantage of the more favourable barter terms of trade in the way stated; by increasing the volume of her im-ports. This enabled her to live better, and there is no doubt that one of the important underlying causes of Britain's rising standard of living in the 1930s was this improvement in her barter terms of trade. But better barter terms of trade did not prove to be an unmixed blessing. More imports could be bought with an unchanged volume of exports; but given the demand for imports, less employment was needed in the trades working for

[1] The following approximate figures give an idea of what took place:

Net income from:	Annual averages in £s m.	
	1927-29	1933-35
Shipping	133·3	68·3
Foreign investments	250·0	171·7
Financial services	64·3	30·0
Other sources	28·3	11·0

export, even in the absence of labour-saving technical improvements. In fact, the demand for imports of foodstuffs and raw materials did not prove to be very elastic; it was in part held down, of course, although not to any very great extent, by tariffs. What people wanted more of was manufactured goods, especially durable consumer goods, including houses. These they had to obtain from home producers, again, in part, thanks to the tariff. Thus there was the problem (which had existed in precisely the same form in the 1920s, and perhaps in the 1880s also), how was the country to take advantage of cheaper imports without wasting some of her productive resources, thitherto engaged in working for export, in idleness and unemployment? How were resources to be transferred, in a word, from the export to the non-export trades?

Improvement in the barter terms of trade was not the only change which enabled Britain to export less and import more (or not much less). There was also the decline, almost the disappearance, of net investment abroad. The figures for new capital issues in the United Kingdom can be summarized as follows (annual averages):

	Home Investment	Overseas Investment
1925-29	£165m.	£115m. (of which in the Empire, £67m.)
1932-36	£124m.	£31m. (of which in the Empire, £28m.)

Thus of the new issues on the British capital market, 41 per cent were for overseas in the later 'twenties, only 20 per cent in the 'thirties; non-Empire issuing declined even more spectacularly, from 17 per cent of the total to 2 per cent. These changes continued the trend set up after 1913, the decline in overseas investment now becoming much more marked. But the figures do not reveal the full extent to which British net investment overseas declined, because countries overseas, especially Empire countries, engaged in extensive conversion and refunding operations in the 'thirties (in order to take advantage of the low rates of interest in London) and repaid a good deal of debt. Thus in 1932, 1935, 1936, and 1938 repayments clearly exceeded the amount of new issues, even when fundings are included in the new issues. Repayments were especially large from Australia, South Africa and India. Thus it is almost certainly correct to say that the nominal value of foreign securities owned in Britain fell during the 1930s, probably by more than £100m.[1] Changes in the 'real value' can scarcely be calculated.

Why did net foreign investment (and it is important to remember that we are talking about the *net* amount; investing abroad went on; the machinery was still there, and it was used; new opportunities were taken, trade in new directions developed)—why did net foreign investment cease after 1929, having gone on in every year (except the war years) since 1820 or before? For a short time it was forbidden. As part of the arrangements for conversion of war loan, all would-be borrowers were 'requested' to keep off the market in the summer of 1932; and when new issues were allowed again after September, issues on behalf of borrowers outside the Empire remained forbidden. There was some relaxation in 1934 and further relaxation in 1938. The idea of control was to prevent a weakening of the sterling exchanges due to large-scale capital outflows. But there is little cause to suppose that in the absence of restrictions any very large volume of funds would have sought an outlet abroad. The reasons are not hard to find. There was a lot of defaulting on foreign bonds in and after 1931; exchange controls made the transfer of capital and of interest payments increasingly difficult in several parts of the world; there was increasing political uncertainty in Europe and war in the' Far East. No wonder that British investors preferred to keep their money in the Empire or at home. In these spheres there was much new development. Capital was found for tin in Malaya, copper in Rhodesia, gold in South Africa, oil in Burma, the Middle East, Trinidad, Venezuela and elsewhere, and for general industrial and commercial development in Australia (the Sydney harbour bridge, for example, was built by a British firm and opened in 1932).[2] But the liveliness of demand at home for new capital was even more striking. As already pointed out,[3] the figures for new home issues in the 'thirties are comparable

[1] The details will be found in a series of articles by Sir Robert Kindersley appearing in the *Economic Journal* from 1930 to 1939.

[2] There was also some capital export in the mid-'thirties in the curious form of the purchase of securities in New York—'a case of one creditor country speculating in the stock markets of another.' (Grant, op. cit., p. 171.)

[3] Supra, p. 97.

with those for the 'twenties—and the prices of capital goods had fallen. The new industries had a lively appetite for capital and they came to the London market in large numbers—a phenomenon of very small importance before 1914. Also, local authorities and public corporations emerged as large-scale borrowers in London, the borrowing of the former chiefly accounted for by slum-clearance and re-housing programmes.

This demand was met by a smaller supply of savings than before. Total net investment (home and overseas) as a percentage of net national income fell from 7 per cent in the years 1924-29 to 6·3 per cent in 1933-38.[1] Personal saving was discouraged by low interest rates and high levels of taxation, and was possibly made less easy by the decline in interest and dividends received on previous overseas investment. Industrial profits were quite good—rather higher in the later 1930s than at any time in the 1920s—but they were heavily taxed; moreover, they took a smaller share, even before tax, of the net national income. The redistribution of income through taxation and social expenditure was in favour of those who saved little or nothing. The result of all these factors was almost inevitably a decline in the volume of savings.

This is not to say that savings were inadequate, still less to say that net foreign investment disappeared because there was no money for it. There would have had to be a great pressure of funds seeking investment before much money was committed to Germany, Japan or even the United States in the 1930s. Admittedly, interest rates rose: 2½ per cent consols rose from 2·89 per cent in 1935 to 3·38 per cent in 1938. But this was not a large movement. It certainly did not suggest a frustrated anxiety to invest abroad. As for the weakness of the current balance of payments, that was an independent consideration which bothered no investors. It is merely an academic observation that trade would probably have shown 'dubious responsiveness . . . to any attempt to transfer large investments'.[2]

The fact that Britain's surplus on her current balance of payments was small or non-existent therefore caused no great anxiety in the 1930s. There was diminished investment over-

[1] Figures from Phelps Brown and Weber, loc. cit. Table III.
[2] A. E. Kahn, *Great Britain in the World Economy*, p. 141.

seas because there was diminished inclination to invest overseas. Britain used the favourable terms of trade to boost consumption; in the circumstances, this course was almost inevitable.
And after all, income from overseas investments during the
'thirties rose from the low level of £150m. in 1933 to £198m.
in 1937; gold mines were doing particularly well, oil investments
were profitable, the foreign exchange position of several South
American countries was improving. It is true that the £198m.
received in 1937 was a good deal short of the £231m. received
in 1929, and that the income was not being re-invested. It is
also true that when trade boomed in 1937, imports rose in
value much faster than exports, due primarily to the great rise in
raw material prices in the first part of 1937, so that the trade
gap widened; and that when raw material prices collapsed, the
balance of payments position improved, but foreigners were
able to buy a far smaller volume of British exports than before.
This difficulty, of achieving both a high level of activity and
balance in the balance of payments was to become all too familiar
after 1945. But in the 'thirties there was not recognized to be a
foreign trade problem except as part of the general unemployment problem. And as far as overseas investments went, Britain
was still benefiting from previous investment to a very satisfactory extent—interest and dividends from abroad accounted
for almost a quarter of the total on the credit side of Britain's
balance of payments in the 1930s.

UNEMPLOYMENT AND GOVERNMENT POLICY

A good number of the measures, and all the most important
ones, adopted by the Government with a view to promoting and
encouraging economic revival have now been mentioned: cheap
money; tariffs and the Import Duties Advisory Committee; aid
to agriculture; self-government for the coal industry; the North
Atlantic Shipping Act.

Perhaps none of these measures was designed simply or
even chiefly to increase employment. This could not be said of
the Special Areas (Development and Improvement) Act
passed at the end of 1934. The existence of areas where unemployment was especially heavy had been noted in 1928, and
Government assistance had been given to help people to move

out of them. During the slump nothing significant was done. But after 1933, when general improvement became obvious but passed these black spots by, the contrast between them and the rest of the country became so conspicuous that it could no longer be ignored. The coalfields of South Wales, Durham and south-west Scotland were the outstanding examples of under-employed localities, with a seemingly permanent contraction of the traditional kinds of labour demand and no other form of local employment available. The shipbuilding districts on the Mersey, Clyde and Tyne also suffered heavy unemployment, al-though some alternative industries did exist in these places. Some of the cotton districts of Lancashire were little better off. Thus in 1934 unemployment in Birmingham was 6·4 per cent, in Oxford 5·1 per cent; but in Greenock and Motherwell it was over 36 per cent, and in Merthyr Tydfil and Jarrow it was over 60 per cent.

The 'natural' remedy for this situation was movement of the population out of the areas affected. This took place at con-siderable speed, aided by the Ministry of Labour; the population of South Wales fell by 115,000 between 1931 and 1938,[1] that of Northumberland and Durham by 39,000. Most of those who moved went to London and the south-east of England, where the unemployment rate in 1936-37 was not much above half the national average. But no such movement could take place rapidly enough to eliminate distress. The 1934 Act appointed two un-paid Commissioners, one for England and Wales and one for Scotland, to initiate and support measures for the 'economic development and social improvement' of the areas. They could not, however, start or assist any undertakings carried on for a profit. There was a grant of £2m. The Commissioners used the money to provide amenities, such as parks and swimming pools, and to help with the capital costs of local services—milk for mothers and children, housing, water supply and so on. None of this expenditure had much to do with reducing unemployment. The Commissioners' powers were in fact too limited to permit them to do much, and they said so. As a result, the Special Areas (Amendment) Act, 1937, gave the Commissioners another

[1] This is no less than 6 per cent of the total population of South Wales in 1931. Few inter-regional migrations in British history can have taken place faster than this.

£2m. and power to make grants to private firms in remission of rent, rates and income tax. The Commissioners were now also helped by the Special Areas Reconstruction Association, set up as an ancillary to the Bank of England in 1936, and the Nuffield Trust; and the Treasury was authorized to make loans to new undertakings in the areas. 'One way and another, it could be said that a new enterprise might hope to escape all capital charges for five years.'[1] The result was the creation and development of the Trading Estates, where firms could lease premises or have premises built, with no trouble about power, services or communications. At last light industries began to be attracted to the areas; by 1939 over 200 factories on the Estates were in production, but the volume of employment which they offered—mostly for women—was not large.

These results were not spectacular, especially considering the amount of attention given to the Special Areas. The number of persons unemployed in the Special Areas fell rapidly between 1934 and 1937, but so did the number of persons unemployed in the whole country, with the result that the unemployment rate in the Special Areas remained about double that of the country as a whole; and workers had moved out of the Special Areas. By 1937, however, new factors were beginning to work in the areas' favour. A scarcity of labour began to be felt in the south-east; armaments contracts began to come, by design, to the Special Areas; the steel-works at Consett and Ebbw Vale were located in favour of the areas. Something substantial had turned up at last. But it was very late. There were 80,000 men over forty-five 'who had become practically a standing army of unemployed'.[2] Worse still, there were in 1936 'too large a number of young men in the Special Areas who are content to live in idleness as State pensioners and are unwilling to make any effort to find work. They have grown up in an atmosphere of idleness . . . [and] are, in fact, demoralized by the seeming inevitableness of unemployment'.[3]

Those whom it could not help to find employment the State could at least help to live. One of the first acts of the National

[1] R. C. Davison, *British Unemployment Policy*, p. 104.

[2] ibid., p. 97.

[3] Commissioners for the Special Areas in England and Wales, Third Report (November 1936).

Government in 1931 was to set up a dual scheme of payments to the unemployed, differentiating between (1) insurance benefit drawn as a right and (2) a secondary assistance scheme on a needs basis. Insurance benefit rates were reduced in amount and duration, and every claimant had to prove thirty contributions in the two years preceding his claim. These restrictions disallowed over a million claimants from further benefit. For them, there were 'Transitional Payments', made only after a means test. This aroused a great deal of resentment. There was the humiliation of official enquiry into private affairs; there was the doubtful justice of helping those who had not saved and compelling those who had saved to part with their savings and so help themselves; there was the ancient stigma of contact with the machinery of the Poor Law. On the other hand, about 200,000 people ceased to be applicants for assistance in any form; most of them, no doubt, 'no longer even regarded themselves as seeking work'.[1] This alone saved about £10m. per annum. This and other smaller savings were the justification of the system, including the means test. 'It was not that it saved money by cutting down the allowances of those poor people who *were* assisted, but that it was a way, perhaps the only way, of keeping off thousands of applications from people who, though not in need, would take advantage of any State "doles" given as a right at fixed rates without contributory conditions.'[2]

In 1934 came the Unemployment Act. This important measure sought to make contributory insurance the main support for the unemployed. It made the scheme more generous (the 1931 cuts were restored), it made it cover more people, and it did something (rising employment did more) to ensure its solvency. But the major feature of the act was what it did for those not covered by insurance. There was set up the Unemployment Assistance Board, which was to take over the work involved in 'Transitional Payments' from the local Public Assistance Committees, and also all their traditional functions relating to the relief of the able-bodied poor. It was, in fact, the nationalization of assistance for the able-bodied. Enquiry into family resources was to continue. The aim was centralized

[1] Davison, op. cit., p. 16.
[2] ibid., p. 24.

control over the expenditure of what was, after all, Government money,[1] and the establishment of uniform principles and equality of treatment throughout the country. The Board was a semi-independent corporation; for its actions the Ministry of Labour had a conveniently remote responsibility. These neat and tidy ideas produced a good deal of trouble. Attempts to impose uniformity led to violent protests, and the Government had to back down. The Board had to work very complicated schemes, and the Treasury had to accept a possible abuse of public funds. In fact, the Government bought its way out of trouble— most of the Board's adjustments were discretionary increases; but its policy was sympathetic, flexible, humane, even imaginative, as well as, by the standards of the day, quite generous.

It may be said that the Government and the civil servants emerged with credit from an exceptionally difficult situation. The Unemployment Act of 1930 'marks the extreme limit of relaxation of benefit rules'.[2] In 1931, when contributory and non-contributory benefit was being paid for unlimited periods as a legal right to all claimants who had ever done a few weeks' work in an insured trade, expenditure was at the rate of £125m. a year; income from employers' and workers' contributions was less than £30m. The fund was over £100m. in debt. Unemployment was higher in 1932 and higher again in 1933. The abolition of unlimited 'rights', reduced benefits (offset a little by falling prices) and stricter administration enabled the authorities to scramble through this period without either breakdown or too great injustice. The fundamentally well-conceived Act of 1934 was a very considerable achievement, and its operation was enormously helped by the basic fact that between 1933 and 1937 there was an increase in the number of persons in employment of about two million. In 1937 the Insurance Fund had £62m. in hand, and compulsory insurance had been extended to over half a million agricultural workers.

There remain two aspects of Government policy which deserve brief consideration; the further development of public corporations, and the acquiescence in monopolistic arrangements in industry.

---

[1] Both insurance and transitional payments were a national charge.
[2] Davison, op. cit., p. 8.

The first of these confirmed the precedents which the 'twenties had created—the BBC (1926) and the Central Electricity Board (1927). The London Passenger Transport Board of 1933 possessed, under the Government, a monopoly of all public passenger transport services in London—tubes, buses and trams. Some such scheme had been suggested by an Advisory Committee as early as 1927, chiefly on the ground that the extension and electrification of suburban railways could be financed only if all London's transport services were centralized. The short-lived Socialist Government brought in a Bill, but had not time to pass it; a very similar measure was accepted by the Tories (with some protest) in 1933. The scheme was a good one, for the imperfect competition of private transport in London was wasteful, and Government backing helped the Board in its investment plans. In 1939 another step on the same path was taken when a Bill was introduced merging the two existing, subsidized but unprofitable companies, Imperial Airways and British Airways, into one public corporation, British Overseas Airways Corporation. This corporation came into existence only in 1940. These were both cases, in effect if not in name, of nationalization; shareholders were compulsorily bought out (i.e. compensated) and Boards set up by authority of Parliament with ultimate responsibility to Parliament *via* a Minister.

The matter of restraints upon competition and the Government's attitude to them is no less important, for certain habits of thought and action became definitely established in the 'thirties, which, although possibly not very harmful then, may have had a deleterious effect upon the efficiency of the economy with the passage of time. Monopolies, or at least firms with monopolistic powers, were of course not new. Monopolistic organizations with a history going back to pre-war days included the notorious Salt Union, the Alkali Combine, the Associated Portland Cement Manufacturers, the Wall-Paper Manufacturers, the Imperial Tobacco Company, and the spinning combine of J. & P. Coats. The 'twenties added some new ones. There was the Distillers' Company, dominant in the industry after fresh absorptions of competitors in 1925. There was Lever Brothers, by 1925 dominating the soap industry (and its ramifications) through the United Kingdom Soap Manufacturers'

Association, possessing 'vast interests in plantations, whaling fleets, shipping companies, oil refineries, cake mills, fisheries, margarine factories, canneries, and many other lines'.[1] Most enormous of all, there was Imperial Chemical Industries Ltd., formed in 1926 by uniting the British Dyestuffs Corporation (created out of wartime needs and fostered by the Government), Nobel Industries Ltd. (with a like history, relating to munitions), Brunner Mond and Company and the United Alkali Company (both interested in the manufacture of heavy chemicals). The result was a company which made most kinds of acids, alkalis, other heavy chemicals, dyestuffs, explosives and fertilizers, as well as possessing special lines such as artificial leather and fabrics, paints, zip fasteners, gas mantles, motor bicycles and locomotive fireboxes. In the field of heavy chemicals, dyestuffs and explosives its influence was dominant. Its creation was justified on the grounds that centralization would make possible better technical guidance throughout the industry, promote expansion at home and abroad, and prevent 'any unnecessary expenditure of capital by duplication and over-lapping'.[2]

It is easy to suspect but impossible to prove that these giant firms had some tendency to inefficiency in the senses of being over-administered, of stifling individual initiative and originality, and of charging too much for their goods. On the other hand, price-competition was not as a rule what was wanted between 1929 and 1936 or so, and at least in the chemical industry there is reason to believe that centralized 'know-how' and research has considerable advantages. The trouble lay, not so much in the existence and possible failings of a few very large firms, as in the pervasiveness of non-competition throughout the economy. Trade associations and price fixing were the rule in British industry between the wars. The Government accepted the situation—it could scarcely do anything else, in view of its own contribution; the Coal Mines Act, the Agricultural Acts, the paternalism of the Import Duties Advisory Committee. Far more surprising, even the law fell silent. The common law was supposed to regard all monopolistic agreements and even all inter-

---

[1] A. F. Lucas, *Industrial Reconstruction and the Control of Competition* (London, Longmans, 1937), p. 191.
[2] Memorandum by Lord Melchett, quoted in Lucas, op. cit., p. 182.

ference with individual liberty of action in trading with disfavour as contrary to the public interest. And yet, nearly all practices

'proscribed by the various anti-trust statutes of the United States as "unfair competition" have been expressly approved by the English Courts . . . on the paradoxical grounds that they are not inimical to public welfare. A group of producers could today [1937] exterminate all competitors with a programme of vicious price-cutting, rigid tying contracts, exclusive dealing agreements, resale price maintenance, deferred rebates and commercial boycotts; they could then proceed to exploit the public through price manipulation and restriction of output; and all the while not only would they be well within their legal rights, but they could successfully defend their policies in the Courts on considerations of public welfare.'[1]

Some of this legal complaisance towards the suppressors of competition can be dated from the Mogul Steamship case of 1892, once described as 'the charter of trade associations'; and it derived some of its strength, no doubt, from the generally bad odour into which 'unrestricted competition' had fallen in the excess capacity economy of the 1920s—'the idea of regulating output by concerted arrangements between producers,' declared an eminent economist in 1927, 'is no longer seriously opposed by economic theory or public policy'.[2]

Thus an attitude which could properly be taken towards some British industries in this period was taken towards them all, and competition was throttled extensively and in detail. How much competition there should be and how it is best preserved and encouraged is never an easy question, and there have always been people too ready to declare that we can never have too much of it and others that we can never have too little. But there is no doubt that the limited, exiguous, emasculated, etiolated competition of the 1930s was too little for good economic health then, and that the economy still suffered years later from the unenterprising habits acquired at that time.[3]

[1] A. F. Lucas, op. cit., p. 352.

[2] D. H. Macgregor, in *International Cartels* (League of Nations, 1927), II, 16, p. 3.

[3] It is instructive to compare the British Government's attitude in the 'thirties with that of the New Deal. Roosevelt began, like the National Government, by condoning and even promoting restraints on competition; but by 1937 the traditional American policy of harassing business men suspected of monopolistic practices had been revived.

THE STANDARD OF LIVING

The standard of living of a community is not a fact but an enormous collection of facts; if it is discussed statistically, it is apt to dwindle to a mere index number. Index numbers, however, are a help; and with them we may begin.

According to the best available series,[1] the national income surpassed its 1913 level in 1927, and then rose to a peak in 1929. It then fell. But in 1931 and 1932, when it was at its lowest, it was only 2 per cent lower than in 1929, and from there it climbed steeply to a new peak in 1937. It is not easy to compare the performance of the economy in the 'thirties with its performance in the 'twenties, because from the beginning of the 'twenties there was a lot of ground to be made up owing to the combination of war-time losses and the set-back suffered in the post-war slump. It is best to make two comparisons; to compare the peak in 1929 with the preceding peak in 1913, and also to compare 1929 with the 'normal' post-slump years of 1923, 1924 (these years, incidentally, had a national income about the same as 1911, 1912): and then to compare 1937 with 1929 and also with 1931, 1932, for there was no post-slump 'normal' in the 'thirties—rapid improvement began at once. The figures are as follows:

Year	Index of national income at 1900 prices (1900 = 100)	Change in per cent	Index of income per head at 1900 prices (1900 = 100)	Change in per cent
1913	120·3		108·46	
1929	132·0	+ 9·7	118·89	+ 9·6
1929	132·0		118·89	
1937	155·4	+17·7	135·18	+13·7
1923-24	115·3		106·0	
1929	132·0	+14·5	118·89	+12·2
1931-32	129·3		115·25	
1937	155·4	+20·2	135·18	+17·3

However the comparison is made, progress was much faster in the 'thirties than in the 'twenties. It may be replied that the 'twenties was itself an unsatisfactory decade. But then it should

[1] A. R. Prest, 'National Income of the United Kingdom, 1870-1946', in *Economic Journal*, 1948.

be remembered that the 13·7 per cent rise in the national income per head between 1929 and 1937 was not only greater than the rise in the 'twenties but was also much greater than the rise between 1907 and 1913 (3·8 per cent) and between 1899 and 1907 (2·7 per cent), and was almost as great as that in the 'nineties—14·3 per cent between 1890 and 1899. From this point of view, the country cannot be said to have been doing at all badly in the 1930s.

But of course figures of the national income, or of the national income divided by the population, give only a rough, aggregative idea of the position. As far as the mass of the people was concerned, things were in one way better and in one way worse than the figures suggest.

They were better than appears because of the redistribution of income, which had begun to be important in the 1920s, in favour of the lower income groups. Taxation, which was probably regressive in the nineteenth century and became progressive only around 1900, was steeply progressive after the war. In the 'twenties and 'thirties, the tax burden was regressive on incomes up to about £300 per annum, moderately progressive on incomes between £300 and £1,000 per annum, and steeply progressive above that level. The burden on the middle incomes, from £300 to £1,000 per annum, was not heavy. But if the distribution of taxation remained approximately constant between the wars, the burden increased. It has been calculated[1] that all compulsory contributions amounted to £5 19s 0d per capita in 1913-14, £20 8s 0d in 1925-26, and £24 16s 0d in 1937-38. These rates of increase, even that for the inter-war decades, are much greater than the corresponding rates of growth of money income. Thus the Government was securing control over the disposal of a larger and larger share of a growing national product. Public expenditure as a percentage of the national income was about 15 per cent in the decade before the war, just over 30 per cent in the 1920s, and almost 35 per cent in the 1930s. And the greatest item in this expenditure, and the most persistently growing, was that for the social services; chiefly education, health, housing, and social security.

[1] G. F. Shirras and L. Rostas, *The Burden of British Taxation* (Cambridge University Press, 1942), p. 35.

The rich did not necessarily pay more towards the cost of these services than the poor; but the rich benefited from them scarcely at all. Thus the real incomes of those who lived in sub-sidized houses, received medical services below cost, drew non-contributory pensions or unemployment benefit, and had their children educated at State schools were higher than their money incomes might suggest. Moreover, the unearned advantages which accrued to the poor were larger in the 'thirties than in the 'twenties. Comparing 1936 with 1923, education was costing the Government another £28m., housing another £28m., public health another £21m. Attempts to estimate the amount of in-come redistributed possess only a dubious theoretical founda-tion; but the amount was substantial, and it increased. It follows that the standard of living of the lower income groups—say, those with incomes below £400 per annum—rose faster than the figures for national income per head suggest in comparing the 'thirties with the 'twenties.

But this statement requires further qualification. Having dis-tinguished the lower income groups from the average, we must also distinguish another group; the unemployed. Disregarding for the moment the personal sorrow and damage which unem-ployment might bring, and considering only income, the un-employed were poor, almost destitute. Weekly benefit rates for adult males from late 1931 to the summer of 1934 were 15s 3d; for adult dependants 8s 0d, and for children 2s 0d. Fancy keeping a child on 2s 0d a week! Of course, prices were low. In the middle of the 1930s £2 10s 0d was an average wage in many large industries; in cotton it was less than £2—most wage earners, indeed, received less than £2 10s 0d a week for most of the 'thirties. Family incomes, of course, tended to be higher. But even by these standards, the unemployed man and his wife and two children were very poor with 27s 3d a week; they were still very poor when the 1931 cuts were restored in 1934, and they began to receive 30s 0d a week.[1] The only men who were prob-ably no worse off whether out of work or in it were those with more than three children; and this is no tribute to the system, for it must be remembered 'that the incidence of poverty is progres-

---

[1] These figures are minima. Some unemployed had other small, possibly occasional, sources of income; and rates of benefit were raised later.

sively greater according to the number of children under working age in the family concerned'.[1] In other words, those families already wretchedly poor could not in decency be allowed to become still poorer when the husband lost his job.

What sort of standard of living was possible 'on the dole'?[2] Fortunately, an unemotional, unpolitical, careful, reliable picture was drawn at the time in a Report to the Pilgrim Trust.[3] A couple of quotations from that Report may suffice.

'In a typical Liverpool [long unemployed] family, where there were two children, aged 4 and 12, the family had nothing but bread, margarine and tea, with condensed milk, for breakfast and dinner, "but we always try to give them something hot for tea. We go to bed early so as not to feel hungry".'[4]

The second case also comes from Liverpool.

'. . . a young couple, [aged] 26 and 23 . . . were visited . . . on a bitter February afternoon. It was snowing outside. The house could hardly have been better kept and both of them were neatly, though not at all flashily, dressed. Yet there was no fire, and so far that day (it was three o'clock) they had had nothing to eat, only cups of tea. They lit the fire when one of us came in, for the man said "his mother had just helped them out with a bit of coal," and so they could manage it. He said his wife "had something for the evening" and that "they weren't starved, though sometimes they had to go pretty short".'[5]

In such circumstances, one of the Report's findings can hardly come as a surprise: 'it was a matter of daily experience to observe the obvious signs of malnutrition in the appearance of the wives of unemployed men with families.'[6] Besides lack of food, any prolongation of unemployment made it impossible to keep

---

[1] *Men Without Work*, A Report made to the Pilgrim Trust (Cambridge, 1938), p. 111.

[2] This phrase came in the 1930s to be applied indifferently to the drawing of both insurance benefits and needs payments.

[3] See footnote 1.

[4] op. cit., p. 115.

[5] *Men Without Work*, p. 121.

[6] ibid., p. 139.

linen and furniture and pots and pans in repair, or to buy sufficient shoes and clothing. The almost inevitable consequence was sale of possessions, resort to the pawnshop, and general shabbiness.

For a time, enormous numbers of people were in danger of falling into conditions like these. Over 2m. men, women and juveniles were unemployed in 1930-31, over 2½m. in 1931-32, and not a great deal short of 3m. in 1932-33.[1] After that, unemployment fell rather rapidly; by 1936-37 over 1m. people had found fresh employment, and the unemployment figure was below 1½m. Moreover, the unemployed were to a considerable extent a revolving army; that 2½m. men were unemployed in 1931 does not mean that they were all out of a job for the whole of that year. But some of them were—over 300,000 of them. This number went on increasing until the summer of 1933, when over 480,000 men and women seeking work had had no work for over a year. This was quite a new phenomenon. Before 1929, most 'unemployed' people succeeded in finding some employment for at least a few weeks in every year. Now this was less often the case. And even when unemployment fell, the number of the long unemployed (out of work for more than a year) fell more slowly. Recovery was failing to solve the problem.

The existence of this army of the long unemployed—still about 250,000 men late in 1936—had a double significance. First, it was these men and their families whose standard of living tended to fall to the levels described above. A brief spell of unemployment might be made more supportable financially by the use of previous savings; the man unemployed for over a year had to live solely on relief. Second, a brief spell of unemployment is a holiday from work; long unemployment, enforced idleness, is demoralizing. '"You see that corner?" said a young man of twenty in the Rhondda. "Well, when I'm on my own, my time is spent between here and that corner." '[2] Men long unemployed suffered loss of skill, loss of physical condition, loss of pride and a sense of place in society, and, at the worst, loss of even the inclination to work. These losses are not reflected in data on the standard of living.

No simple verdict is thus possible on the 'thirties. Probably

[1] The actual figures were 2·2m., 2·6m. and 2·8m. for the years referred to.
[2] *Men Without Work*, p. 150.

a simple verdict distorts the truth for most decades. But the decade of the 'thirties was more mixed than usual. The overall standard of living rose; there were more houses, more cars, more wireless sets, food was cheaper and more abundant. But the average unemployment figure for the decade was about 2m. And this unemployment was particularly heavy in certain districts. And, especially in these districts, there was a lot of long term unemployment. In the Rhondda in 1936 over a quarter of those unemployed were long unemployed and they had on the average been unemployed for no less than fifty six months. No society, even with standards of living rising faster than they were in Britain in the 'thirties, could be satisfied or happy with a social problem and a personal tragedy of this character in its midst.

CHAPTER V

The War Economy, 1939-1945

THE British economy from 1939 to 1945 can be studied from two points of view. One can concentrate upon the organization and the achievement of the economy in these years, dwelling upon the methods by which military requirements were met and civilian requirements held in check, examining the history of the development of new aircraft or new weapons, laying bare the administrative processes which allocated scarce resources between competing uses: alternatively, one can attend chiefly to those developments which turned out to be significant not so much for the wartime economy of the day as for the peacetime economy which was to follow it. How the economy provided the sinews of war is a study in itself. The concern of this book is rather with the general course of development through several decades, and the war economy is therefore treated here as an interlude to be studied not so much for its own sake as with regard to the influence which it had upon the shape of things to come.

Great Britain declared war on Germany on September 3, 1939, and upon Japan on December 7, 1941. Germany capitulated in May 1945, and Japan in August. These six years of war were an unprecedented interruption in the normal course of Great Britain's economic development. For this was total war—something which the world had never seen before. And for no country was the war more total—if the phrase may be permitted—in an economic sense, than for Great Britain.

What is meant by saying that Great Britain's war effort was an unexampled exhibition of total war? Simply this: that everything that could usefully be sacrificed in order to build up and maximize the military strength of the country for the time when it was possible to strike back against Germany in Europe (in

1944-45) was sacrificed. Foreign investments were sold, women conscripted, capital was run down and not replaced, civilian consumption was drastically reduced, exports were cut back. Of course, a balance had to be struck in all these matters. To have realized all foreign assets as soon as possible would have resulted in sales at knock-down prices; there were obvious limits to the conscription of women; most difficult of all, 'might not the war effort be better served by maintaining the supply of tobacco, horse-racing, cinemas, ice-cream or flowers—things which would strengthen the will to work or brighten dreary lives? . . . The reduction in the standard of living was throughout determined largely by a process of trial and error and by the prevailing balance of opinion about public psychology.'[1] Nevertheless, this reduction was persistent and went very far. Comfort in the present and economic security in the future were alike abandoned. The war effort could not have been greater.

Production for war required the contraction of innumerable industries and the expansion of two in particular: agriculture and engineering.

Agriculture was expanded in order to conserve shipping space. To begin with, in 1939 and 1940, in 'a mood of muddled cheerfulness',[2] the authorities thought that there were plenty of ships, and earlier ideas of a food production campaign designed to increase the output of food for direct human consumption at the expense of other kinds of food were quietly dropped; instead, a general increase of agricultural production was encouraged— even the production of import-expensive foodstuffs like beef and bacon. A subsidy for ploughing up grassland was given in 1939, and by the middle of 1941, encouraged by generous price increases as well as the subsidy, farmers had nearly 4m. more acres under crops than in the summer of 1939. But an agriculture planned to save as much shipping space as possible would have had little room for meat-producing livestock, which compete with human-beings for food; yet livestock farming was widespread in Britain in 1940. By the end of that year, however, it was obvious that ships were scarce, and that the methods of

---

[1] W. K. Hancock and M. M. Gowing, *British War Economy* (HMSO, 1949), p. 492.

[2] Hancock and Gowing, op. cit., p. 126.

allocating importing capacity were thoroughly unsatisfactory. As a result, a campaign was launched to plough up a further 2½m. acres for crops, and prices were at last adjusted so as to encourage the production of milk and potatoes, and to discourage the production of pigs, fat cattle and sheep. After 1940 almost no feeding stuffs were imported, and animal feeding stuffs were rationed early in 1941. Agricultural output continued to rise, but at the same time its composition began to coincide more closely with national needs. By the end of the war, the value of net agricultural output at constant prices was about 35 per cent higher than in 1939. British agriculture had become intensively mechanized—the number of tractors in use rose from 60,000 to 190,000—and output per man increased by 10 to 15 per cent. Farmers, moreover, became prosperous. The spur to increased production was higher profit. Many farmers had done little more than cover their costs in the 1930s, but the increase in prices during the war was more than sufficient to meet the further increases in costs which took place. Juggling with price differentials, providing a stimulus for the marginal producer, and tempering the wind towards the farmer in lines of production now less popular, the Government was unable to avoid being more generous than the case often required. Farmers discovered that farming for the nation to Government order was a profitable proposition.

The engineering industry (using the term in its widest sense to cover metal manufacture and working, motors, vehicles, aircraft, shipbuilding and ship-repairing) was obviously the backbone of war production. In all departments it had to be converted and expanded. Many of the firms which had specialized in work for the War Office and the Air Ministry had been all but ruined in the 'twenties and 'thirties by the run-down of the armed forces; when rearmament began in 1936 and especially when, in the middle of 1938, orthodox financial limitations on its pace were removed, many of these firms were hard put to it to keep up with Government orders. Before 1939 arrangements had fortunately been made to put work out to firms not normally engaged in making armaments—the car industry was almost the first to be affected—and production facilities were extended, especially for the manufacture of aircraft. But demand grew at a tremendous pace after the debacle in France in the early summer of 1940, at a pace which no one would have thought reasonable or possible even in 1939. Thus in August 1940 it was assumed that the number of armoured divisions (there were three in the spring of 1940) was to be raised to ten; early in 1941 this figure became twelve; in the spring it became sixteen; and by the end of July, eighteen. This meant that, whereas in August 1940 industry was expected to produce 6,000 cruiser tanks in the next fifteen months, in May 1941 it was expected to produce 14,000 cruiser tanks in the next eighteen months. Similarly with aircraft. The 1938 plan was to produce 12,000 aircraft in two years, with a potential of 2,000 aircraft per month; in September 1940 the Air Council was wanting to raise actual production, with all ancillary equipment, to 3,000 per month as soon as possible, and the 'target' for the third year of war became 2,550 aircraft per month.

Inevitably, great difficulty was experienced in meeting these colossal demands. There were three main sources of trouble. First, there was the technical problem of producing good, up-to-date designs of new weapons, tanks and aircraft. Much was hoped of the Whirlwind, for example, in 1941 and 1942; but few people ever flew one. The Churchill tank, designed and developed in an enormous hurry in 1940 and ordered 'off the drawing board', turned out to be most unreliable, and two years had to be spent on its further development before it became a sound weapon of war. The Navy spent years working on a radar set for aircraft which ultimately had to be abandoned as useless. Secondly, there were recurrent shortages of raw materials and semi-manufactured goods. The supply of light alloys was at one time inadequate. With the entry of Japan into the war, serious concern was felt for supplies of rubber, tin, sisal, tungsten, and some other materials. New sources of supply could be, and were, found; but it took time to develop them; and in any event shipping losses became so severe in 1942 that in March the Raw Materials Department of the Ministry of Supply 'had to act on the dismal assumption that the quantity of materials to be received by sea would only be 75 per cent of the forecast in November 1941. At this level imports would be considerably less than the amount below which, it was thought, they could not fall without creating a serious situation.'[1] Fortunately, production was never interrupted or even slowed down by failure in the supply of basic raw materials, although in order to maintain that supply, ships had sometimes to be diverted from military uses. Shortages continued to be felt, however, in the supply of semi-manufactured goods—rolled products, castings, gauges, drop forgings. Surprisingly, the supply of machine tools held up well. In 1940 and 1941 the United States was supplying to the United Kingdom four times the number of machine tools supplied in 1939. But the British machine tool industry was itself responsible for half the total increase in supplies in 1940 and for all of it thereafter. The industry more than doubled its output in two years. This was a remarkable achievement. Lastly, and most important of all, there was a growing and chronic shortage of labour, especially of skilled labour. This did not appear immediately—more than 1m. people were still unemployed in April 1940, this despite a very large number of vacancies. But as soon as war production got into its stride, the shortage of skilled workers became serious, especially of skilled tool-makers and machine-setters. 'Towards the end of 1940 and in the early months of 1941 new factories and expansions planned before Dunkirk were approaching their full rates of production. And most of them were now threatened with hold-ups through shortages of skilled labour . . . In the shipbuilding industry the supply of electricians, turners and fitters was becoming difficult at the end of 1940,'[2] and the movement of men in these trades out of shipbuilding into other branches of the munitions industry made matters worse. The solution lay in up-grading and training labour, standardizing designs, pooling key men. Remarkable results were achieved; for example, by mid-1942 the number of people in the engineering industry drawing skilled rates of pay had doubled. But by 1942 the problem had changed into an acute shortage of manpower in general. It was this which set the ultimate limit to production. In 1944 the manpower problem 'was no longer one of closing a gap between demand and supply by subtracting at the demand end and adding at the supply end. Nothing was left to add. The country was fully mobilized and all

[1] M. M. Postan, *British War Production*, p. 213.
[2] ibid., op. cit., pp. 148-9.

that remained was to change the distribution of manpower as the strategy of war demanded.'[1]

Yet the goods were delivered. An industry able to produce just over 2,000 fighters and light bombers in 1939 was producing between 2,000 and 3,000 a quarter—and more complicated aircraft at that—in 1942, 1943 and 1944; more tanks were produced in any one quarter of 1942 than in the whole of 1940; and so on. Of course, the capital of the industry had been greatly increased—it had more floor space, more handling equipment, more tools—and mass production techniques had been extended and developed. In the shipbuilding industry the gain was especially noticeable. Pre-war doubts about the shipyards' efficiency proved as a rule only too well founded. There was general obsolescence of plant, tools and power supplies, and methods of work were not all that modern either. A substantial programme of re-equipment and modernization had to be undertaken, largely at the Government's expense; modern methods of welding, in particular, were introduced to a backward and distrustful industry.[2]

How was it all done? The labour force in agriculture rose from 711,000 in 1939 to 887,000 in 1945. The labour force in engineering (as previously defined) and in chemicals (including explosives) rose from $3 \cdot 1$m. to a peak of $5 \cdot 2$m. in 1943. And meanwhile the armed forces increased from 480,000 in 1939 to $5 \cdot 1$m. in 1945. How was it possible to find these 6 to 7m. extra people, get them into the right jobs, supply them with equipment, feed, clothe and house them, and simultaneously keep the rest of the economy going?

The actual business of moving people and keeping everything going was of course a triumph of centralized organization. But the fundamental principles involved in the headlong expansion of the armed forces and the supply of food and arms were two: the contraction of everything else; and the conscription of women.

In allocating manpower and scarce resources between the

[1] Hancock and Gowing, op. cit., p. 449.
[2] It is only fair to add that the Admiralty, before the war, was as obscurantist about welding as was the industry. The Admiralty had, of course, the precedent of its attitude to steel in the nineteenth century.

Services, industry working for the Services, and everything else, it was everything else which always came last. There were of course minimum standards to be preserved—it was Churchill himself who once reminded his colleagues that Great Britain was 'a modern community at war, and not Hottentots or Esquimaux'.[1]

Standards were, however, reduced a long way. Some goods ceased to be made altogether. Food was rationed. Civilian clothing for adults was available to the extent of half the pre-war level. Furniture was made only to utility specifications, and not much of it. Production of a host of goods was restricted, and the goods themselves standardized and vulgarized. The civilian petrol ration disappeared in 1942. Sometimes these cuts went too far. Pots and pans became lamentably scarce. The Government, perhaps forgetting that this was still, in at least one sense, a dynamic economy, reduced the supply of perambulators to a level quite unequal to the demand. Most serious error of all, the coal industry was allowed to run down. When France collapsed in 1940 her large demand for British coal disappeared, and miners became unemployed. They wished to leave the pits; and the Government removed the restriction which prevented miners being called up or volunteering under the age of thirty. Miners went into the forces and into other branches of industry; and the labour force in the mines fell by about 10 per cent, and production fell rather more. Coal began to be rationed in 1941, but difficulties were encountered and in 1942 (when the fuel situation seemed much more threatening) the scheme was abandoned. The country scraped through owing to a combination of fuel economy and mild winters (although there were a good number of instances of firms obliged to stop production temporarily due to lack of coal). Output per man in the coal industry steadily fell, absenteeism (mostly voluntary) increased, and mechanization and reorganization made little headway.

The standard of living was not the only victim of war demand. Foreign assets, capital at home and current earning power in foreign markets were all to some extent sacrificed. The first of these is the most easily measured. Britain began the war with capital assets overseas of the order of £3,000m., and gold

[1] Quoted in Hancock and Gowing, op. cit., p. 491.

reserves amounting to about £450m. Until the Lend-Lease Act was passed by America in March 1941, Britain had to pay for everything she received from the United States. But the Lend-Lease Act was passed only after the British had paid over almost all their available dollars; and most other countries, of course, still wanted payment even after March 1941. The final result was that Britain emerged from the war having sold over £1,100m. of capital assets, reduced her gold and dollar reserves by £150m., and increased her external debt by almost £3,000m. The export trade suffered in a similar fashion. There was an attempt at an export drive in 1940—aimed mostly at earning dollars—but it had scarcely begun when it was swamped in the war crisis and emergency military orders, while the prospect of US financial aid late in 1940 led to concentration on war production. By the time lend-lease began, the volume of British exports was half what it had been in 1938; by 1944 it was less than one third; when the war against Japan ended it was rather less than 40 per cent. South America, in particular, was virtually turned over to US exporters in this period. Lastly, certain kinds of capital were badly run down between 1940 and 1944 or 1945. Permanent-way on the railways was barely maintained. Plant used for generating electricity, and plant and equipment in basic industries like chemicals and iron and steel was, even before the end of the war, in a condition which necessitated a greatly increased effort at overhaul and repair in the very near future. As to housing, the situation was at least as serious. Even before the attacks by flying-bomb and rocket, well over 3m. families were living in bomb-damaged houses or in houses which in peacetime would have been condemned as slums. The amount of over-crowding is incalculable. Bad housing conditions were 'one of the worst of the social and economic legacies of the war'.[1]

The devices by which the Government secured this marvellously rapid and far-reaching re-orientation of the economy were many and various, but they all came under the heading of what later became the magic phrase 'central planning'. As soon as war was declared an outcrop of new Ministries appeared—Home Security, Economic Welfare, Information, Food, Ship-

[1] Hancock and Gowing, op. cit., p. 497.

ping, Aircraft Production. (The important Ministry of Supply had already arrived in the summer of 1939.) Several of these Ministries rapidly acquired wide powers; for example, by the beginning of 1940 the Ministry of Shipping was well on the way to complete requisition of ocean-going shipping. Old Ministries were no less active. Thus at an early date most raw materials, as well as iron and steel and machinery, could be obtained only from the Board of Trade or through a Government department on licence. Less direct but equally effective controls over civilian consumption were both numerous and ingenious. Points rationing for food and clothing, whereby each individual could make up his total ration as he wished (out of a limited choice; and of course he still had to pay for it), was introduced in 1940 and 1941. The utility schemes, already mentioned, were introduced in 1941 and 1942. But the essence of control lay, not in these things, but in manpower budgeting. In May 1940 the Minister of Labour acquired extraordinary powers:

'He might direct through his National Service officers any person in the United Kingdom to perform any service required in any place. He might prescribe the remuneration and conditions of such services and the hours of work. He might require persons to register particulars of themselves; he might order employers to keep and produce any records and books.'[1]

These powers were in fact used very sparingly, especially to begin with. The last thing the Government wanted was a row with the trade unions—trouble had arisen in the 1914-18 war, and was not forgotten. Bevin, as Minister of Labour, aimed to preserve a good degree of freedom of wages, earnings and movement of labour while at the same time securing all the benefits of industrial conscription. This worked up to the middle of 1941. But after that, compulsory transfer became commoner. It was not always needed. Shortage of raw materials caused unemployment in 'unessential' industries, and the workers took jobs where they could get them, in essential industries. But by late 1941 it was becoming clear that there simply were not enough men to go round; so, with marked reluctance, the Government agreed to an unprecedented step—the conscription of

[1] Hancock and Gowing, op. cit., p. 298.

women between twenty and thirty years of age. The majority of these women, however, turned out to be already at work or to have domestic responsibilities. Accordingly, in October 1942, the age limits were altered to 18½ and 45½. And then, in 1953, resort was had to the so-called grandmothers—women up to fifty.

. Control of the largest possible labour force was thus secured. Its disposition rested upon the War Cabinet's 'Manpower Budget'. This calculation rested upon the estimated requirements of the fighting services for men, and their requirements for equipment translated into terms of labour;[1] and upon the estimated requirements of the Board of Trade for exports and essential home requirements, similarly translated. The resulting total was then squared with available supplies. Towards the end of the war, this manpower budgeting 'had become a very powerful instrument . . . the only method the War Cabinet ever possessed of determining the balance of the whole war economy by a central and direct allocation of physical resources among the various sectors . . . At the end of the war the manpower budgets were the main force in determining every part of the war effort from the numbers of RAF heavy bombers raiding Germany to the size of the clothing ration.'[2]

The financial incentives to work and to change one's work were not of course altogether lacking in these years. But from the start the Government was alive to the dangers of rising prices. Prices did, in fact, begin to rise even in 1939, as a result of rising commodity prices and a rise in freights. Pressure for wage increases promptly followed—the coal-miners put in a claim as early as October 1939, and the owners and the Government agreed to an increase. Naturally, other wages followed suit. The Government talked about the need for sacrifices and the dangers of inflation; but the General Secretary of the TUC replied that no trade union leader could expect to stay in office who asked his men to accept a lower standard of living. The cost of living rose by 12 per cent between the outbreak of war in

---

[1] Not an easy calculation. The aircraft and motor vehicle industry reckoned that it needed a labour intake of 117 per cent in order to fulfil its programme from mid-1939 to mid-1940. Its labour force rose by only 22 per cent; but it fulfilled its programme. Things were better in later years.

[2] Hancock and Gowing, op. cit., p. 452.

September and the end of the year. But early in 1940 the principle of subsidizing a wide range of foodstuffs began to be accepted, the implication of this policy being that wage claims based on rising prices would lose most of their justification. This policy did slow down the rise in the cost of living; and after Dunkirk the need for sacrifices was scarcely arguable. Throughout the war years the subsidy policy was strengthened and extended; subsidies rose from £72m. in 1940 to £215m. in 1944. At the same time, taxation was sharply increased. An Excess Profits Tax of 60 per cent appeared in 1939; in 1940 it became 100 per cent. The standard rate of income tax, 7s 6d at the start of the war, became 8s 6d in 1940 and 10s 0d in 1941. Purchase tax, at $16\frac{2}{3}$ per cent and $33\frac{1}{3}$ per cent, was introduced in 1940.[1] Post-war credits began in 1941. These measures were in turn supported by the National Savings Movement. This was important, because rationing had a part to play not only in protecting poorer people from scarcity prices, but also in preventing surplus income from being used to call forth a greater supply of scarce goods or a supply of goods of higher quality, i.e. embodying more resources. The utility schemes, with fixed maximum prices and fixed margins, contributed to the same end.

These policies did not succeed in stopping the rise in the cost of living, nor did they stop the rise in wages. In 1941 the cost of living was 26 per cent above its 1939 level; but by mid-1945 it had advanced only a further three points. Wage rates, however, 20 per cent higher in 1941 than in 1939, continued to rise. They overtook the cost of living in 1942, and by 1945 were almost 50 per cent above their 1939 level. Earnings, of course, rose still faster: Mr Bevin, it is said, stated flatly that he did not mind how much a man drew so long as his pay reflected his output. All these changes were probably inevitable. Higher pay was an incentive to harder work, in war as well as in peace. Industrial transference was made easier when wage differentials were increased; and higher wages in some trades are always apt to lead to higher wages in the others. Coal-miners took the opportunity to revive old claims and grievances and went a long way to reinstating themselves as among the aristocrats of labour. In 1942

[1] Over half the cost of the war was paid for out of taxation; in the 1914-18 war it was less than one-third.

they secured—at last—a national minimum wage; in 1944 the Ministry of Fuel carried through an extensive overhaul of the entire wage structure in the mines; and the miners, who in 1942 had been in the lower half of the earnings league, reached 1945 with a level of earnings among the highest in the country. Nevertheless the verdict must certainly be that it was a remarkable achievement to multiply the size of the armed forces tenfold, keep the volume of civilian employment almost steady, reorganize the entire structure of production, reduce civilian consumption by over 16 per cent, and have the cost of living rise by less than 50 per cent.

The economic relations between Britain and the United States from 1939 to 1945 were very close and very complicated. Britain depended upon foreign trade for her survival, and she depended especially upon the United States for much of her power to retaliate against German aggression. To begin with, the United States was perfectly willing to trade, so long as Britain paid in cash (i.e. in dollars) and shipped the goods herself. The British and French spent their dollars in 1940 at a rate which meant the exhaustion of their dollar reserves long before the war could possibly be won—although not before it might be lost. This expenditure produced not so much weapons and aircraft as an extension of America's capacity to produce them. By the summer of 1940 France was defeated and Britain, assisted by a United States Administration 'fertile of suggestions to the British of stripping themselves bare',[1] had almost run out of dollars. Then the American attitude began to change. At last it was appreciated that this was not a European quarrel, that America should not and probably could not remain neutral. It was seen that Britain was fighting not only for her own liberty, but for liberty everywhere. 'Defend America by helping Britain now'; 'All aid short of war' were the new slogans; and American 'neutrality' rapidly became a very one-sided affair. Lend-lease came in March 1941. For a time it made little difference—Britain was still paying dollars for the greater part of the supplies she received up to the end of 1941. But in the end it made a vast difference. In 1943 and 1944, at its peak, lend-lease provided a quarter of the armaments received by British and Empire forces.

[1] Hancock and Gowing, op. cit., p. 233.

No less important were the lend-lease supplies of food and raw materials. British industry was kept going with large amounts of American steel; food represented an important and considerable item in almost all lend-lease shipments. In the final reckoning, America sent to Great Britain about $27,000m. of goods (about $11,000m., incidentally, went to Russia); and Britain responded with reciprocal lend-lease aid to America valued at about $6,000m. This enormous account was settled by a final British payment to the United States of £162m. or about $800m.

This settlement may have been generous or it may have been no more than just. In what was, and was recognized to be, a common cause, certainly, the British made far greater sacrifices than the Americans. The war caused the British standard of living to fall, the American standard of living to rise; it caused a contraction of British exports, an accumulation of external debt, and a run down of capital; in America it had, on the whole, the opposite effects.[1] But whether it was generous or only just, the American decision not to demand payment was beyond question wise and helpful. Trouble arose, unfortunately, from two other elements in the lend-lease arrangements. These concerned British exports and British gold and dollar reserves. The difficulty over British exports was that lend-lease materials might be used in British exports which sold in competition with similar American exports. It was certainly rather hard for the American producer to pay taxes to help the British producer to compete with him. Accordingly, anxious to please, the British Government undertook in September 1941 not to allow lend-lease supplies to have any favourable influence upon their export trade; and the Americans shortly afterwards kindly set up an organization 'for policing observance of the terms' of this undertaking. At the time this arrangement made little difference; Britain could afford to forget about her exports as long as lend-lease was working and the war was on. But in 1943 the position grew difficult. It began to be observed in Washington that the British gold and dollar reserves, all but exhausted in 1941, were rising, largely as a result of expenditure by American troops in the United Kingdom. Influential American opinion held that lend-lease was

[1] Net United States foreign investment fell from 1942 through 1945.

to provide the United Kingdom with the sinews of war, not to help her build up depleted reserves. As a result, in October 1943, the United States administration declared that industrial equipment, machine tools, materials and equipment for the petroleum industry were no longer available under lend-lease. Britain must start spending her dollars again.[1]

Late in 1944 discussions were held on these points. The American administration conceded the desirability of Britain entering the post-war world with reserves a good deal greater than she possessed in 1944; but it did not prove possible to do much to supply the needed dollars, and British reserves were not built up to the level agreed to be desirable. The export question was, however, at last settled, it being agreed that Britain had full freedom to run her own export trade as from the beginning of 1945.

British exports were not the only post-war matter to receive attention while the war was on. As early as 1942 a Committee was set up to review the transition from war to peace made in 1918-19. In 1943 a Minister of Reconstruction was appointed, and in the same year the Ministry of Town and Country Planning came into existence, partly because planning was fashionable and partly because bombing and the need to build a lot of houses after the war made the disposal of land of unusual importance. New plans for education appeared in 1943, and in this case the necessary legislation was passed before the end of the war. The future of agriculture was also considered. As early as 1940 the Government announced that a system of fixed prices and a guaranteed market for agricultural produce would be maintained for at least one year after the war and moreover proclaimed 'the importance of maintaining after the war a healthy and well-balanced agriculture as an essential and permanent feature of national policy'. In 1944 it was agreed that the fixed prices/guaranteed market principle should continue until the end of the 1947 harvest. In 1942 there appeared the Beveridge Report, dealing with workmen's compensation and the unification and nation-wide extension of insurance for sickness, unemployment and old age. The Government's proposals, based on the

---

[1] Britain always paid for quite a large range of American goods, most conspicuously for tobacco.

report, were published in 1944. Perhaps most important of all, the white paper on Employment Policy, more or less pledging the Government to maintain a satisfactory level of employment after the war, appeared in 1944.

Alongside these hopeful schemes for internal reform came discussions and proposals on future international economic policy. These stemmed from Article VII of the Mutual Aid Agreement signed in February 1942, which laid down that the final settlement of lend-lease should

'include provision for agreed action by the United States of America and the United Kingdom, open to participation by all other countries of like mind, directed to the expansion, by appropriate international and domestic measures, of production, employment, and the exchange and consumption of goods . . .; to the elimination of all forms of discriminatory treatment in international commerce, and to the reduction of tariffs and other trade barriers.'

The British Government was bound to welcome the general idea of these proposals, all the more so once it had accepted responsibility for the maintenance of full employment at home. Discussions continued from 1942 to the end of the war. Keynes's suggestion of a new international money of account with extensive overdraft facilities at a new international central bank ('to allow debtor nations to live indefinitely beyond their means', according to an American critic) was made and rejected, but at Bretton Woods in 1944 the forms of an International Monetary Fund and an International Bank for Reconstruction and Development were agreed. A scheme for stabilization of commodity prices through internationally managed buffer stocks was provisionally agreed. Commercial policy received even lengthier attention. On this topic British and American views diverged more than was often admitted. Why, the British were wont to ask, were men to work for the *elimination* of preferences (which were characteristically British) but only for the *reduction* of tariffs (which were characteristically American)? No satisfactory answer was ever returned; America, indeed, adopted from the start a 'holier than thou' attitude, the only justification for which appeared to be that whereas the British had put on duties in the

1930s the Cordell Hull tariff reduction programme had at that time been making very small (bilateral) reductions in the formidable American tariff, a tariff which had exacerbated the difficulties of repaying war debts in the 'twenties and was to make more intractable the dollar earning problems of Europe and the sterling area after 1945. General agreement in favour of a multilateral international convention to limit protective measures and to outlaw discriminating practices was nevertheless reached—America had succeeded in exporting her views on trade policy along with the lend-lease supplies. But no binding Government decisions had been reached on any of these subjects when the German war ended in May and a General Election was held in Britain in July 1945.

British preparations for a three-year war in Europe began seriously late in 1938. Six years later, after five years of war, the date of the ending of the war in Europe was still uncertain. The industrial war effort, however, began to be reduced once adequate stocks had been built up; the peak rates of production of small arms ammunition, tanks and some kinds of bomb had all been passed in 1943. Employment in the munitions industry declined accordingly: from a peak figure of 5·23m. in mid-1943 the labour force declined to 5·01m. in mid-1944. Once the end of the German war could be definitely foreseen, the plan was—having regard to the requirements for war against Japan—to run down the munitions industry at as fast a rate as was compatible with an orderly transition to civilian production. Shortly after the end of the German war the 'munitions' labour force was down to 4·35m; and an increasing proportion of these workers was engaged on production of civilian rather than of military goods.

In 1945, with the end of the German war certainly approaching, economists in the Cabinet Offices began to reckon up the damage and to assess the prospects. The obvious losses, in terms of real capital, export trade, foreign assets and gold and dollar reserves have already been recited. The only obvious material gain to set against them was the creation of buildings, plant and machinery, largely paid for by the Government and intended for war production, which could be used by post-war industries; over £1,000m. was spent between 1936 and 1945 on fixed capital for the munitions industry. There were also less obvious gains, such as the virtual elimination of German and Japanese competition in international trade, at least for a few years, the rise in the labour force of the engineering industry, with its great export potential, and the spread of new skills among the working population. But the prospect was not encouraging.

'Assuming an export and import price level double pre-war, a very rough calculation suggested that the deficit in visible trade which had been about £300m. in 1938 might be £650m. in 1946. Government expenditure abroad which had been £16m. in 1938 might be £300m. in 1946 and net invisible income might shrink from the 1938 figure of £248m. to £120m. Altogether, the estimate . . . was that the deficit in the balance of payments in 1946 might be £750m. even with a very austere import programme . . . the hypothesis then held was that the adverse balance would diminish until equilibrium was reached, possibly in 1951.'[1]

[1] Hancock and Gowing, op. cit., p. 549.

CHAPTER VI

Since the War, 1945–1966

·

THE years from 1945 to 1966 are not a unified whole—a 'period' —in the sense that the 'twenties and the 'thirties are: the phase of economic development which began in 1945 has not yet come to an end. This stretch of just over twenty years has been dominated by extremely full employment, a continuous and occasionally alarmingly rapid rise in the price level, an unprecedented volume of decision-taking and cajolement by the Government in economic affairs, and repeated crises on the foreign exchanges.

These years can be divided into three sections: late 1945 to late 1947; late 1947 to late 1951; and late 1951 to the present time. Towards the end of 1947 the nature of the post-war world and its problems began to be recognized on both sides of the Atlantic. For twenty-four months from the end of the war the Americans went on persuading themselves that a few deft institutional adjustments would bring into being a world of 'normal' trade, and that a moderate amount of lending would soon produce equilibrium; while the British lived in a fool's paradise of a different kind, nationalizing industries and inaugurating the Welfare State to the accompaniment of apathy, low productivity, shortages, suppressed inflation and borrowing from abroad. This phase came to a sudden end when the dollar loan ran out in August, 1947, and interest rates began to rise. There followed four years of genuine if modest progress; 'disinflation' became at least moderately respectable (although prices continued to rise), productivity began to increase, exports soared, and Marshall Aid was pumped into western Europe. Around 1950 or 1951 the world entered a new phase. In most countries (except for Germany, Italy and Russia) recovery from the war was now complete, in the sense that industrial production was approximately back to 1938 levels; Germany, Italy and Russia were beginning to make rapid progress; and international trade and competition began to increase along 'normal' lines. This meant that the 'fifties brought new opportunities but also new difficulties for Great Britain. Late in 1951 a Tory Government came to power, and there began the years of Tory socialism, marked especially by the re-establishment of monetary control and sporadic resistance to continual inflation. In the later 'fifties and early 'sixties Britain's international economic situation gradually deteriorated, and the Tory party lost the election in 1964. But no decisive change in economic circumstances or policies is yet discernible.

Although there are these three different phases in the post-war years down to 1966, they have in common two very important characteristics. First of all,. they were years of repeated if not continual crisis; years of acute difficulty and the imminent danger of still greater difficulty, even of collapse. There were too many debts, and there were grave shortages, especially of coal and dollars. Collapse through inability to pay for sufficient imports, especially dollar imports, was always a danger. Secondly, Government economic policy assumed an importance such as it had never before possessed in peacetime, partly because of the adoption of specifically Socialist measures between 1945 and 1951, partly because of the persistent economic difficulties themselves, partly because of the responsibility which the governments now acknowledged—and seemed eager to acknowledge—for the maintenance of full employment, and, latterly, for .economic growth itself. Thus for a variety of reasons the economic activities of Government became and remained crucial and pervasive, and economic policy became a grander theme for political debate than it had been for a hundred years. There are therefore good reasons for treating the years 1945-66 *en bloc*: rising prices, important Government measures and crisis or near-crisis are common to almost every one of them.

GOVERNMENT PLANNING, MONETARY POLICY AND THE
BALANCE OF PAYMENTS

During the war money was kept cheap. Apart from a brief

spell at the very beginning of the war, Bank Rate was held steady at 2 per cent. This policy, combined with the direction of labour, other physical controls, patriotic response to a savings campaign, and the general shortage of anything to spend money on, was successful. Costs and prices, after their initial increase, rose fairly slowly, and while the Government never wanted for money, its tremendous effective demand produced a minimum of economic dislocation through rising prices, and the increase in the burden of the national debt was also minimized.

When the Labour Government took office in the early autumn of 1945, Dalton became Chancellor of the Exchequer, and a policy of still cheaper money, operating alongside continuing physical controls, of which the most important were building licences and the controls on imports, was almost immediately introduced. In October, the interest on Treasury Deposit Receipts—virtually compulsory loans from the banks to the Government—was reduced from $1\frac{1}{8}$ per cent to $\frac{5}{8}$ per cent; and in the course of 1946 the deposits of the eleven clearing banks were made to rise from £4,729m. to £5,629m., an unprecedented rate of increase and one well in advance of the rise in the national income. At the same time, the purchase of existing securities was stimulated by official prognostications of further falls in the rate of interest still to come; such purchase drove up prices and drove down yields; and the opportunity was then taken to issue new securities bearing lower rates of interest. In this way the yield on irredeemable Consols was driven down from less than 3 per cent in August 1945 to just over $2\frac{1}{2}$ per cent in January 1947. 'So long as the Chancellor was prepared to borrow from the banks at $\frac{1}{2}$ per cent or $\frac{5}{8}$ per cent any money he could not borrow from the public on the terms he offered, he could continue to force the pace. But it took a credit expansion of £900m. to bring the rate down by under $\frac{1}{2}$ per cent to $2\frac{1}{2}$ per cent.'[1] Inevitably, prices rose, especially the prices of fixed interest bearing securities—'No Tory Chancellor could have done better for the city than Mr Dalton'[2]—but due to price controls on almost all articles of general consumption the cost of living did not rise especially rapidly. What did happen was that the excess of

[1] F. W. Paish, *The Post-War Financial Problem*, p. 28.
[2] *The Economist*, April 27, 1946, p. 675.

purchasing power created by this quite novel policy of *forcing down* interest rates could not, due to price controls, be used by consumers to bid up the prices of and so attract resources into the production of the commodities they really wanted to buy; instead, it was used to encourage production in lines of secondary attractiveness where prices were not controlled, and to raise the general level of costs and hence the prices of British exports.

As time passed, increasingly grave doubts about the wisdom of this policy began to be expressed. It was asking a good deal that physical controls, effective enough in wartime, especially when combined with virtual direction of labour, should discipline a mounting excess of liquid purchasing power; it was asking still more that incentive and initiative on the one hand, and the willingness to save on the other, should survive in peacetime unimpaired by easy profits for inessential work, complicated controls, and a steady fall in the value of money. By the spring of 1947 investors were beginning to show reluctance to buy 'Dalton's'—$2\frac{1}{2}$ per cent Treasury Stock 1975—commended as they were by nothing else than the Chancellor's repeated assertion that $2\frac{1}{2}$ per cent (or less) was the 'appropriate long-term rate'.

It was in the balance of payments, however, that trouble became acute. Lend-lease was brought to an abrupt and unexpected end in August 1945. Next week, there was an exchange crisis. Imports, excluding munitions, were coming in at the rate of about £2,000m. per annum; exports amounted to a paltry £350m. plus some £450m. of mostly non-recurring items. Some such situation had been foreseen before the end of the war, but it had been supposed that time would be available to arrange to meet it. An export drive had been begun, with the aim of increasing exports to 150 per cent of the 1938 volume; but the first fruits of this policy were hardly yet to be seen. Discrimination against the dollar and exchange control all round seemed inevitable, unless some arrangement could be reached with the United States.

Hurried negotiations produced the famous Dollar Loan Agreement. This Agreement contained five important provisions:

(1) The United States was to lend Great Britain $4,400m. of which $650m. was to settle outstanding debts under lend-lease. There was thus a net credit of about £930m.

(2) There was to be no interest and no sinking fund for five years. Thereafter, interest was to be paid at 2 per cent, and the loan was to be repaid in fifty years. This meant that Britain would have to pay combined annuities of 3·18 per cent or about £35m. per annum.

(3) Interest payments would be waived, upon request, if in any year Britain's earnings of foreign exchange fell below the 1936-38 average.

(4) Britain was to seek 'adjustment' of her debts to other countries such as Argentina and India.

(5) Britain was to ratify the Bretton Woods Agreements forthwith and was to undertake the full obligations of the system, including that to make sterling fully convertible, within a year.

The Loan Agreement was the cause of much disappointment and friction. The British negotiators, headed by Keynes, expressed themselves as satisfied; certainly they had done their best. But public complaint and criticism were widespread. It was admitted that the terms, for a commercial loan, were generous; and while the amount of the loan was widely thought to be barely sufficient, the common expectation at the time was that it would just suffice. What was objected to was the fact that the loan was a commercial one, and that Britain, in order to get the money which she could not do without, was compelled to accept American ideas about how to reorganize international trade— ideas which certainly looked as if they were designed to benefit the United States and would disadvantage Great Britain. The *Economist*, in particular, did not mince words. The agreement, it declared, was 'a bitter pill to swallow'; but there was

'no real option. There is, however, one compulsion to which we are not subject. We are not compelled to say we like it . . . Our present needs are the direct consequences of the fact that we fought earliest, that we fought longest, and that we fought hardest. In moral terms we are creditors; and for that we shall pay $140m. a year for the rest of the twentieth century. It may be unavoidable; but it is not right.'[1]

[1] *The Economist*, December 8, 1945, p. 821.

Making the lion swallow the Bretton Woods scheme before he got his rations was also bitterly resented. This scheme was designed to liberalize trade without delay—a hazardous programme—although nothing was said about the illiberalism of American tied loans or the necessity for the United States to arrange an import surplus; above all, exception was taken to the proposals to abolish preferences (which were British) but only to reduce tariffs (which were American).

> 'We are undertaking to pay America, to pay our other creditors, to accept limits on the power to devalue sterling and to put no check on complete convertibility for current transactions . . . [This scheme of ideas] is based on the underlying assumption that Bretton Woods will automatically solve many problems of world employment and trade which would otherwise fall to the proposed International Trade Organization . . . The nearer the conditions of trade return to complete competitive freedom at this moment, the larger is the advantage they confer on those who (through no merit of their own) are ready to start.'[1]

Britain's export target was promptly raised to 175 per cent of the 1938 volume; and in July 1946 President Truman signed the Loan Agreement.

This American loan was supplemented by a Canadian loan for $1,250m., made on the same terms as the American loan. The identity of the terms was dictated by political necessity. In all other respects the Canadian agreement was generous, and the amount of free dollars made available to Britain was rather more than one quarter of that afforded by the US loan, although Canada's national income was hardly one twentieth the size of America's.

Early calculations suggested that the loans plus the gold and dollar reserves minus special needs (including the need to keep an 'ultimate' reserve) would provide a fund of about £700m. for current purposes; and that the prospective commercial deficit was £60m. a month in 1946, falling to £20m. a month in 1947-48. But, to begin with, prospects improved. Exporters, given priorities for materials, manpower and shipping, did extraordinarily well. There was a seller's market in western Europe,

[1] *The Economist*, December 8, 1945, p. 821.

Africa and India, and in July 1946 the long and unexpected boom began in America. In the first half of the year British exports were not far short of £70m. a month, and observers began to think that 'it should not be an impossible task for the controlling authorities to keep the aggregate deficit over the next three years within the total of the American and Canadian credits'.[1]

But in 1947 the situation deteriorated. In January it was officially admitted that the loan was being drawn upon 'considerably more rapidly' than had been expected. In March came the coal crisis, causing a partial shut-down of industry which lasted for several weeks and which Cripps subsequently reckoned to have cost the country some £200m. in exports. In spite of this, the *Economist* reckoned at the end of May that the dollar credits would 'even on the worst supposition . . . last through the next winter'.[2] But when, on July 15th, twelve months after ratification of the Loan Agreement by the United States, sterling became convertible, the situation was obviously most unpromising. The size of the dollar deficit, already considerable, increased immediately; on August 10th sterling convertibility had to be stopped; and with convertibility there disappeared the sanguine American hopes of the early creation of a 'normal' world of 'liberal' trade.

What happened to the dollars? Most of them were used by Britain herself. Buying almost exactly three times as much from the western hemisphere as she sold there, Britain had a deficit of over $1,000m. in the first half of 1947; over 70 per cent of the dollar credit was used directly by Great Britain. Convertibility merely made a bad situation worse. The holders of sterling balances were allowed to convert them into dollars at a rate which was scarcely prudent; and then, in August, European countries lost faith in the arrangement and turned pounds into dollars as fast as they could while there was still time. The capacity of Great Britain to earn dollars had been perhaps overestimated; her capacity—or willingness—to do without them had certainly been overestimated. Also, the prostration of western Europe, and the need for exceptional measures to re-

[1] *The Economist*, July 20, 1946, p. 82.
[2] ibid., May 31, 1947, p. 833.

create earning power in Belgium, France, Italy, Norway—to say nothing of Germany—were far more serious than at first was realized.

1947 was a year of crisis in more ways than one. The Moscow Conference in April ended the phase of post-war history in which the victors clung to the belief that they could work out agreed policies. In June the American Secretary of State, General Marshall, spoke at Harvard:

> 'The rehabilitation of the economic structure of Europe quite evidently will require a much longer time and greater effort than has been foreseen . . . The truth of the matter is that Europe's requirements for the next three or four years of . . . essential products—principally from America—are so much greater than her present ability to pay that she must have substantial additional help.'

Food prospects for Europe in the coming winter were grim.

In this world of American prosperity, European poverty and Russian hostility, Britain was comfortably—or uncomfortably—keeping herself on that standard to which she had been accustomed in 1938. Productivity was low, but, as the labour force had increased, output was already higher than in 1938, and the difference went to exports; the only trouble was, that this difference was not enough. The Government's 'policy' was to ask for more output; but voices began to be heard suggesting that what was needed was less consumption. To this it was objected that productivity was low because there was no incentive, and that there was no incentive because the goods which people wanted could not be got. Others thought that the rate of capital creation was excessive. But the commonest object of criticism was the cheaper money policy. Resistance to 2½ per cent had grown during 1946 despite the Chancellor's assurance in June that the danger of inflation had 'nearly—well, largely—passed away'.[1] In 1947, a few months after introducing a slightly inflationary budget, Dalton found 'the contrast . . . most remarkable between the great difficulty of the overseas position . . . and the relative ease of the purely domestic financial position'. But he was shortly reminded that 'what are politely called

[1] *The Economist*, June 22, 1946, p. 1015.

"balance of payments difficulties" do not drop like a murrain from heaven . . . any nation which gives its mind to it can create them for itself in half an hour with the aid of the printing press and a strong trade union movement'.[1] After the convertibility fiasco in August, nothing more was heard of cheaper money.

Abandoning cheaper money did not provide the Government with a policy; but it went some way towards doing so. The shortage of manpower (relative to demand) attracted a lot of attention.

> '. . . the crux of the whole matter is that generally speaking, except when occasionally they roll upon the floor, the housewife's shillings and pence can be relied upon to go where they are told, and generally speaking the Minister of Labour's men and women cannot. "Ask yourself", whispered [a] very highly placed person [Dalton] into the ear of each one of us one evening, "ask yourself whether you are doing the kind of work which the nation needs, in view of the shortage of labour. Your job may bring you in more money, but be quite useless to the community." It is not recorded that on the following morning a gigantic game of conscience-stricken general-post took place.'[2]

The arts of persuasion failing, the Government resorted to the desperate expedient of the direction of labour, hitherto used only in the extremity of war; this was through the Control of Engagement Order (1947), destined to have a life of two and a half years but to be very little used. An autumn budget was introduced (the accidental prior revelation of some of its contents causing Dalton's resignation) and capital cuts of £180m. were proposed. Agreements were made with India, Pakistan, Egypt—the largest holders of sterling balances—and some other countries about the rate at which these balances could in future be drawn on for conversion into dollars or for other purposes. Beyond the sterling area, the situation began to alter as the Marshall offer turned into a definite plan; at the very end of 1947 the Truman administration (already providing 'interim

---

[1] D. H. Robertson, *Utility and All That* (London, Allen & Unwin, 1952), p. 56.
[2] ibid., pp. 50–51.

aid' to Europe) produced its Bill proposing the expenditure of over $17 billion on European recovery in the next four years, a scheme of aid entirely without precedent in the history of the world, generous to a degree, visionary and yet practical, not devoid of political considerations and yet an act of philanthropy more than of self-interest.

It was by now painfully clear that Britain needed further subventions. And no wonder. The management of the economy in the first ten months of 1947 had shown an unparalleled incompetence. At the beginning of the year a White Paper described the situation as 'extremely serious'. Late in February there appeared the famous *Economic Survey for 1947*, which declared that, even with the help of controls, 'the task of directing by democratic methods an economic system as large and complex as ours is far beyond the power of any Governmental machine'; but which failed to produce any new ideas for dealing with an economic crisis which the *Economist* declared in August was 'reaching desperate proportions'.[1] Convertibility came and went. And in February 1948, the Government published the results. The 'plan' in the 1947 *Survey* had been to spend £350m. of gold and dollars during 1947; the actual expenditure was about £1,000m. As a result, the gold and dollar reserves, which had fallen by $226m. in 1946, fell in 1947 by no less than $963m. Gold and dollars in hand now totalled only about $2,400m. against a current rate of expenditure of about $160m. a month. There were some excuses for these dreadful figures. Invisible earnings were disappointing in 1947; other countries had run off with some dollars while sterling was convertible; capital exports had been allowed to the tune of £180m.; above all, the terms of trade had deteriorated so severely that two-thirds of the increase in the import bill was accounted for by rising prices; £329m. out of £482m. All this Ministers might plead in extenuation. But the fact remained that the country was going bankrupt while personal expenditure on consumption goods rose above the level of 1946 (and 1938), and that nothing was done about it for at least ten months. The facts lend colour to the view that Ministers, by doing nothing to make the balance of payments balance in

[1] *The Economist*, August 2, 1947, p. 177.

1947, deliberately promoted the failure of sterling convertibility, forced on them by the Americans. But this is scarcely credible, for the consequences of the 1947 policies were wholly bad. Here was a country with over 1m. men in the Forces, over 2m. in Government service, no coal to export, a flowing tide of monetary inflation, foreign exchange reserves being used up at a rate which would completely exhaust them in fifteen months, and apparently no new ideas about what to do. Foreigners drew their own conclusions: 'The intervals between the recurrent rumours of sterling devaluation', wrote the *Economist* in March 1948, 'are becoming shorter. Perhaps for that reason the official denials are becoming increasingly explicit and emphatic. Asked last week whether he considered sterling devaluation to be inevitable during the course of this year, Sir Stafford Cripps [now Chancellor of the Exchequer] replied bluntly, "No, I certainly do not".' But on the Continent such denials merely 'added fuel to the flames of speculation'.[1]

Sterling was not devalued in 1948. Instead, severe import restrictions were imposed, the export drive—greatly assisted by boom conditions abroad—was intensified, and imports were switched, as far as possible, from dollar to non-dollar sources. At least as important, these changes of policy now worked in conditions of disinflation—or at least of markedly diminished inflation; 'no system of economic controls', it was at last officially admitted, 'can be wholly proof against strong and persistent inflationary pressure working against the general objectives of economic policy'.[2] The substance of the Government's case for maintaining the apparatus of controls had always been its alleged determination to prevent inflationary disorder. But in this it was not succeeding. The more controls there were, the more manpower was needed to operate them, the more was business enterprise frustrated, and the more devious became the routes by which the ever-growing mass of purchasing power, dammed up here, broke out in some other direction. By the end of 1947 people were tired of living in the enervating and debilitating conditions of suppressed inflation. Hours were short— the average number of hours worked weekly in industry in 1938

[1] *The Economist*, March 13, 1948, p. 427.
[2] *Economic Survey for 1948.*

was 46, in 1947 it was 45—and jobs were plentiful; but harder work, or a better job, although it might bring in more money, brought very little prospect of being able to choose among a wider range of better goods. Extras were to be got through influence rather than with money. Business efficiency was equally affected—'the way to thrive, too often, is to know which way the official cat will jump'.[1] People were tired, too, of the humiliation of repeated borrowings from the United States. It had become clear that the country did not want what the Government offered—comfort (of a sort), security, shortages and controls, with the constant uneasy knowledge that what was consumed was not all earned. The moment was an important one in economic history, for it was the beginning of the end for the post-war experiment of running a 'mixed' economy by means of an extensive apparatus of physical and fiscal controls, coupled with exhortations, but with a minimum of monetary restraint. From a narrowly economic viewpoint the experiment had been anything but a success; what was worse, people did not even like it.

At the same time that financial conditions in Great Britain changed, major alterations were effected abroad. The Marshall Plan was approved by Congress in April 1948, and in September allocations of this aid and mutual aid between the European countries were agreed at Paris. In October the first Intra-European Payments Scheme began, designed to promote trade by enlarging international credits. Out of this there grew the European Payments Union of 1950, involving the grant of mutual credits among members, the interchangeability of members' currencies, and the settlement of debts, to a limited extent only, in gold. This was designed to increase freedom of trade and of payments within Europe, despite the dollar shortage from which all members except Belgium suffered. It was an ingenious scheme, and with the initial help of Marshall Aid it worked well. Industrial production in Europe in 1948 was 25 per cent above the 1947 level. In the same year gross national product in the United States registered its first post-war increase.

It was in conditions of a world boom, therefore, that Cripps in 1948 budgeted for a 'true' surplus of no less than £300m. This

[1] *The Economist*, July 31, 1948, p. 171.

was to work alongside drastic import restrictions and a gentle rise in the long-term rate of interest. There were also some new incentives to effort in the shape of small tax reliefs, and the trade unions, in response to appeals from the Chancellor, contented themselves with wage increases considerably less than could have been obtained had they used their bargaining advantage to the full. The results were remarkable. At least partial equilibrium between demand and supply began to appear. During the summer it was found possible to relax several controls which, only a few months before, had seemed likely to be permanent. Furniture rationing largely disappeared; clothes rationing was much relaxed; and even some foodstuffs began to prove not quite so scarce as had been thought. This was the 'miracle of disinflation'.[1] It was followed by the celebrated 'bonfire of controls' in November, in the course of which perhaps nothing very important was burned, but which was in turn followed by further steps towards freedom of internal trade.[2] There was parallel improvement in external relations. Assisted by a reduced rate of release of the blocked sterling balances, by improved invisible earnings, by slightly better terms of trade, and by exports running in the last quarter of 1948 at 147 per cent of the 1938 volume, sterling strengthened and talk of devaluation disappeared. The change in the position of sterling, said the *Economist*, was 'almost magical'.[3]

This was, indeed, the start of a better period as regards Great Britain's international accounts. The current overall balance of payments was unfavourable in only two years between 1948 and 1957, and the surpluses exceeded the deficits in these years by almost £1,000m. Money was thus available for lending abroad or strengthening the reserves. Most of it was usually used to make loans. The table opposite[4] summarizes the position.

[1] *The Economist*, August 14, 1948, p. 249.

[2] Controls were now of three types: (i) statutory regulation of the manufacture and supply of an article, by a licensing system related to the pre-war pattern of the industry, so working that unless a firm produced certain types of goods before the war, it could not produce these types after the war; (ii) Government allocation of scarce materials; (iii) licensing of imports and exports, and public purchase in general.

[3] loc. cit., December 25, 1948, p. 1049.

[4] Figures derived from Table 31 of the *Report of the Committee on the Working of the Monetary System* (Cmd. 827, 1959).

Balance of payments and changes in reserves, 1948 to 1957 (£m.s)

	Current balance of payments (surplus + deficit −)	Balance of long-term capital (assets: increase − decrease +)	Reserves at beginning of year
1948	+ 1	1	457
1949	+ 3	1	512
1950	+300	1	603
1951	−403	1	1,178
1952	+168	−134	834
1953	+148	−194	659
1954	+121	−191	899
1955	−157	−122	986
1956	+209	−187	757
1957	+216	−106	799

But the position of the economy was not so comfortable as these figures suggest. The dollar deficit was a constant anxiety, which an overall surplus did not necessarily remove. And if the reserves increased, so did the liabilities. And while it was good that the country was able, as it had not been before the war, to earn a substantial surplus on current account, the pressure to invest this surplus abroad was very great. The result was that insufficient was available to strengthen the reserves. They were always inadequate. And time and again a comparatively small change in British prices, in foreign confidence in sterling, in the level of activity at home, in the willingness of markets overseas to buy British goods, or in the terms of trade caused hasty internal adjustments because the reserves were not large enough to permit the authorities to watch heavy inroads being made upon them without anxiety. The balance of payments on current account—with the exception of 1951—has never deteriorated by more than £300m. in a single year. This is no very great change in comparison with the total for transactions on current account, credit and debit, which is in excess of £10,000m., but is 'far from negligible when compared with reserves that have generally been less than £1,000m'.[2] This undue exposure to

[1] The balance of long-term capital transactions was not separately distinguished until 1952.

[2] *Report of the Committee on the Working of the Monetary System* (Cmd. 827, 1959), para. 636.

influences operating through the current balance of payments goes a long way to explaining the many sharp changes of course made by successive Chancellors in the years after 1948.

In 1949 Cripps budgeted for a much smaller surplus; only £14m. as compared with the £352m. realized in the year just ended. This was done partly because of the recovery in 1948, partly because there were widespread fears of a (long-awaited) American 'economic blizzard' later in the year. The budget proposals also contained one decisive change of policy; in future the cost-of-living subsidies,[1] which on a pre-budget basis would have gone to £568m., were to be limited to £465m. 'When I hear people speaking of reducing taxation', said the Chancellor, 'and at the same time see the cost of social services rising rapidly, very often in response to the demands of the same people, I wonder whether they appreciate to the full the old adage, we cannot have our cake and eat it.' Unhappily, the world conditions which would have suited this budget did not appear. There was a mild recession in the United States,[2] and selling in dollar markets became more competitive. At the same time, demand within Britain held back exports, the rate of increase of which was already declining at the start of the year. Complaints began to be heard of the high cost of British goods, and by the end of April, everyone—except in Great Britain—was talking about 'currency adjustment'. Devaluation at this point would have been a wise move, a helpful and well-timed adjustment to circumstances. But nothing was done. The trade position of the sterling area continued to weaken, and speculative pressure against sterling mounted *pari-passu* with the world-wide expectation that sterling would soon *have* to be devalued. The dollar deficit almost doubled between the first and second quarters of 1949, and in September, about six months late, sterling was devalued.

This was in every way a serious blow—perhaps it was in the

[1] See above, p. 151.

[2] In real terms, the gross national product of the United States fell by 1 per cent between 1948 and 1949, and the volume of imports by 3 per cent. The value of imports fell by 7 per cent, however, and manufacturing production by 6 per cent. Trimming of inventories exerted fairly heavy pressure in commodity markets, and therefore upon sterling.

end a fatal blow—to the policies and prestige of the Government. In 1947 a serious mistake had been made about the consequences of introducing convertibility; and now another mistake had been made about the timing of devaluation. Devaluation was taken to be, as it was, a confession of failure. Industrial production was going well, there was reasonable wage restraint, new Price Control Orders introduced in March 1948 were slowing down the rate of retail price increases. Even the trend of import prices, which so often in these years appeared to be the decisive consideration, was favourable. Yet a comparatively mild American recession had to be met by a devaluation of no less than 30 per cent. After this, nothing could be the same. Price control and wage restraint could no longer be effective. The cost of living was now bound to go up. The TUC, to which devaluation came as a serious shock, gallantly if mistakenly recommended a wage standstill; but in June 1950 it had to retreat from this hopeless position as the policy of wage restraint gradually crumbled before a gradually and then more rapidly rising cost of living. To some extent, indeed, it was now economically desirable that wages and prices should rise, for the extent of devaluation was greater than was required having regard to price and cost considerations alone. For that, 20 per cent would probably have been ample. To devalue by 30 per cent, therefore, was to cause the terms of trade to move more adversely than was necessary, and a rise in the British wage and price level was needed to offset the 'excess' of devaluation which was designed to end speculation against the pound.

For a time, all went well. The gold and dollar reserves began to recover—as they were more or less bound to do—immediately, and, from $1,425m. at the end of September 1949, they reached $2,422m. in the middle of 1950. Wages rose only slowly to the autumn of 1950, although the limit on the food subsidies was reduced from £465m. to £410m. in the spring. The virtual ending of the allocation of steel came in May 1950, and petrol rationing ended in June. Dollar spending was held down, and exports to the dollar area rose slowly. By the summer of 1950, average consumption was probably about as high as in the summer of 1938, income being more evenly distributed. Between 1947 and 1950 national output had risen at almost 4 per cent per annum—a very satisfactory rate of growth—and almost one-third of the increase had gone to fixed investment. In spite of constant vicissitudes and the making of many mistakes, both tactical and strategic, much had been accomplished since the war, and especially in the preceding three years, and for a short time it looked as if a solution to the country's difficulties had been found, and that the future was secure.

But fresh difficulties now arose in the field of international politics. At the end of June, 1950, the Korean war broke out, and Truman at once announced his epoch-making decision: 'I have ordered United States sea and air forces to give the Korean Government troops cover and support.' Stockpiling began. Prices of tin, rubber, wool and other commodities reached fantastic heights (tin prices rose from £300 a ton in June to £1,280 in November) at which prices there were scarcely any supplies; everyone was competing with the American Munitions Board. Trade boomed; American purchases of sterling area commodities sent the gold and dollar reserves to $3,300m. by the end of 1950 and to a peak of $3,867m. by the middle of 1951; but Britain's terms of trade deteriorated and shortages of coal, steel and other commodities began to hamper some important industries. In February 1951, a new and costly defence programme was introduced. And in March the Government gave way on a wage demand by the railwaymen, and a big round of wage increases was triggered off. In these unpromising circumstances Gaitskell, the new Chancellor of the Exchequer, introduced a budget which surprised everyone by its confident optimism, its ingenuity, and its leniency to the taxpayer. Government expenditure was to increase by £973m. (mostly on defence); yet new taxation amounted to only £138m. This budget was a serious mistake, although it was admittedly very difficult at the time to foresee the course of events. It was bad luck that a few weeks later the Iranian Government took over the Anglo-Iranian Oil Co. at Abadan, in which £350m. of British capital had been sunk, and which was the source of over a quarter of Britain's crude oil supplies in 1950; it was excessive optimism which ignored the probability of large wage increases, permitted the level of home consumption to be maintained in a year which required large additions to be made to stocks, and made no allowance for a serious deterioration in trading conditions. It is also the case that the terms of trade moved very unfavourably. Between April 1950 and May 1951 import prices rose by 41 per cent, export prices by 17 per cent; by the summer, commodity prices were falling, but stocks had been run down in 1950 and had to be replaced in 1951 at unfavourable prices. The rise of import prices alone was sufficient to account for the swing in the balance of payments from a surplus of £300m. in 1950 to a deficit of £400m. in 1951. But the change in the terms of trade had been foreseen, it is said,[1] early in 1951. It was not this which caused the deficit. It was the failure to foresee any decline in export earnings, especially in the earnings of the overseas sterling area from sales of raw materials (very large in 1950), plus very heavy stock-building, which brought on the third post-war economic crisis. Fundamentally, it was caused by failure to anticipate all the consequences of renewal of international warfare—hardly an easy thing to do. Too much effort went into rearming; having to substitute dollars for Persian oil (reckoned to have cost about $300m.) and a gold loss to EPU did something to make the difficulties greater. But domestic policy did little to help. 'This summer', said the *Economist*, 'the country has lived almost as far beyond its income as it did in 1947, at the peak of post-war dislocation.'[2] In the second half of the year the gold and dollar reserves fell from $3,867m. to $2,335m.

The Government's proposals to deal with this crisis were even more astonishing than the manner in which they had helped to create it. These proposals were for dividend control and price control. The latter had already been tried, had led to inefficiency and rigidity in the pattern of production, had made inflation worse, and had clearly failed; the former could be thought of only as a political gesture, because dividends had increased by only one tenth or £240m. since 1947 compared with an increase of one quarter or £800m. in wages and salaries. It seemed that the planners in Whitehall had now tried every club in the bag without success. Fortunately, a General Election

[1] J. C. R. Dow, *The Management of the British Economy, 1945-60* (Cambridge 1964), p. 63.
[2] loc. cit., September 22, 1951, p. 663.

was held in the autumn, and late in the year the country had a new Chancellor of the Exchequer.

No time was lost in resorting to monetary control. Nor was there time to lose. Wage increases in the first seven months of 1951 were for over £200m. compared with £25m. in the same months of 1950. The gold and dollar reserves fell by $600m. in the third quarter of the year, and when the new measures were introduced were falling at a rate which was to result in the loss of $1,000m. in the last quarter, easily the largest quarterly loss ever experienced. These new measures consisted of substantial import cuts, and monetary changes as follows:

(i) Bank Rate was raised from 2 to 2½ per cent.
(ii) the ½ per cent market rate for Treasury Bills, pegged since 1945 by the operations of the 'special buyer', was abandoned.
(iii) the possibility was thus opened up of the market being driven 'into the bank', i.e. of having to cover its excess commitments at Bank Rate.
(iv) the Treasury announced funding loans for £1,000m. against outstanding Treasury Bills.
(v) Public Works Loan Board rates were raised from 3 to 3¾ per cent.

This amounted to a carefully thought out programme for re-creating flexible monetary control. The change in Bank Rate was in itself so small as to be almost insignificant. Also, the banks possessed such a large supply of Treasury Bills or call loans secured by Bills that they were in a position to finance new advances for a long time to come without having to sell gilt-edged securities at a loss. This was where the funding loans came in. By mopping up Treasury Bills these loans destroyed the excessive technical liquidity of the banking system and reduced the banks' ratio of liquid assets (cash and Treasury Bills) to deposit liabilities nearly to that 30 per cent ratio which convention regarded as the safe minimum. It is this convention which ensures that, if the monetary authorities try to hold down bank deposits by restricting cash reserves (i.e. Treasury Bills), the banks will not thwart the authorities' intentions by turning some of these short-term assets into cash instead of restricting their long-term investments or their advances.

These measures, announced early in November 1951, re-introduced the whole apparatus and idea of monetary control. From that date to the end of 1957 there took place an irregular but persistent increase in Bank Rate to 7 per cent, a movement fluctuating in response to changes in the balance of payments position but with a trend—interrupted only in 1953–54—always upwards as successive Chancellors ventured or were forced to take stronger measures against internal inflation. The last Chancellor who was content 'to cheer on any steps towards dearer money . . . taken by anybody but himself'[1] voiced the objections which made his successors so reluctant to push the policy to the lengths needed for success: monetary policy, he said, would not bring down prices 'unless it was pushed so far that it created losses and unemployment'.[2] This argument con-tinued—and still continues—to exert an all-but-decisive in-fluence on public policy in spite of the fact that experience has shown that persistent losses of output and occasional increases of unemployment are inseparable from the broadly alternative policy of free spending and 'easy money'.

One corollary of the re-introduction of a positive monetary policy was the further and final dismantling of the system of physical or direct controls. On this question the two political parties did not differ nearly as widely as is often supposed.[3] Export quotas, control over capital issues, and even some price controls were continued by the Conservatives; after all, it was nothing new for British businessmen brought up in the 1930s to accept, even to welcome, Government restraint upon private competition. What existed was 'a congeries of many separate controls . . . [each] sharing out supplies on its own principles of compromise or "fair shares".'[4] Experience had shown that direct controls were clumsy instruments, often nearly useless (building controls had worked particularly badly) 'far more

[1] *The Economist*, April 4, 1951, p. 302. The Chancellor thus described was Gaitskell.
[2] ibid., May 5, 1951, p. 1053.
[3] See P. D. Henderson in G. D. N. Worswick and P. H. Ady, *The British Economy in the Nineteen-Fifties* (Oxford 1962), pp. 334–6.
[4] J. C. R. Dow, *The Management of the British Economy, 1945–60* (Cambridge 1964), p. 16.

effective in sharing out what supplies were available, than in altering the quantities that were to be shared.'[1] Economic growth and decontrol, it was agreed, went together. Import controls, the easiest to administer and perhaps the most effective, gradually disappeared between 1952 and 1960. By 1955 the Government had almost completely withdrawn from the business of buying raw materials abroad. Building licensing and food rationing both ended in 1954, and the last important allocation scheme, that for coal, came to an end in 1958. Thus from about the middle of the 1950s the price system was left to operate virtually free of rationing, licensing arrangements, and systems of physical allocation. Monetary policy and fiscal policy were again supreme.

To begin with, the new policy had no visible effects on the balance of payments position at all. In the first two months of 1952 the run on the reserves reached fever pitch, and Britain lost gold and dollars at the rate of $63m. a week. Further import restrictions were introduced, especially on trade with Europe, only recently liberalized; restrictions on the hire purchase terms for consumers' durables were for the first time introduced; and deliveries of plant, machinery and vehicles to the home market were ordered to be cut by one sixth—a policy described as 'salvation by not investing'. In the spring the rearmament programme was scaled down. Then, in the budget, came cuts in the food subsidies, reducing them from £410m. to £250m., and some reductions in income tax. These changes passed on to the consumer some £200m. in higher food prices, and reduced the disincentive of very high taxation. The net result was to reduce the prospective surplus from £540m. to the still enormous figure of £510m. Critics called it a budget of income redistribution; but this was the necessary consequence of encouraging production and discouraging consumption. At the same time, Bank Rate was raised from 2½ to 4 per cent, producing 'violent effects in Lombard Street'.[2]

For a while the reserves continued to fall, but very slowly. They reached bottom at the end of August, when they were

---

[1] J. C. R. Dow, *The Management of the British Economy, 1945-60* (Cambridge, 1964), p. 16.

[2] *The Economist*, March 15, 1952, p. 688.

£1,672m., almost exactly half what they had been at the end of August 1951. But the balance of payments recovered much more quickly. The deficit with the non-sterling area fell, chiefly due to a reduction in imports, and the surplus with the sterling area rose, chiefly due to an increase in exports. The recovery was much more rapid than anyone had thought possible. It was helped by an improvement in the terms of trade, despite the fact that a textile recession began in the first half of the year and that in the second six months a buyers' market existed throughout a considerable range of engineering products. Industrial production fell by a little over 3 per cent (its first fall since the coal crisis), employment fell less, but short-time working affected more than 5 per cent of the workers in manufacturing industry.

The financial outcome was that the prospective budget surplus of £510m. became a realized surplus of only £88m. The Chancellor responded by planning for a surplus of £109m. in the financial year 1953–54, with reductions of income tax and purchase tax. Consumption rose, and the terms of trade continued improving until mid-summer, after which they changed little. The second post-war American recession began in the third quarter of the year, but in Britain, Bank Rate was reduced, rather surprisingly, to 3½ per cent in September. By the end of the year the reserves had picked up by some $700m. in twelve months. The Chancellor produced a 'no-change' budget and, in May 1954, Bank Rate was reduced from 3½ to 3 per cent. The area within which sterling might be automatically transferred was considerably extended, and a free gold market and genuine foreign exchange market was opened in London. The City began, at last, to resume its position as a leading centre of international finance. This was certainly desired by the Government. There were earnings of foreign exchange to be got, and the Government was also interested, for political reasons, in promoting foreign investment. It was hoped, too, that investment in the Commonwealth would help to solve the dollar problem:

'The United Kingdom Government are determined that the flow of capital from London for sound development throughout the Commonwealth shall be maintained and increased.

This will only be possible if the United Kingdom can sustain the necessary level of internal saving and can achieve a surplus on overseas account additional to that required to meet its heavy existing commitments.'[1]

In June 1954, the Chancellor threw out his famous challenge: 'Why should we not aim to double our standard of living in the next twenty-five years, and still have our money as valuable then as now?' To a nation which had spent nine inflationary years struggling to get rid of the worst shortages and the most irksome controls, in which real personal consumption per head of population had risen by only a couple of per cent between 1948 and 1953, the idea was new and exciting. Was rapid economic progress possible, after all, even for Britain?

Certainly the last eighteen months had seen big improvements. Production had risen by almost 10 per cent, and despite an American recession considerably more serious than that experienced in 1949 the gold and dollar reserves at the end of June were $3,017m., the highest since American stockpiling had sent them very high in the autumn of 1951.[2] The rate of increase of retail prices had slowed down from $9 \cdot 1$ per cent in 1951 and 1952 to an average of $2 \cdot 5$ per cent in 1953 and 1954. The rate of private saving had increased very rapidly since 1951, and this was presumably helping to finance the boom in industrial investment which was well under way at the beginning of 1954. In February 1955 a form of *de facto* convertibility for non-residents of the sterling area was introduced, and signs multiplied that the Government's general aspirations to making sterling truly and generally convertible as soon as possible were

[1] Communiqué of the Commonwealth Economic Conference, December 1952.

[2] 'Nothing could have demonstrated more clearly the distance which had been travelled since 1949 than the profound difference in the international repercussions of the United States' recessions of that year and 1954. A somewhat larger decline in national output in 1954 than in 1949, instead of resulting in serious balance of payments difficulties in the rest of the world, coincided with a lifting of restrictions on dollar imports by a number of western European countries. And far from touching off a wave of speculation against sterling, as had occurred in 1949, the fall in United States' import demand was actually accompanied by a surge of confidence, expressed in a sharp rise in private capital outflow, both to the United Kingdom and elsewhere, which in total sufficed to offset virtually all other elements of decline in the dollar supply.' *World Economic Survey*, 1956 (United Nations), p. 27.

maturing 'into a definite intention to do so'[1] before the summer.

But most of this progress proved to be temporary and deceptive. From the middle of 1954 the gold and dollar reserves fell (with periods of recovery) to the abysmally low point of $1,850m. at the end of September 1957. Prices began to rise faster again (although not as fast as in 1951 and 1952). Industrial production had to be held almost steady from 1955 through 1957. And in September 1957, Bank Rate was raised to 7 per cent. Why was the apparently favourable trend of 1953 and 1954 thus reversed, and why was there a fourth post-war crisis, and a bad one, in 1957?

The answers to these questions are numerous. Some of the adverse factors at work were extraneous and adventitious. The most obvious of these was the British attack on Egypt in November 1956. This resulted in the blocking of the Suez Canal, and a certain amount of dollar expenditure was incurred partly to make good the oil losses. The Suez affair also caused a temporary flight from the pound, and a massive fall in the gold and dollar reserves; this was largely made good, however, in six or seven months. Other factors, which had caused difficulties in the past, did not operate adversely. That old bogey, the terms of trade, caused very little trouble. Having improved from May 1951 to the summer of 1953 and then steadied, the terms of trade deteriorated about 5 per cent in 1954; in 1955, however, they were down by only 1 per cent and in 1956 they improved. As to trading conditions, they were on the whole good. Activity in Europe was at a high level, and in most European countries production was actually rising fairly rapidly during these years. Signs of the third post-war recession in the United States began to be visible in the late summer of 1957; but up to that time America was extremely prosperous, and the recession, when it came, was not very serious. On the whole, therefore, the background conditions in which the British economy operated from 1952 through 1957 were more favourable than those which had existed earlier.

There are two reasons why, in these favourable conditions, serious difficulties were experienced. The first relates to the level of internal activity and the level of stocks. The private in-

[1] *The Economist*, June 12, 1954, p. 869.

vestment boom, which began late in 1953, was at its height from the spring of 1954 to the autumn of 1955. This boom was occasioned by greater freedom for business, improved expectations, greater availability of supplies—especially coal and steel—and of investible funds, Tory exhortations to 'invest in prosperity' and the very real stimulus of the investment allowances restored in the 1953 budget. In 1955, capital expenditure by manufacturing industry was from 15 to 20 per cent higher than in 1954; and business plans at that time suggested that it would rise by a similar amount in 1956. All this caused pressure on the balance of payments, especially because imports of raw materials had been held down at the beginning of 1954 by false fears of an approaching American slump. Inevitably, imports on a larger scale had now to be obtained; and heavier importing to build up depleted stocks helped to turn the terms of trade against the United Kingdom in 1955, and converted the balance of payments surplus of the first half of 1954 into a small deficit in the first half and a plunging deficit in the second half of 1955.

This situation the authorities endeavoured to correct almost exclusively by monetary and fiscal means. Their first move indicated their general approach. Bank Rate was raised from 3 to $3\frac{1}{2}$ per cent and then to $4\frac{1}{2}$ per cent at the beginning of 1955. The 'credit squeeze' had begun. In October, Butler presented an interim budget, which involved some increases in purchase tax and a few cuts in Government expenditure, notably a stop to Exchequer subsidies on much future local authority house building (local authorities at this time were doing almost 25 per cent of the nation's investment). In February, Macmillan, the new Chancellor, raised the Bank Rate to $5\frac{1}{2}$ per cent, the highest figure for 24 years, replaced the investment allowances by less generous initial allowances, reduced the food subsidies, cut the investment programmes of the nationalized industries, and imposed new restrictions on hire purchase. These measures were at least a partial success. The deficit in the balance of payments —which had, incidentally, been particularly bad with the dollar area, and which the remaining sterling area countries had, contrary to the usual experience in a bad year, done nothing to worsen—disappeared, and was replaced by a modest surplus (which would have been larger had it not been for Suez) in 1956.

Investment in the overseas sterling area also recovered (from £119m. to £150m.) but industrial production stood still and total production scarcely increased. This was the price which evidently had to be paid for international solvency.

'How soon will output begin to rise? This question . . . shoulders its way into any discussion of disinflation in Britain today. In terms of extra goods and services deliberately forgone this year to trim the economy, it is becoming a several hundred million pound question.'[1]

The edge had been taken off the demand for labour; but the rise in wages and prices was at best only moderated. Early in 1957, for largely technical reasons, Bank Rate was lowered to 5 per cent and there was a cautious budget. By the summer industrial output was rising, especially in the car industry, which had suffered a serious fall in output in 1956. These increases were not large, and the balance of payments position was not seriously prejudiced by them. Disregarding special items, the reserves were approximately stable during the first half of 1957. Thus the September crisis seemed to come like a bolt from the blue.

Among the crises of the '50s, this 1957 crisis was unique in that it was not caused by nor accompanied by a deficit in the current balance of payments. It was caused by persistent capital withdrawals, an ebbing away of the reserves. It was thus entirely a crisis of confidence in sterling, and the question which has to be answered is why holders of sterling lost confidence in it at this juncture. Was the loss of confidence due to misgivings about the consequences of persistent inflation ('the value of the £ at home and the value of the £ abroad is, in the last resort, the same thing'[2]) or was it due to uncertainty about the future of exchange rates, without any particular reference to British domestic policy?

It was widely believed at the time that the explanation of the crisis, and also of the underlying weakness in Britain's position revealed by other periods of difficulty in the 1950s, was to be found in the fields of Government expenditure and of monetary

---

[1] *The Economist*, September 1, 1956, p. 735.
[2] Mr Thorneycroft, in the House of Commons, October 1957.

conditions. While this is almost certainly not the whole truth, it is hard to believe that there is not a good deal of truth in it. It is not so much that Bank Rate was not raised high enough until the autumn of 1957, as that the combination of a higher Bank Rate and the various funding operations which took place, along with the hire purchase controls, adjustments of investment spending in the public sector, and other modifications and refinements of the system, did not work or was not made to work so as to get rid of inflation, open or suppressed. It was frequently claimed, of course, that this had been achieved. The first—and most absurd—of these claims was advanced in the notorious *Economic Survey for 1947*; the corresponding document for 1953 alleged that 1952 had seen 'the checking of inflation in the United Kingdom'; in 1954 even the *Economist* began to think that the thing had at last been done—'Inflation has, to all intents and purposes, been eradicated . . . The miracle has happened—full employment without inflation.'[1] Yet prices went on rising. From 1948 to 1952 retail prices rose by 26 per cent; from 1952 to 1957 they rose by 14 per cent. In short, money income persistently rose faster than output.

Essentially, the difficulty was that while the Government was anxious to keep down the flow of money demand from private sources, it was as a rule most unwilling to exercise any noticeable restraint on those expenditures for which it was itself responsible, directly or indirectly. And that meant not only that the Government utilized resources and created incomes by its own expenditure, but that it was always apt to be creating money for these purposes, and that this creation of money served as the basis of credit which could never be completely withheld from the private sector.

This phenomenon was noticeable from the very start of the new monetary policy in 1951. Bank advances, which went mainly to the private sector, were cut down early in 1952, but this reduction was substantially off-set by increased Government borrowing from the banking system on a scale which, said the *Economist*, 'has taken even well-placed domestic observers by surprise'.[2] For the year as a whole there was a decline in the

[1] *The Economist*, Banking Supplement, June 12, 1954.
[2] loc. cit., July 5, 1952, p. 41.

net deposits of the London clearing banks, but these deposits were rising from May. This was largely due to the need to provide banks and persons overseas with the sterling counter-part of Britain's considerable external surplus. In 1953 the trend was continued, and deposits rose by £168m.; in 1954 they rose by £213m., and advances, which had fallen in 1953, also rose. In 1955 policy changed; it became, for a time, what the nine-teenth century would have regarded as orthodox. When Bank Rate was put up to 3½ per cent in January, Treasury Bill rates and other short rates were put up to match; instead of going on lending to the market at fixed rates, of which the lowest was the same as the very low rate allowed on deposit accounts, the banks opened a margin between their deposit rate and the basic rate for short money by raising the former by ¼ per cent but the latter by ½ per cent. The results were not magical—Bank Rate had to be raised again in February and there was an emergency autumn budget—but the situation improved to the extent that net deposits fell and fell sharply. This was a sudden, even a violent reversal of the trend. Advances, on the other hand, did not fall to begin with; but when a Government directive was issued to the banks in the summer of 1955, advances fell by 10 per cent in the following twelve months. Thus there was a reduction in the total stock of money—and yet, to most people's surprise, prices went on rising. This was possible because idle money was drawn into use—businesses had large reserves of liquid funds early in 1955—and because the velocity of circula-tion increased very markedly. As to the banks, after selling securities very largely in 1955 and thus tending to raise long-term interest rates, they discovered in 1956 that pressure on bank liquidity was disappearing again; liquid assets grew by an extraordinary amount, and the banks' liquidity ratio, down to 33·1 per cent in March, rose to 37·1 per cent in October. This was the result of borrowing by the Treasury. There began to get about 'a widespread impression that the monetary regulator has been tried and found wanting'.[1] In the first half of 1957 the position grew worse: advances to all borrowers other than the Boards of the nationalized industries increased almost three times as fast as in the first half of 1956.

[1] *The Economist*, July 7, 1956, p. 50.

It was the practice of successive Chancellors of the Exchequer, having issued enormous numbers of Treasury Bills, to appeal to the banks to act with moderation in extending further credit, i.e. to act as if these Bills had not been issued. This 'policy' was already customary when the Labour Government went out of office in 1951. In 1955 the banks were peremptorily informed that it was their duty to effect a 'positive and significant' reduction in their advances in the next few months; advances were to be made only when they were 'in the national interest'. In 1957 this sort of request was still being reiterated. But, as the Chairman of Barclay's Bank said in 1955, the banks were put in a very difficult position:

'Further reductions in advances will become correspondingly more difficult, for the obvious candidates have been tackled already, and from now on decisions will involve increasingly complex discussions of what is, and what is not, in the national interest. All such discussions tend to be wearisome, and must, at times, resemble medieval disputations.'

Lots of Government spending made a buoyant demand, and a buoyant demand made lots of credit-worthy would-be borrowers. As was said at the time, the banks thus had the task of 'planning' thrust upon them by a Government which declared all 'planning' to be impossible.[1]

Appeals being, in the nature of the thing, of no avail, the only course was for the Government to reduce its own expenditure. Why would it not do so? There were obvious but extremely deep-seated reasons. The Government—any British Government—stood or fell in these years by its success in maintaining a high level of employment. The easy way to do this was to have excess monetary demand. This meant inflation, which caused social injustice and was always threatening the country's ability to earn its daily bread in foreign markets; but Government after Government gambled with social justice and national economic security for fear of a little more unemployment. Also, Governments had support from voters for ambitious medical, educational and other social schemes; the political parties vied with one another in seeing who could divert more of the

[1] *The Banker*, September 1955, p. 154.

nation's resources to building houses; there were large projects in every post-war year for capital expenditure on electricity supply, coal and transport; latterly, atomic energy was added to the list. All these things were popular, and Governments took a pride in them—sometimes justifiably. But the attempt to do them all at once, while private industry repaired and then increased its capital equipment and consumers raised their standard of living was bound to cause something to give way. And what gave way was the value of money.

Foreign observers had less difficulty in seeing the dangers of British policy than had the British themselves. From 1945–57 sterling was seldom strong and was often weak. Fear of devaluation was seldom far away in foreign exchange markets, and sterling was often near the lower gold point. The large sterling balances, a little larger in 1957 than in 1951, were a source of weakness, although one which was probably overestimated abroad. Sometimes, no doubt, dealers in foreign exchange were excessively nervous—or speculators were excessively optimistic: large sums of money must have been lost from time to time in operations against sterling. But the important point is that the run on sterling which developed in the summer of 1957 was based on much the same sort of fears, only a little better founded, as those which well-informed observers had felt, for example, at the beginning of 1955 and in the autumn of 1956. Because, fundamentally, of the excessive demands which Britain was making on her own resources, and which were always apt to spill over into excessive demands on other people's resources, sterling was not a safe currency and Britain was not a safe economy. The main difference in 1957 was probably the contrast which Britain then made with Germany. Germany's recovery had been spectacular, and by 1957 Germany had huge surpluses with EPU. It was not clear that Britain would be able to hold her own in a world which contained a new, dynamic Germany. Expectation of an imminent upvaluation of the D-mark caused pressure on sterling. Half of Europe expected that an exchange realignment would be announced at the meeting of the International Monetary Fund in September, and that this would include sterling devaluation. The situation was further aggravated by the fact that even British investors were showing themselves anxious to get out of sterling. Financial circles in Britain—as well as abroad—were beginning to feel alarm, and to doubt the value of a currency controlled by economic policies such as had been pursued in the preceding six years.

There was no devaluation. Instead, Bank Rate went to 7 per cent. This was the highest rate for thirty-seven years, and the sensation it caused was tremendous.

'After a year of passive neutralism, suggesting at times almost an abdication of monetary leadership, the Bank has reclaimed the initiative with a thrust of wholly unexpected boldness.'[1]

The psychological effect alone was very great. It was accompanied, however, by a request to the banks to put a ceiling on advances and by instructions to the nationalized industries, the Government departments and the local authorities to undertake no increased expenditure for two years. Above all, 'there was substantial effect in raising long rates and making people hesitant in their planning;'[2] all previous changes of Bank Rate had been too hesitant and too readily reversed to have more than minimal effects on long rates. But now it seemed different. Thorneycroft, Chancellor of the Exchequer, was apparently among those who thought that a new turn to economic policy was required. 'The Government', it was officially stated, 'are determined to maintain the internal and the external value of the pound', and it was indicated that the way to do this was to control the supply of money:

'What is needed . . . is for the Government to be prepared to deny the extra cash, whatever other painful consequences may follow. . . These measures . . . will be effective. They will be pushed to the lengths necessary for that purpose . . . If an attempt were made to take out of the system in money income more than is put in by new effort and production, the only result would be a reduction in activity and the employment of fewer men.'

[1] *The Banker*, September 21, 1957, p. 953.
[2] *Report of the Committee on the Working of the Monetary System* (Cmd. 827, 1959), para. 497.

How far the Chancellor intended his new policy to go was never revealed. It was interpreted by many as an attempt to subordinate the aim of full employment to that of maintaining the value of the currency; and this was probably correct. Left-wing politicians became alarmed at the Chancellor's objective ('really to declare war on the trade unions'[1]) while many economists expressed incredulity at the implied revival of the quantity theory of money. As things turned out, neither had much cause for alarm. Four months after introducing his new measures the Chancellor resigned, ostensibly on the ground that his colleagues in the Cabinet would not agree that current government expenditure should be held absolutely constant in money terms. This was hardly a realistic aim—a rising population required a rising expenditure unless standards were to fall; and acceptance of Mr Thorneycroft's 'principle' would, as Mr Butler put it, have overturned 'in the course of a few days, policies in social welfare to which some of us have devoted our lives'. It may well be, as has been suggested,[2] that Thorneycroft resigned because the Cabinet would not accept a policy of putting price stability as the number one aim.

The economy recovered from the 1957 crisis fairly rapidly, both the reserves and the balance of payments showing improvement early in 1958. The crisis measures had restored confidence. Nevertheless, disillusion about the effectiveness of monetary policy began to spread (its critics had their field-day in the rather one-sided Radcliffe Report[3] published in 1959) and the realization grew that managing the British economy so as to achieve its peace-time ambitions was, if anything, an even harder task than organizing its recovery from the war. On the other hand, it was possible to believe that the crises so far encountered were largely in the nature of accidental misfortunes: thus the events of 1951 would have been very different had it not been for the Korean war, while those of 1957 could be explained as being due at least partly to changes in the position of the franc and the West German mark—the latter itself a reflection of the enor-

[1] Mr Gordon Walker in the House of Commons, October 1957.
[2] A. Shonfield, *British Economic Policy since the War* (Penguin, 1958), pp. 248–9.
[3] *Report of the Radcliffe Committee on the Working of the Monetary System*, Cmd. 827, 1959. For contrasting views, see *Not Unanimous* (Institute of Economic Affairs, 1960).

mous change which had taken place in the position of West Germany in the 1950s.

Unfortunately, in the next ten years the pattern, expansion—balance of payments crisis—recession, became chronic, with no fewer than three crises taking place in the seven years 1960 to 1966—as many as had occurred in the whole of the 1950s. Worse still, these crises became more and more severe, partly because experience increasingly showed that the British economy seemed unable to change direction, and that the capacity of the pound to withstand pressure on the foreign exchanges therefore remained small. Precisely because the balance of payments of the United Kingdom had shown marked weakness throughout the 1950s, the crises of the 1960s were worse than those which had preceded them. Over the seven-year period from 1958 to 1964 the current account of the U.K. was, on average, just in balance; it follows that current earnings made no contribution to the financing of long-term capital exports which averaged about £175m. a year during the same period. And as a result, the reserves were under £1,000m. by mid-1964, lower than they had been seven years earlier; and this was *before* they came under intense pressure in the autumn of that year.

Balance of payments and changes in reserves, 1958 to 1965 (£m.s)

	Current account (surplus + deficit −)	Balance of long-term capital (assets: increase − decrease +)	Reserves at beginning of year
1958	+330	−193	812
1959	+132	−251	1,096
1960	−273	−185	977
1961	− 14	+ 77	1,154
1962	+ 93	− 93	1,185
1963	+105	−162	1,002
1964	−406	−363	949
1965	−136	−218	827

That the difficulties of the economy were so deep-seated was certainly not appreciated in 1958. Crises were to be avoided (the new Chancellor was 'determined to spare no effort to see that we do not have another'[1]) and inflation was to be held in check.

[1] Mr Amory, House of Commons, April 1958.

The 1958 budget was mildly expansionary, and a general fall in commodity prices enormously improved the terms of trade, leading to the largest balance of payments surplus since the war. But the year was one of recession, with slowly mounting unemployment of both plant and labour. As a consequence, Bank Rate was reduced to 4 per cent by November, and various steps were taken to encourage both investment and consumption. In spite of these measures, unemployment reached 2·8 per cent in January 1959, the highest level since the war.

The time had clearly come to inject additional purchasing power into the economy—how much, it was difficult to calculate. The outlook for the balance of payments was not too encouraging; on the other hand, there was unused capacity, and many observers feared that if under-utilization kept holding down the returns to investment, industrialists' confidence would be undermined, net investment would decline, and a large-scale recession occur. In the event, the stimulus given by the 1959 budget turned out to be excessive. Investment allowances were reintroduced, there were cuts in indirect taxation, and the standard rate of income tax was reduced by no less than ninepence (this last item alone cut revenue by £229m. in a full year). The economy promptly revived. During 1959, final expenditure rose by 6 per cent, national output by about 4 per cent, and industrial production by 10 per cent. Most surprising, prices remained stable, in spite of the fact that wage rates rose by 3 per cent; this was because import prices fell slightly, and output per man rose, so that, 'for the first and only time since the war labour costs per unit of output actually fell'.[1]

Thus 1959 took up the slack which had been generated in the second half of 1957 and in 1958. But obviously the question was whether the economy could now continue on this upward path. The reserves of labour and of capacity had been used up. Moreover, the balance of payments surplus had smartly declined from £345m. to £140m., in spite of the fact that world trading developments had been favourable to British exports; for internal expansion had brought about a substantial rise in imports. Bank Rate was raised in January 1960, there was a cautious budget, and, for the first time, the device was used of

[1] G. D. N. Worswick in Worswick & Ady, op. cit., p. 66.

requiring the banks to make special deposits with the Bank of England, deposits which reduced their liquidity ratio and hence their capacity to lend. Production began to level off, exports started to decline, and the balance of payments again went into deficit. As the year went on, further restrictive measures had to be taken, but most of them, unfortunately, appeared to 'hit that section of demand which was just on the point of receding in any case'.[1] The rise in private consumption was halted. But private non-housing investment went ahead throughout the year, reaching a record level for 1960 as a whole, while investment in stocks, that wretchedly unpredictable magnitude, rose by more than in any year except 1951. Consequently, there was yet another serious deficit in the balance of payments; but this time the reserves were supported by a large inflow of foreign capital, most of it short-term. This made the situation supportable. But it was not sound.

By the spring of 1961 it was clear that the brakes would again have to be applied. The balance of payments in the second half of 1960 had turned out more serious than anything since 1951. Labour costs per unit of output, stable from the spring of 1958 to the spring of 1960, were rising rapidly. And so were prices. The budget accordingly made some tax increases; but their effect, on the whole, was not so much to dampen demand as to raise industrial costs and cut down distributable profits—a policy ill-calculated to benefit exports. More important, the Chancellor's measures included the introduction of powers which would permit him or his successors *at any time of the year*

1. to apply a special charge or rebate on all the main consumption and excise revenue duties and purchase tax, by a single alteration with a maximum of 10 per cent;
2. to impose a surcharge on the employer's contribution to National Insurance, with a maximum of 4s. per employee per week.

Each of these powers could, if utilized to the full, affect revenue by ±£200m. This would be—and is—a significant figure from the point of view of management of the economy, and it was

---

[1] I. M. D. Little in Worswick & Ady, op. cit., p. 271.

unquestionably a wise move to take powers to act decisively and swiftly without having to go through the lengthy and complicated procedures associated with a Finance Act. Finally, and perhaps equally important, the need was proclaimed for a 'pause' in pay rises, to be achieved, seemingly, by direct intervention in the process of wage-bargaining.

These measures turned out to be, not very surprisingly, quite insufficient to reduce the rate of growth of money income to anything resembling the rate of growth of production. The reserves continued to fall while short-term liabilities rose, and the deficit on current account continued. Another serious sterling crisis developed, its timing closely affected by revaluation of the Federal German and Dutch currencies. It was therefore, in some ways, not dissimilar to the crisis of 1957; but the situation was less easy to deal with, because this time the balance of payments was seriously adverse. The Chancellor announced his new measures in July. There was to be a 10 per cent increase on a wide range of indirect taxes (he thus used the power obtained a few months before), intentions—somewhat vague—to reduce Government expenditure were declared, and there were proposals to hold down wages in the Government sector, starting with teachers. As the second step in a wages policy (the first had been taken in April) this was significant; but its practical effects were, for the time being, extremely small. What mattered a great deal was that short-term assistance for the UK was obtained from European Central Banks to a total of £323m., while a large credit of £535m. in addition to a smaller stand-by credit of £178m., was secured from the International Monetary Fund. This temporarily relieved the pressure exerted upon sterling as a result of the highly illiquid state of Britain's international assets. At the same time, as the IMF credit had to be repaid in from three to five years' time, it made the necessity of finding a permanent solution to Britain's problems more urgent than ever.

This crisis was a depressing event. Not only did it make a mockery of Mr Amory's resolution of only three years before 'not to have another'. It also cast serious doubt on the technical competence of those in charge of economic policy. Expert observers felt acute disappointment.

'The boom of 1955 had been encouraged by policy; policy was reversed very late in the day; and when it was reversed, policy remained restrictive for three years. After this experience, it seemed reasonable to hope that intervention on this scale could in future be avoided; that—while demand would doubtless have to continue to be controlled—small adjustments made in good time would suffice; and that expansion could be allowed to proceed—now rather more, now rather less rapidly —at a fairly steady pace. Yet the expansion induced in 1958 and 1959 had to be severely checked barely fifteen months after it got under way. By 1960, national output was 14 per cent, and output per head 12½ per cent higher than in 1955. But Britain's neighbours on the Continent had been growing at something like twice that rate; and by 1960, this was being made one of the major criticisms of British economic policy.'[1]

The July budget, coupled with measures already taken, had the desired effect, and economic growth slowed fairly abruptly; most important, exports during the year as a whole rose more than imports, and the terms of trade moved in Great Britain's favour. The 1962 budget gave no stimulus to demand, being aimed rather at holding down the persistent rise in wages and prices by keeping home demand moderate, in the apparent hope that this policy would be of sufficient help to exports. The *Economic Survey for 1962* seemed to state the Government's position; in two important respects, it said,

'the Government can help. They can regulate the strength of total home demand which would otherwise compete with export demand for the use of skilled labour and other scarce resources. They can also influence the level of incomes, and, therefore, the cost of production.'

The Government also found another way to help; they set up 'Neddy', the National Economic Development Council. Neddy was charged with these responsibilities:

1. to discover the growth plans of the different sectors of the economy;

[1] J. C. R. Dow, op. cit., p. 111.

2. to enquire how far these plans are consistent with one another;

3. to seek agreement on ways of improving the plans.

In the course of 1962 the number of unfilled vacancies fell quite sharply, the reserves did well, and—world trade in manufactures being good and the terms of trade exceptionally favourable—the balance of payments was reasonably satisfactory. But production scarcely moved upwards. Therefore, as in the summer of 1958, cautious reflationary moves began. In November 1962 indirect taxes were reduced and investment was encouraged by means of the investment allowances. But unemployment continued to rise, reaching 815,000 by January 1963. (It had been 260,000 just before the emergency measures taken in July 1961.) This in itself was bad. There was much idle capacity in industry—it was reckoned by the spring that perhaps 10 per cent or 15 per cent more output was possible even with the *given* labour force. Thus output was being lost, and the 4 per cent target rate of growth not being achieved. The trend in Government policy was 'clearly in the expansionist direction';[1] but the measures so far taken were having little effect upon either output or consumption. Further stimulus appeared to be in order.

The aim of the 1963 budget was described by the Chancellor as 'expansion without inflation . . . to do the Government's part in achieving the rate of growth broadly described as the 4 per cent target, which we have already accepted in the NEDC'. This target was for the years 1962-66, and as growth in 1962–63 had been less than 2 per cent, the requirement was now for growth rather above $4\frac{1}{2}$ per cent per annum. Many looked on this 'target' with extreme scepticism, pointing out that the British economy had hardly ever achieved a 4 per cent growth rate, except for very short periods of time. Others appeared to believe that the thing could now be done. The Government's contributions took the form principally of tax remissions to the extent of some £250m. This was certainly going to stimulate the economy, and it was anticipated that some strain was going to be placed on the balance of payments; but the risk was deliberately taken

[1] *London and Cambridge Economic Bulletin*, March 1963.

that a short-term call on the reserves might have to be made 'in order to get the economy moving again'.

This was clearly a chancy policy; and in the end it failed. But the reasons for its failure were complicated. One fundamental reason was the rather absurdly optimistic view taken in the NEDC about the probable relation between demand for imports and the trend of exports. In 1963 the NEDC put forward the view that its 4 per cent target rate of growth for GNP was consistent with a 4·7 per cent per annum increase in imports. (A rather lower figure had previously been suggested.) The NEDC also suggested that it was consistent and reasonable to look for a growth of exports (in volume) of about 5 per cent per annum. These expectations appear to have been the basis of Government economic planning in the final years of the Tory administration. They looked at the time, to say the least of it, extremely optimistic. Since 1961, imports had risen by about 6 per cent per annum, while exports had increased by only about 2 per cent. There were grounds, certainly, for expecting some improvement on both sides of the balance; but it looked as if policy had suddenly shifted from great caution to rash optimism.

For a time, the effects of the 1963 budget, allied to the preceding measures, were not apparent; and fears were even expressed in the summer that the steps taken to reflate the economy had been inadequate. This shows how difficult is the task not only of forecasting a future situation but even of assessing that which already exists; for GNP rose by no less than 7 per cent between the fourth quarter of 1962 and the fourth quarter of 1963. This possibly still left some industrial capacity idle; but it was clearly not a 'sustainable' rate of growth.

The situation which the Chancellor faced in the spring of 1964 was therefore a very difficult one. Consumer expenditure had risen rapidly and exports had done well. On the other hand, it could still be argued that 'the rise in GNP has exceeded 4 per cent a year only because it included a substantial element of recovery from a depressed position'.[1] And at the back of many minds—too many—was the anguished thought that the current rate of growth was not much more than was necessary if the magical target of 4 per cent per annum by 1966, on average, was

[1] *London and Cambridge Economic Bulletin*, March 1964.

to be achieved. The Chancellor, still hoping for the best, brought in a budget which made little change in the position. Always assuming that the fundamental strategy was reasonable —namely, that a higher level of activity, once sustained, would cut costs, increase efficiency, encourage investment, and boost exports—this budget might be described as a bold gamble. As Professor Robinson wrote near the time,

'Mr Maudling is prepared this year to operate near to full stretch, using reserves, and, if necessary, borrowings to permit stock building and to attempt to set us on the path of 4 per cent growth. How to give ourselves that extra bit of elbow room that we require is the problem.

'The optimists of NEDC believe that it can just be done within the total of our constraints, on the assumptions—two very important assumptions—that improvement of competitiveness is sufficient for 4 per cent growth, and that growth itself does not multiply the number of bottlenecks which can be relieved only by imports . . . One can only hope that they are right.'[1]

But it soon became apparent that they were wrong. A few months later the figure for unfilled vacancies was the same as it had been in 1960, imports were running at a very high level, and exports were doing conspicuously less well than was required. The balance of payments surplus of £70m. for the first quarter of 1963 was converted into a deficit of £54m. for the same period of 1964, and in the second quarter all the signs were that the situation was growing worse.

	Balance of payments, 1964			£ million
	1st quarter	2nd quarter	3rd quarter	4th quarter
Current balance	−54	−60	−182	−78
—seasonally adjusted	−77	−102	−110	−85

Still the Chancellor, Mr Maudling, held on. Unemployment was fractionally over 1·5 per cent, prices were rising, consumption was rising quite rapidly, and output per man-hour in manufacturing industry was no greater than in 1964. As the summer

[1] *London and Cambridge Economic Bulletin*, June 1964.

passed, the grounds for action to stem the tide of inflation and prevent yet another sterling crisis shifted swiftly from prudence to necessity. Yet nothing was done. The third and gravest sterling crisis in nine years was allowed to develop without the authorities taking a single step to avert it. For this, Mr Maudling and his economic advisers must take the full blame. And it is to be feared that the course which was followed was not unrelated to the fact that a General Election was to be held in October. No Government relishes going to the polls on the morrow of announcing unpopular economic measures. But history, as well as common sense, strongly suggests that it is better, even when appealing to the electors, to face unpleasant facts than to try for an easy popularity.

The historian's advantage, one which he can too easily abuse, is that of hindsight; the man who knows how and when the battle was lost finds it easy to point out the mistakes of the general in the field. In the writing of very recent history this advantage, such as it is, largely disappears, and into its place there step the hazards of imperfect information, over-hasty judgment, and bias about events and personalities of immediate concern to the writer. Nevertheless, it seems worth while to bring this narrative almost up to date, for the events of the last twenty-two months strongly suggest that the advent to power of Mr Wilson's Labour Government in October 1964 was not the opening of a new chapter in Britain's affairs as so many people expected it to be.

The Tories lost the election by an exceedingly narrow margin. Had their conduct of affairs in the preceding two years shown more flexibility and imagination, they might well have retained office; but the image of the party was gravely harmed first by the sordid Profumo scandal and then by the undignified and ill-managed squabbling over the leadership which took place when Mr Macmillan announced his resignation. The Tories appeared tired, dreary, old-fashioned, and out of humour with one another. Mr Wilson, on the other hand, exuded confidence and energy, and he skilfully allied his cause with the ideas of modernity and progress. There was to be a 'new Britain'. Modern technology, instead of being regarded as a menace or a nuisance, was to be

198

harnessed to the ends of social justice. The faltering 'stop-go' policies of the past were to be replaced by economic planning, guided by Socialist priorities and worked out by Socialist dons. There was to be a Minister of Technology and a Ministry of Economic Affairs. Best of all, there was to be an economist as Prime Minister.

From the point of view of the Labour Party, they could scarcely have come into power at a more unfortunate time. From the moment of taking office they had an incipient and already serious balance of payments crisis on their hands. Their electoral promises had included the renationalization of steel, which was absurdly irrelevant to the real problems of the day, reform of taxation, which was wanted, repeal of the Rent Act, which would do nothing to raise productivity, or increase the supply of house room, and legislation to prevent rising land values from falling entirely into private hands. But none of these steps, even when in the right direction, could have a quick effect on the situation.

The crisis which existed in October was, like the previous one, largely the result of earlier policy measures. In 1963, consumer expenditure had risen by over 4 per cent. In 1964 it rose a little less rapidly, but investment expenditure gathered speed, and achieved the phenomenal increase of 16 per cent during the year. From the autumn of 1963 onwards, each successive survey of business investment plans showed an upward revision in response to encouraging demand prospects. Public investment excluding housing was on a rising trend in 1963 (+7 per cent) and this item increased still more rapidly in 1964 (+15 per cent). Investment in house-building was much higher in 1964 (+25 per cent) and public investment programmes were substantially increased. Only for stock-building was the rate of increase rather less than might have been feared.

The ever-widening deficit on current account was possibly added to by the mere fact of a Labour Government having taken office. On the other hand, Continental bankers were accustomed to seeing Socialist parties in power in their own countries, so it is doubtful if much weight should be attached to this argument —except in so far as Socialism frightened home investors. Also, it is now known that the current balance of payments situation was tending to improve by October. But it is beyond question that the new Government inherited a fundamentally bad situation, and that by tactical errors they soon made it very much worse. 'Not many people seem to have thought devaluation likely until the Government itself began drawing attention to the seriousness of the external deficit. But once they had been convinced, the Government's efforts to correct the situation looked a bit half-hearted.'[1] Worse still, they bore the signs of, and were indeed announced as being, panic measures. Small export rebates were introduced and petrol tax was raised. Direct aid was given to the balance of payments by a 15 per cent surcharge on imports, which approximately doubled the average rate of import duties in Britain except on food and basic raw materials. (Britain's partners in EFTA were not consulted before the surcharge—in any case contrary to GATT—was announced. This aroused understandable hostility in a world in which Britain badly needed friends.) These measures were bound to help the balance of payments. But nothing was done to affect total domestic demand—indeed, the granting of higher pensions and other benefits, also hastily announced by the Government, was calculated to raise demand. As for raising Bank Rate, it was emphasized by the Foreign Secretary in Washington late in October that the British Government had no intention of doing any such thing. The result of these unwise pronouncements and inept and inadequate measures was that although the balance of payments steadied, the withdrawal of funds from London increased, and assumed the most alarming proportions.

'By late November confidence in sterling and in the authorities' intentions had been so effectively shattered that a two point rise in Bank Rate to 7 per cent only accelerated the capital flight, and even the announcement of a record $3,000m. of emergency credit facilities from foreign central banks did not bring it to an immediate halt.'[2]

This crisis lingered on for many months, but the worst was, for the time being, over. The most significant feature was the unprecedented co-operative rescue operation on the part of the

[1] *London and Cambridge Economic Bulletin*, March 1965.
[2] ibid.

central banks of Europe and North America to save the pound from collapse as an international currency. Under the leadership of Lord Cromer, Governor of the Bank of England, and the Federal Reserve Bank of New York, eleven foreign central banks, together with the Export Import Bank of Washington and the Bank for International Settlements, put $3 billion, mainly short-term, at the disposal of the United Kingdom. This was not a disinterested gesture of goodwill, but an indication of the importance of sterling in the international structure of exchange. For if sterling were devalued, other currencies would follow suit. World trade would be seriously affected. And the problem of world liquidity, one of the most serious and deep-seated problems of the decade, would grow worse.

The fall in the sterling area's reserves from mid-September to the end of 1964 cannot have been much less than £500m.; and for some of this flight of capital UK residents were themselves responsible. To make matters worse over £500m. had been drawn from the emergency credits. The situation was thus now bad beyond precedent, and it was therefore of the utmost importance that substantial surpluses should as soon as practicable be achieved in the balance of payments. But these surpluses proved extremely reluctant to appear. The current balance had not deteriorated as much as in 1958–60, but the initial surplus position in 1962 had been much smaller than in 1958; and therefore the final deficit was now much bigger.

| | Current Account | | £ million |
	Visible balance	Invisible balance	Current balance
1958	+ 41	+304	+345
1960	−386	+128	−258
1962	− 72	+187	+115
1964	−519	+115	−404

Through the winter the Government tinkered with the situation, chiefly by putting restrictions on bank lending, and in April the Chancellor, Mr Callaghan, introduced his second budget. Some indirect taxes were raised, capital gains were to be more extensively taxed, the import surcharge was reduced to 10 per cent, and a new, complicated, and uncertain corporation tax was introduced. In the way that the budget was presented the Government seemed to lay more emphasis on social justice than on solvency (just as it had insisted on raising pensions as well as discouraging imports in October), and it was perhaps hardly the moment to take steps which would unsettle business without increasing its efficiency; but the budget was, on the whole, deflationary. The question was, however, whether it was deflationary enough. National incomes had risen considerably faster than real output in 1964 and the rise in wages and salaries appeared to be accelerating. It was absolutely vital to check the price rise and to improve delivery dates for exports. Yet the Chancellor still seemed to be aiming for a high growth rate and full employment—in the inflationary sense of that phrase. In other words, the Government evidently still believed that 'the deadly sin was to check the growth of the economy',[1] and that it was better to take the gravest risks with sterling (supported by other people's money) than see unemployment rise to 2 per cent.[2] This was Mr Maudling's policy of the summer of 1964 all over again—a policy based on the so-called 'over-spill thesis', that if only the economy was active enough at home, then exports would benefit automatically from the new products and rising productivity generated by home demand. But at least Mr Maudling had not borrowed $3 billion.

In the Government's defence it must be added that they appeared to attach great importance to their proposals for an incomes policy and a national plan. The former was designed to achieve voluntary restraint in the matter of wage increases, so as to keep the increase in money wages more or less in line with increases in productivity. This amounted to asking the trade unions not to use their bargaining powers to the full, and employers not to bid against one another for scarce labour. It was arguable that success in this field could make a significant contribution to achieving sustainable growth in the medium term. But the Government was either incapable of understanding or deliberately shut its eyes to the limitations of such a policy. The aims of an incomes policy, they were reminded by the OECD, 'are unlikely to be achieved unless the economy is run

---

[1] *The Statist*, April 15, 1965.

[2] Unemployment in the first quarter of 1965 was 1·4 per cent—an almost record low.

with a lower pressure of demand than that prevailing recently and in previous peak periods.'[1] However successful, not much effect on prices could be expected before 1966; and the effect was in any case unlikely to be more than a short postponement of the upward march of wages. The trade unions disliked the policy, and Mr Cousins was clearly correct in condemning the Government for believing 'that a policy of restricting wage increases is a substitute for an economic policy'. Worse still, if voluntary restraint failed there was likely to be resort to compulsion, and this would set the Government on the path to more and more 'planning' by controls, quotas, and quantitative restraints.

The national plan, devised by the Department of Economic Affairs during 1965, was also a medium-term proposition, calculated to show what sectoral and other rates of growth would be required if the economy as a whole were to grow by 3·8 per cent from 1964 to 1970. Planning—although few people were very clear just what the word might mean—was fashionable, partly because it appeared to have been very successful in France, and the public was led to believe that the national plan would solve many difficulties. The plan, when it appeared, was an elaborate and ingenious document, and the fact that it had been constructed through the co-operation of businessmen and trade unionists, as well as economists and civil servants, meant that a process of extremely valuable mutual education had gone on, and that attention was drawn to potential bottlenecks and to the idiosyncrasies—perhaps the failings— of individual industries. But the publication of the plan achieved nothing and could achieve nothing. At the most, it pin-pointed areas of particular difficulty if there was to be 'a steady expansion of industrial production year by year' at the stipulated rate, and it provided a useful frame of reference for forward-planning by firms, Government departments, or nationalized industries— always provided that the 3·8 per cent 'target' rate of growth was practicable; but it did nothing, and suggested nothing, to solve the problems of how to achieve a better allocation of resources, increase exports, or raise industrial productivity. In a sense, it was a largely academic exercise. Had 3·8 per cent been a realistic rate—and all the evidence was that it was not—the

[1] *Economic Surveys by the OECD: United Kingdom* (OECD 1965), p. 29.

plan would have been marginally helpful. As it was, the plan distracted attention from real difficulties, and was held up as a solution to problems not all of which it even professed to face.

In addition to the incomes policy and the national plan, the Government introduced a number of measures to raise economic efficiency. There were to be better training facilities for work-people, severance payments for those made idle by technological change, more ambitious regional development schemes, and Economic Development Committees ('Little Neddies') to study means of improving the efficiency of firms in particular branches of industry. These were good moves, but they could have little immediate effect. The current balance of payments remained adverse until the last quarter of 1965, when there was a small surplus, and the balance of current and long-term capital trans-actions was unfavourable throughout the year. A number of deflationary measures were taken, including, at long last, some reduction in Government expenditure. But in the autumn came the break with Rhodesia. A few months later the Government gave way in connection with a pay award on the railways (where rising productivity was conspicuous by its absence) and it was obvious that although their policies were holding up price increases, at least for a time, they were having virtually no effect on earnings, which had risen, under the Labour Government, by no less than 9 per cent per annum.

There was a General Election in March. And once again it seems not too cynical to conclude that the Government's policy had been to keep up employment and the rate of growth at least until they were returned to power for another five years. The May budget was notable for its introduction of the Selective Employment Tax, to fall on the so-called 'service industries'. This considerably broadened the base of taxation, was arranged so as to reduce liquidity in all sectors of the economy, and to have a substantial deflationary effect. On the other hand, this effect would not be felt for another six months, and the tax would do nothing to discourage the hoarding of labour in industry or the civil service. Steps were also taken to reduce directly the net outflow of long-term private capital to non-sterling area countries. This budget, like its predecessor a year before, was little calculated to resolve the endemic emergency from which the country was now suffering. Its misplaced ingenuity served chiefly to increase the confidence-sapping uncertainty which Government actions had now induced over wide sectors of the economy. In June, the September credits were renewed, and growth was about 2 or 3 per cent. But as it became clear that there would be no balance of payments equilibrium by the end of 1966, possibly not even in 1967, sterling again came under pressure, and in July came the biggest 'stop' of all time. The May budget had been calculated to take more out of the economy in a full year than any budget since 1951—perhaps over £300m. Now came a set of measures calculated to reduce demand by another £500m., enough to cause a complete standstill in home output for twelve months. Even public sector investment was to be reduced. Most serious of all, a 'freeze' of wages, dividends and prices was introduced, a policy unpopular with all sections of the community and one bound to produce anomalies and injustices, and to discourage enterprise and innovation throughout the economy. This was a crisis measure if ever there was one, a confession of failure even more complete than devaluation in 1949. But no economic system can be expected to do well which is subjected to five budgets in twenty months. The trouble was made at home. For it must be acknowledged that these budgets betokened, as was said at the time, 'not so much a sequence of unexpected and unavoidable disasters as a lack of comprehension, wisdom, courage, and will. The story of the past twenty months brings little credit to the Prime Minister, or to the ingenious but impractical men from whom he has chosen to take advice.'[1]

At the time of writing, the situation is gloomy, not only in respect of the immediate outlook but also in respect of the fact that the past two years have been almost completely wasted. The reserves/liabilities situation is worse than it was in the summer of 1964, and the economy is farther away than ever from a path of rapid and sustainable growth.

Provided that world trading conditions remain as good as they have been, on average, over the past ten years, the steps now taken are probably too severe, and some reflation will have to be attempted in the next twelve months. But so long as a 1·5

[1] *The Statist*, July 22, 1966.

per cent unemployment rate is regarded as an indispensable objective policy, and so long as a high rate of growth is also made an immediate aim instead of being seen as the natural outcome of economic activity in an economy in which innovation and competitive efficiency are widely and enthusiastically sought, so long will disappointment, indebtedness and failure be the lot of Britain.

INDUSTRIAL DEVELOPMENT AND FOREIGN TRADE

In the decade after the war there were very considerable changes in both the structure and the organization of British industry. To begin with, it was the organizational changes which attracted much the greater part of public attention. The Labour Government which was elected in 1945 was pledged to carry out various schemes of nationalization, of which very high hopes were entertained by a number—perhaps the majority—of its supporters. These schemes, in accordance with Socialist thinking, included the large and basic industries of coal mining, electricity, transport and iron and steel. Nationalization of these industries meant that a very large part of the British economy came under more direct Government control than hitherto, and was run not on a profit-making basis but in the public interest. It was soon seen, however, that the difference between making money and acting in the public interest was smaller than most people had imagined, and that nationalization raised some difficult problems of its own. It also became increasingly clear that Britain's future was not going to be secured so much by re-organizing basic industries as by developing new and existing industries which could sell their wares in competitive markets overseas and produce for home consumption the goods which a people growing rapidly richer after 1952 wanted to buy—motor cars, television sets, nylon stockings and the rest. The changes in industrial structure thus required were a continuation of those changes which had taken place in the 1920s and the 1930s. Such change is continuous; but in periods of very rapid scientific development (such as the post-war decade) there is the opportunity of especially rapid industrial transformation; and if at the same time there is difficulty in selling enough abroad, even in a seller's market, to pay for essential imports, this opportunity becomes one which the economy is compelled to accept. Beside these changes, the scope for improvement which nationalization offered was decidedly limited, especially in the short run. Yet the stimulus of Government pressure and activity, as well as some of the nationalization measures themselves, almost certainly helped the economy to put up a better performance in the 'fifties than it had put up between the wars. There was waste and extravagance. But the important fuel and power situation became better, and there was encouragement everywhere for imagination and enterprise.

The Labour Government began its brief nationalization career by nationalizing the Bank of England. Probably no change could have made less difference to the economy than this. No doubt there are 'ineffable mysteries'[1] in the relationship between the Bank of England and the Treasury, but no one had ever suggested that the Bank had no co-operated loyally with whatever Government was in office for at least a hundred years. The change, indeed, was entirely one of form. The stock of the Bank came to be held by the Treasury, and the private shareholders— distressingly anomalous in the new, logically constructed world —received fair compensation. 'Nothing,' said the *Economist*, 'could well be more moderate.'[2]

In December came an important measure, the Coal Nationalization Bill. This was the first major instalment of the Government's Socialist programme. The Bill brought into existence the National Coal Board, consisting of nine members appointed by the appropriate Minister, and charged with the business of running and reorganizing the industry. The Board was given very wide powers, and £150m. of new money to spend on the re-equipment of the industry. Its financial obligation was vague and not onerous: the books were to balance 'on an average of good and bad years'. Compensation was on the basis of reasonable net maintainable revenue. The country was divided into eight divisions, and the Board took over on the first day of 1947, encouraged by mass meetings and colliery bands in the mining

[1] The phrase is applied by Sir Dennis Robertson in his *Economic Commentaries* (London, Staples Press, 1956), p. 156.
[2] *The Economist*, October 13, 1945, p. 513.

areas The Bill was reasonable, and put an end to the political quarrel in the industry which had gone on for a quarter of a century. But the circumstances were in many ways not propitious—coal was scarce and dear and the miners were pressing for a five-day week. The Bill left a lot undecided. Everything now depended on the Board—on the speed and efficiency with which it carried out the long-overdue reorganization of the industry—and on the miners.

Further measures of nationalization followed extremely rapidly. In April 1946, after little serious discussion, the Government announced that it intended to introduce 'a large measure of public ownership' for iron and steel. In August it set up, as a first step, the Steel Board. This Board had two main functions: to supervise the development and reconstruction of the industry and to act for the Government in cases where the continuation of control over production, distribution and prices was deemed necessary. The Board was therefore to perform much the same duties as had been performed by IDAC and other bodies for over ten years. In November came a far more important measure, the Bill for the nationalization of the railways, the canals, and London Transport. Compensation, this time, was on the basis of the market values of the relevant securities on the Stock Exchange at a specified date. The sum involved worked out at about seven times the price paid for the coal mines. A Railway Executive came into existence to run the railways, and a Road Executive to run road transport—and the Transport Commission became responsible for the whole business.[1] Thus little could now sail or crawl within Britain in the name of transportation for which the Transport Commission, and virtually the Minister of Transport, was not responsible. The undertaking was enormous; and the units of organization were, to say the least of it, big; the Railway Executive, for example, had three times as much on its hands as the largest previously existing railway company. Competition was almost entirely eliminated. The whole scheme was certainly logical. Critics had spoken for years about the 'integration' of transport, about the need for 'rationalization', about the

[1] It was at first proposed that no privately owned lorries should be allowed to operate more than forty miles from home. This would have made all long-distance transport a Government monopoly. This clause was cut out in discussion of the Bill.

'wastes of competition'. It did, and sometimes still does seem that there is a strong case for unifying transport services and reducing overlapping. If the arguments were sound, the Bill was an almost ideal answer. If they were not—and, as opponents pointed out, there had never been a public inquiry to find out what the possible economies really were and whether they were likely to outweigh the inevitable diseconomies of a gigantic monopoly—the Bill was a mistake and a serious one.

Four weeks later came the Town and Country Planning Bill, designed to give powers to local authorities to permit or pro-hibit building and rebuilding without having to worry about the financial consequences, and powers to acquire land compulsorily up to ten years in advance of need and put up anything. The idea was excellent. But, as was remarked at the time, 'the belief that a public authority . . . will automatically act for the public good has by now worn very thin;'[1] and experience has shown that hideous buildings and the misuse of sites are as common as be-fore the war, the chief difference being that it now takes three years to do what used to be possible in one. The week after the Town and Country Planning Bill came the Electricity Bill. This was to nationalize the supply and distribution of electricity. The existing Central Electricity Board owned the Grid, but not the generating stations, nor the distribution systems. Further econ-omies of scale were agreed to be available, if there were single ownership by areas. This the Bill provided for, giving power stations and the Grid to the new British (later, the Central) Electricity Authority and the distribution systems to fourteen Area Boards. Compensation was again on the basis of Stock Ex-change prices. There was a good case for the Bill, and the public took it calmly, perhaps because, as the *Economist* remarked, 'after the revolutionary proposals of the Transport Bill and the intellectual gymnastics necessary to comprehend the Planning Bill, the mere proposal to take the electricity industry into public ownership looks almost tame.'[2]

Last of all, in November 1948, came the Steel Bill. This Bill aroused intense opposition. There had been general public sup-port for the nationalization of the mines, there was a very strong

[1] *The Economist*, February 1, 1947, p. 179.
[2] ibid., January 18, 1947, p. 92.

case for nationalizing electricity, and many people believed when it was done that there was a strong case for nationalizing transport. But steel is a manufacturing industry making a great variety of complex products. It is impossible to draw a clear line between the steel industry and the engineering industry. In this case, therefore, nationalization raised quite a different set of questions. Moreover, Government after Government had had a say in the running of the industry ever since 1934. And the industry was making cheap steel, cheaper than in most countries. If there was not enough of it, that was hardly the industry's fault. Complaint could be made about the pre-war cartel arrangements in the industry, which had kept up costs (and therefore prices) by protecting and preserving inefficient producers. But if that was the charge against the industry, the question immediately arose, would a Government-sponsored corporation be any more willing than the private Iron and Steel Federation had been to force people out of business? And the answer, on the face of it, was no, because a public corporation would be even more reluctant than the Federation to close down inefficient plants (because of political, chiefly trade union, pressure), and would be excellently placed to subsidize the inefficient out of the profits of the efficient. There therefore seemed little reason to suppose that nationalization would tend to increase efficiency in the industry. The strong argument for nationalization was that it might lead to larger, more imaginative schemes of development for the industry as a whole—in the long run; but in the 1940s the long run mattered less than the short. What was wanted in the post-war years, was not a lower-cost industry, but more steel as soon as possible; and while there were legitimate doubts about nationalization lowering costs, it was quite clear that it could do nothing to increase output in the short run, and might even reduce it. Also, there were strong political-economic arguments against nationalization in 1948-49. Any nationalization proposals were bound to delay the industry's plans for expansion and modernization; any radical new proposals were bound to cause conflict and perhaps bitterness, as well as to distract attention from really urgent problems like the balance of payments; lastly, there was little evidence to show that the country wanted the steel industry to be nationalized and a good deal of evidence to show that it did not want it. But the scheme went through. The Iron and Steel Corporation of Great Britain was created and in 1949 it took over 107 major steel companies along with a fair amount of their engineering activities. The companies did not lose their identity; the Corporation simply took over the shares (at Stock Exchange valuation) and assumed responsibility to adopt such measures regarding the industry 'as may seem to the Corporation best calculated to further the public interest in all respects'.

These four important Bills—Coal, Electricity, Transport and Steel—were the Labour Government's contribution to economic reorganization after the war. How far were they a success? This is obviously a very difficult question to answer. How do we measure success? What is our standard? Even if the industries did well (or badly) might they not have done better (or worse) in private hands? Whatever is said is a matter of judgment.

Coal is the least arguable case. The mines *had* to be nationalized. Nationalization was the inevitable political outcome of a quarter of a century of wrangling, incompetence, indecision and frustration. Given that nationalization was inevitable, did the Coal Board do a good job? Only an expert could answer such a question with any confidence; but to the interested observer the Coal Board seems to have done reasonably well in conditions of exceptional difficulty. It was bad luck for the Socialist Party that its nationalization policy had to begin with coal mining. The Coal Board inherited a dwindling and discontented work force, and a desperate shortage of coal. Production in 1946 was less than 190m. tons and output per manshift was 1·03 tons—in 1938 it had been 1·17 tons. Almost before the Board could sit down the coal crisis broke. Power stations and industrial concerns, living for months from hand to mouth, finally ran out of coal in the first week of February. Exceptionally bad weather prevented the replenishment of stocks, and within a week about 4½m. workers were idle. Power did not begin to be switched on for industry in the Midlands until late in February, and it was still intermittent in the first two weeks of March. This had nothing to do with the Coal Board, although it cast very grave reflections upon the quality of the Government's so-called economic planning. 'Profoundly depressing', the *Economist* called it; and so it was.

The Board began by hoping for 200m. tons of deep-mined coal in 1947, and it got 196m. tons. This was not bad, especially in view of the five-day week introduced in May 1947. To shorten working hours in a big industry in 1947 was, of course, absolute economic nonsense; but the hope was that the men would work better if the Board gave in to them on this issue. Output per man, undoubtedly, was the key to the problem, for labour was scarce both in and out of the mines, and new recruits to the industry were hard to find. The Board, of course, could not hope for quick results. It had to reorganize production and increase investment in pits where increased investment seemed likely to produce more coal. But it soon became clear that the Board, and the country, might have to wait longer than at first was expected. In the spring of 1948 the production director of the NCB spoke with unusual frankness:

'We are putting into the pits day by day great masses of machinery, and it does not seem to matter what we do—output per man is not rising. The Board are very much concerned. There is something wrong somewhere . . . We think that there is a slackening off all over and we are not getting the advantage of the machinery.'

Over £1½m., Sir Charles Reid went on, had been spent on machinery by the Northern Division of the Coal Board alone since 1945; and the result was negligible. The miners, in other words, did not feel like producing more coal; and who shall blame them? Theirs was a traditional occupation, dirty, unenviable. For decades they had fought the owners and for years, during the war, they had been tied to the industry. Their wages were now high, and they were better off than they had ever been. They did not want to work harder; and they did not want more money. For a time, the miners' perverse preference for leisure to cash was a popular theme for economists and psychologists. But gradually old habits broke down. Machinery became accepted, and miners learned to want more goods—enterprising car manufacturers, for example, toured the mining districts with the latest models and caused, at the time, a mild sensation. Output per man gradually rose. In 1950 it exceeded the 1948 level for the first time, and in that year the Coal Board produced its long-term plan for the industry. It proposed to put £520m. into the industry in fifteen years, plus £115m. into auxiliary activities. The result, it was hoped, would be 18 per cent more coal raised by 80,000 fewer workers. The export target was 25-35m. tons by 1961-65. This was not a very startling plan; and it was not fulfilled. In 1956, having invested almost £350m. since nationalization, the Board was obliged to defer its hope for 240m. tons in 1965 to 1970. In 1957 deep-mined output was still only 210m. tons—much what it had been in 1951; opencast was 13m. tons. Industry did not suffer—it was continually changing over to oil. What suffered was the balance of payments. Coal was imported for a time after the fuel crisis in 1947. Imports began again in 1950 and were still coming in in 1957. There were exports, and in the 'fifties Britain was on balance a coal-exporter, but only to the tune of 2m. or 3m. tons a year. By 1957 coal was no longer king. But appreciable results from the reconstruction programme were to be seen. In pits where major schemes of modernization had been completed, output was beginning to rise rapidly. Production by power-loaders doubled between 1955 and 1957. There was always opposition to closing down inefficient or high cost pits, and every move of this kind became a political issue. Costs rose, and consumers turned to substitutes. Under the Coal Board the industry became more profitable, but less important.

The nationalization of electricity is a simpler story. Here, the mistakes of the past were more easily put right. The economies to be obtained were of a technical character, and it was not difficult for the Authority to obtain them. Problems arose not over reorganization but over expansion. How much electrical power was going to be wanted by industry and the domestic consumer over the next five, ten or fifteen years? The Authority made the best estimates it could, starting with a situation in which demand far outran supply. A large programme of capital investment was at once begun, and sales of electricity to industrial consumers rose by 46 per cent between 1946 and 1951. Still the supply seemed inadequate. Critics complained that demand would always exceed supply so long as the Authority failed to charge prices sufficient to cover the costs of production (including plant replacement) and did nothing to discourage excessive consumption by domestic consumers at peak hours. Unabashed, the Authority came forward in 1956 with a capital investment programme of £1,250m. in the next six years, designed to raise sales capacity by a further 45 per cent, i.e. to 25·5m. kW by the end of 1959. Thus between 1945 and 1960 provision was made to double the supply of electricity in Great Britain. This very ambitious programme probably made, especially in the early years when men and materials were scarce and quick returns from investment were, or should have been, at a premium, an unduly large demand upon the nation's resources. It does not prove anything that the Authority paid its way 'taking one year with another', but at least it had the satisfaction of doing so; by 1957 it had realized surpluses totalling £88m.

No such satisfaction came the way of the Transport Commission. After only a few years of operation, a Tory Government was returned to office, and one of its first acts was to denationalize road transport, selling British Road Services' fleet of lorries in parcels to private hauliers. Simultaneously—this was in the spring of 1953—the publicly-owned railways were reorganized. A large measure of decentralization of management was the intention; and there was also a scheme to increase the railways' competitive power by making charges more flexible. A lot of railway legislation from 1854 onwards had been designed to protect the trader against exploitation by the railway 'monopoly'; what this legislation now did was to prevent railways from competing with road transport. These new moves were certainly moves in the right direction. But the railways also needed new equipment, of which they had been starved for twenty years. In 1955 the Commission produced a modernization plan which proposed the spending of £1,200m. on a programme of capital works, starting within five years and to be completed within fifteen years. Half of this expenditure was reckoned to be necessary merely to maintain existing services. The rest was to modernize track and rolling stock, and to introduce diesels and extend electrification—'The end of the steam era', the Commission announced, 'is at hand.' It was also proposed to put an end to branch line services where fares bore no relation to economic costs. This was a large plan, and inevitably some time passed before any results could be seen. They were, to begin with, disappointing. The reason was that the railways turned out to be harbouring some human problems not unlike those in the coal industry. Morale among the railway staff was low— equipment was old, the railways were subject, partly as a result, to constant criticism, and railwaymen's wages were no longer well above the national average. New chances to share in increased productivity through doing new jobs were viewed with suspicion—for example, a protracted quarrel went on over the unions' insistence that diesel and electric locomotives should have two men on board just like the steam engines, although it was clear that there was work for only one. And there were other restrictive practices. The decentralization of management also took time to bring about and to show results, and the task of producing a new scheme of charges was enormous. Politics, as in the coal mines, also played a part. Closing a branch line always produced public complaint; and railwaymen's wages were a constant source of friction and occasionally a matter of Government concern. It is perhaps not surprising that by the end of 1955 the Transport Commission had an accumulated deficit of £70m. and a deficit on British Railways to the end of 1956 of £57m. The only hope of solvency was that the return on the £1,250m. to be spent on modernization would suffice to pay interest on old debts as well as on the new borrowing.

By the end of 1958 about 200 main line diesels had been delivered, and the railways at least began to look a little more modern. Then, in 1961, the Government persuaded Dr Beeching to leave ICI for a time in order to undertake the gigantic task of radically reorganizing the whole railway system. His labours were herculean, and his Report, published in the spring of 1963, was a masterly document. It proposed, not to make the railways pay, but at least to take a long stride in the direction of cutting their losses, and to spend an additional £250m. for more diesels, liner trains, and the reorganization of 'sundries' freight traffic. Out of 4,293 passenger stations on British Railways, 2,363 were to be closed; 5,000 route miles of passenger services, most of them making large losses on lightly loaded rural routes, were to be withdrawn entirely; the handling of freight traffic, especially coal, was likewise to be simplified so as to reduce losses; and 70,000 jobs on the railways were to disappear by 1966. This was a bold effort to keep within bounds the running of the railways as a social service provided below cost. Much progress was made in the next couple of years, in spite of rural protests and the dismally sectarian and shortsighted attitude of the railway unions.

But with the advent of the Labour Government Beeching departed, and visions of the railways as a vehicle for the subsidization of consumers revived. An integrated transport system —a phrase often heard in the later 1940s—was the new panacea. It was only sensible to use the railways to take pressure off the roads; but only if marginal costs were no higher on the former than on the latter. And the pressure on the roads was so severe because successive governments had shown no grasp of the importance of road-building, so that investment on roads was far too little in the 1950s, reaching only £80m. per annum by 1959. The 1960s saw a larger road building programme, but by the middle of the 1960s, although expanding faster than any other major programme, it was officially admitted that road building would not match the growth of traffic expected in the next ten to fifteen years.

Lastly, steel. The Tory Government lost little time when it came to power in 1951 in denationalizing the steel industry, but it did not go so far as to leave the industry to its own devices. (Even as it acted the Socialist Party promised (or threatened) that it would renationalize the industry as soon as possible. The opportunity has not yet presented itself, but it seems almost certain to come.) The steel industry had thus worked under four different forms of Government peacetime control in the past twenty-five years. In the 'thirties the British Iron and Steel Federation (the industry's own organization) co-operated with IDAC to 'secure the systematic planning of the industry as a whole' and to eliminate 'unrestricted' competition while 'avoiding the evils of monopoly, safeguarding the public interest, and fostering efficiency'. In 1946 came the Steel Board, to oversee plans of expansion and to maintain supplies and the wartime policy of price control. This was followed in 1950, after prolonged uncertainty, by nationalization, and a holding company, the Iron and Steel Corporation of Great Britain, appeared. The

Corporation had wider power and greater authority than the Board, but its main tasks were the same—price fixing and investment planning. It did not live long enough, however, to show whether or not it was likely to bring to its tasks insight, imagination and drive superior to what had been shown by its predecessors. In 1953 arrangements were made to sell the steel firms back to private ownership, and a new Iron and Steel Board —a Tory one—was brought on to the scene, 'to provide for the reorganization of the iron and steel industry under free enterprise with an adequate measure of public supervision'. The new Board had wider powers than the Socialist Board of 1946, its interests including prices, raw material supplies and their distribution, capacity, research and training, safety, health and welfare, and joint consultation—'an amalgam', said the *Economist*, 'of the general duties laid on the Corporation by the 1949 Act with the main functions of the British Iron and Steel Federation'.[1]

How did the industry fare under this perpetual but ever-changing Government supervision? Its course seems to have been hearteningly—or, from a more critical standpoint, disheartengly—uniform. Demand for steel outran supply, and was always rising; this reflected chiefly the growth of the car industry and the large plans of capital investment throughout the economy. Steel was cheap, because labour productivity was at a good level and coal and scrap prices were artificially low. What was most wanted, therefore, was rapid expansion of the industry. In 1945 the industry presented the Government with a seven and a half year modernization plan to cost £168m. Furnace capacity was to rise from 14·1m. tons to 15·95m. tons, 3·99m. tons being scrapped in the process. The money was spent, although not in the ways planned, and steel production rose with encouraging rapidity, exceeding 16m. tons in 1950. There were still shortages, however, and in 1952 a new plan was produced. Capacity was to be raised from 17m. tons to over 20m. tons. Expenditure was to be over £60m. per annum for several years. Like its predecessor, this plan erred on the side of modesty. Blast furnace developments in particular lagged, and there were shortages of flat steel in 1952 and 1955. These shortages had serious repercussions on the balance of payments,

[1] *The Economist*, February 2, 1952, p. 297.

not only by necessitating more imports of steel, but also by reducing the capacity of the metal-using industries to produce for export. Moreover, the general expansion of all existing plants did nothing to concentrate output on the most efficient plants or sites. Labour productivity rose, however, and there was improved fuel economy. 'Within the pattern of what was done, much was impressive.'[1]

Nationalization of the steel industry, therefore, was an interlude which had little effect upon its organization or production. Nationalization of coal, electricity and the railways, on the other hand, came to stay. The whole programme made a big difference to the economy. Great improvements in these fundamental industries were made; the old sense of hopelessness and stagnation disappeared. Moreover, something like 18 per cent of the country's gross domestic capital formation in the 1950s was done by the nationalized industries, and modification of their programmes, therefore, could make a perceptible difference to the employment situation, to the degree of inflationary pressure, or to the general level of demand and availability of resources; and modification could fairly easily be brought about by the Government. It is far from clear, however, that this increased share of Government investment helped to produce economically efficient working or stabilize the economy. Long-term investment and output plans cannot be maintained 'when Government decisions are changed from month to month on the basis of short-term reappraisals of the current situation';[2] and these short-term reappraisals and changes of policy have now been perpetual for twenty years. Moreover, Ministers and civil servants have constantly interfered with the actions of the various Boards in drawing up investment plans, redeploying labour, fixing prices, reaching wage agreements, and generally conducting their affairs. These interventions, made by persons not directly accountable to the public for their actions, have usually been the result of political calculation, and have invariably produced embarrassment for the Boards concerned which found that they did not, after all, have freedom to charge

[1] D. L. Burn in *The Structure of the British Industry* (Cambridge University Press, 1958), ed. Burn, vol. I, p. 291.

[2] D. L. Munby in *The British Economy in the Nineteen-Fifties*, p. 389.

their own prices, reach wage agreements which they thought viable, and act commercially.

And there were other disadvantages. The nationalized industries borrowed in the market (until 1956) under Treasury guarantee; they were voracious devourers of loanable funds (especially the Electricity Authority) and many observers thought that they got a larger share of the nation's resources than was economically justifiable; as they were monopolistic, investment criteria were hard to find and harder to apply. The position of wage-earners within the nationalized industries also caused difficulty. The trade unions in coal and the railways were in a very strong position in what was, at least until 1957, a very insecure economy. They could shut down essential industries and cause crippling losses; and the responsible employer was, in the last resort, the Government. Wage demands in the nationalized industries were therefore liable to put political pressure on the Government, and settlements were apt to be reached on political as much as on economic grounds.

Outside the nationalized sector of the economy, the Government was far from powerless or inactive. In three very important fields, indeed, its influence was paramount; these were agriculture, house building, and atomic developments.

The chief object of post-war agricultural policy was increased output. Food was scarce in the post-war world—for a time, very scarce. Cereal imports had to be cut in 1946, and in the summer bread and flour were rationed. This had not been necessary even during the war. Nevertheless, the total area under crops continued to decline from its 1944 peak and the area under temporary grass continued slowly to increase. In 1947, when it was seen that dollar (and therefore food) imports would have to be kept to a minimum for several years, came the Agriculture Act. This set up the post-war framework for agriculture: an annual price review along with guaranteed markets for the most important farm products. 'The twin pillars upon which the Government's agricultural policy rests,' it was declared, 'are stability and efficiency. The main method of providing stability is through guaranteed prices and assured markets.' In the early years the price guarantees were on the whole invariant with respect to the amount produced; but after 1952, when the pattern of production had gained in importance partly because further increases in the mere volume of production had fallen in importance, the guaranteed price allowed fluctuations to occur in market prices and some of these to be reflected in the prices received by farmers for the ten products[1] scheduled in the Agriculture Act, 1947. 'The price guarantee schemes, therefore, act as a form of sieve, holding back some price changes and allowing others to trickle through to influence farmers' incomes and their production plans.'[2] Everything turned on how much stimulus to food production the Government wanted to give—always assuming that higher prices would lead to a larger output. Prices for eighteen months ahead (or longer) were settled at the annual price review. This review took into account farm costs, aggregate farm income, and the distribution of that income between different types and sizes of farm. Estimated requirements of different kinds of product were made, and, finally, guesses as to the changes in individual prices needed to bring forth the additional output. The whole performance became, in practice, a tug-of-war between officials of the Ministry of Agriculture, trying to keep costs down, and officials of the National Farmers' Union, doing their best for farmers as a whole and—like any trade union—trying to keep all groups of their constituents happy. The system certainly produced more home-grown food. The Government's five-year plan for farming, announced in 1947, called for a 20 per cent increase in output, i.e. to 150 per cent of the pre-war level. This was not achieved, output in 1951-52 being 141 per cent of the pre-war level at constant prices. In 1953-54, however, the figure was 155 per cent, and in 1956-57 it was 160 per cent.

As for the farming community, it grew, if not rich, at least prosperous. Agricultural income rose from 100 in 1946-47 to 314 in 1956-57. The value of the final output of the economy as a whole, of course, rose too, but it did very little more than double between 1947 and 1957. Farmers therefore improved their position, and were well off. There were inefficiencies in the

[1] These ten products were wheat, barley, oats, rye, potatoes, sugar beet, fat stock, milk and eggs, and wool (the last was added in 1950).

[2] E. H. Whetham, *A Record of Agricultural Policy*, 1954–56 (School of Agriculture, Cambridge, 1957), p. 20.

in the system. Some resources drawn into agriculture could possibly have produced more food, indirectly, if used in the export industries instead; this was certainly the case, sometimes, in the 1950s. Some investment in agriculture did not produce more output so much as reduce the farmer's work and worries. The greater part of the payments made by taxpayers under the guaranteed price scheme went to farmers 'whose farm structure [was] sufficiently flexible to take advantage of changes in relative profit margins',[1] and these farmers were the already prosperous ones, those who sold more and hence obtained more of the payments made on guaranteed prices. An attempt was made to remedy this by means of grants—grants for specific products, or to help pay for equipment or improvements. By the mid-1950s these grants were running at £80m.-£90m. per annum; but the farmer remained poor on many a small dairy, upland or hill farm. Nevertheless, the agricultural industry as a whole had never fared so well; or if it had, one must go back probably to the first decade of the nineteenth century. Total estimated food subsidies were about £235m. by the end of the 1950s. This sum was 'of the greatest importance to farmers, for it is equivalent to about three-quarters of recent annual net farm incomes . . . and the manner in which the sum is distributed, and expectations about future changes in its size or distribution, affect greatly many individual farmers' entrepreneurial decisions'.[2]

In house-building, likewise, the call was for production and more production. Even before the end of the war it was obvious that a big effort was needed to make up accumulated arrears in house-repairing and house-building, and it was accepted that this effort would be largely the Government's business. House rents had never been completely free since 1915, and the house-building of the 1930s was mostly carried through by Government pressure on local authorities and supported by extensive Treasury subsidies. One of the Government's first considerations after the war, therefore, was to move men and resources into the building

[1] E. H. Whetham and J. I. Currie, *A Record of Agricultural Policy*, 1956–58 (School of Agriculture, Cambridge, 1958), p. 11.
[2] J. R. Raeburn, 'Agricultural Production and Marketing' in *The Structure of British Industry*, vol. I, p. 13.

industry. In 1946, with a labour force of only 190,000, the industry completed 60,000 permanent and 90,000 temporary houses. By the end of 1949, 1m. houses had been built new or reconstructed. It was reckoned that one more year of building would make good the cessation of building in the war years, i.e. would bring housing standards back to about where they had been in 1939. But the shortage of houses seemed to be as bad as ever. This was partly because the standard of what was reckoned acceptable had risen, but chiefly because the subsidies made house-room—subsidized house-room—so very cheap. There was plenty of demand—insatiable, it seemed—for a good article rented at a price which gave a derisory return on the capital invested. By the spring of 1951 1¼m. houses had been built or rebuilt since the war, and Great Britain had more dwelling units per head of population than ever before. Moreover, these postwar houses were for the most part bigger than pre-war houses and they were better equipped. Most of them were built by local authorities, whose output was about double the pre-war level. Private builders, on the other hand, were producing only one tenth of what they had produced in 1938. The combined result was a high, but not astonishing, rate of building, little more than half the high pre-war level. As for the cost of living in a rent-controlled house, it had increased by only 13 per cent since 1938. Average money income per family after tax was about 80 per cent higher, so house-room was very cheap by any previous standards. The cost of repairs, moreover, had about doubled since 1938, so that rents did not enable landlords to keep up their property, and many privately owned houses were undoubtedly falling into disrepair.

The Tory Government of the 1950s responded to this situation in two stages. First of all, it set out to show that what the Labour Government could and would do, it could and would do better. Had the Labour Government built 1m. in six years? Very well; the Tory Government would build 300,000 houses per annum. Did the economists complain that the country could not afford so much unproductive investment? Never mind; the people loved men who built houses, and voted for them. And the Government was as good as its word. In 1951, 195,000 houses were completed; in 1952, 240,000; in 1953, over 300,000. This was quite a triumph of effort and organization, partly made possible by encouraging the private builder and by having local authorities build some houses with two bedrooms instead of all of them with three—a sensible innovation. During the boom years of the mid-1950s about 1½m. men found employment in the building industry. Then, late in 1956, with a post-war achievement of 2½m. houses behind it, the Government took its courage in both hands and introduced a Rent Control Bill. This Bill removed some 810,000 houses from control, and allowed rent increases for 4·3m. which remained controlled. Inevitably, those accustomed to good plain accommodation at anything from 7s 6d to £1 a week protested; but the illogicality, to say nothing of the wastefulness, of random income redistribution brought about by subsidizing anyone who had secured a subsidized house was too clear to be gainsaid. Under the new system no spectacular rise in rents took place. The majority of controlled houses continued to be rented at less than £1 per week, about a quarter of them at less than 10s 0d. The measure did a little to improve labour mobility, by making people less afraid to leave their house for fear of not finding another one so generously subsidized, and the available accommodation became better used as people moved into houses that suited them instead of staying at all costs in those which they already had. Also, higher rents enabled landlords to halt the gradual deterioration of rent-restricted property.

From about 1957 the housing shortage was no longer a serious issue. But a high price had been paid for its disappearance. House-building accounted for about 22 per cent of gross fixed capital formation in the United Kingdom from 1948 to 1957; in 1953 and 1954 it accounted for 26 per cent. Some of these resources could have been used to swell exports and so strengthen the reserves or to build and equip factories. The taxation which paid for the houses discouraged effort, and thus tended to diminish the national product, while below-cost houses left those who lived in them with money to spend which they would not have had had they been paying an economic rent; and this contributed to inflation. From an economic point of view, the story is instructive but not edifying. Nor was the situation satisfactory from a social point of view. Those who occupied local authority or private rent-controlled housing were paying, on average, about half what was paid for similar accommodation in the free market sector of owner-occupied and uncontrolled rented dwellings. But controlled tenants

'are simply those who happened to live in a house below a certain rateable value before a certain date. There is no reason to believe that their need for low rent dwellings is greater than that of many other householders. Local authority tenants are, on the average, somewhat poorer than owner-occupiers, but by no means uniformly.'[1]

The rents charged by local authorities are usually about one half of the economic rent, and this means that their tenants pay about 9 per cent of their incomes in rent. Indiscriminate subsidization thus continues, and the mobility of labour is still gravely impeded. It is perfectly clear that the housing situation will continue to be unsatisfactory until the level of local authority and controlled rents is raised to or near that of the free market sector.

The third field of Government-sponsored activity, atomic development, was of course a heritage of the war. When the newly created Atomic Energy Authority took over in the summer of 1954, experimental stations and plants already had over 20,000 employees all told. Development was pressed forward at a rapid pace. This was chiefly for prestige reasons. Britain had played a major part, perhaps the major part, in the early work on nuclear fission. The United States had taken over during the war, and was now the chief manufacturer of nuclear weapons. But Great Britain had sufficient knowledge and resources to have a good chance of pioneering the peace-time uses of atomic energy. Besides, the coal industry's performance was far from satisfactory and it was easy to be too dependent on Middle East oil. Early in 1955 the British Electricity Authority announced that it would soon start work on its first two atomic power stations, and that it hoped to complete twelve atomic power stations within ten years. The expenditure would be in the region of £300m. per annum, and the result, it was hoped,

[1] D. C. Paige in *The British Economy in 1975*, p. 386.

would be that by 1965 one quarter of the authority's modern
generating capacity would be atomic-powered. This news caused
a considerable sensation. There were no precedents anywhere
for the commercial generation of atomic power. The Atomic
Energy Authority (which, it was explained, would give all possible help and would continue to be responsible for basic engineering research) had its own power station at Calder Hall,
but it was not yet completed. It went into operation the following year and gave promise of being not very much more costly
to operate than orthodox stations. By this time, technical knowledge permitted a sizeable upward revision of the scale on which
future stations were to be built, and it was calculated that
the Electricity Authority's demand for coal might level off in the
1960s. This enormous programme caught the public imagination. Britain had not led the world in the commercial application
of new discoveries very often in the twentieth century; this time
she seemed to be well ahead with the biggest discovery of all.
The credit was the Government's. Cabinet Ministers had not
discovered atomic power, but they had taken the risk of inducing
the Electricity Authority to devote huge sums to the construction of power stations—costing, say, £40m. each—about the
running costs of which no proven information was or could be
available. This was a very bold step, and in 1959 we still do not
know whether or not it will be economically justified. But the
country is proud, not without reason, of the huge, inaccessible,
incomprehensible, white fortresses of power that are arising
here and there along the edge of the sea.

Now, having surveyed that part of the economy where the
Government gave the orders, albeit indirectly, or called the tune,
what remains? House-building and capital expenditure by the
public corporations accounted in the mid-1950s for between 40
and 45 per cent of total gross fixed capital formation. Adding
agriculture, the steel industry, and central Government expenditure on capital account (roads, schools, hospitals) the
figure would exceed 50 per cent. But who was responsible
for the rest? What private industries were big creators of capital,
employers of labour and exporters?

Many industries prospered and expanded in post-war Britain.
To begin with, even the cotton industry did well. It was looked

P

to to make a big contribution to the export drive, and it succeeded. There was a great back-log of demand throughout the world, and German and Japanese competition was for a short time negligible. Exports of British cotton goods, only 85 per cent of the 1938 level by value in 1945, were three times as great by 1949, and four times by 1951. The industry's work force rose from 287,000 in 1946 to 370,000 in 1951. Production was more concentrated, and the utilization of capacity higher than before the war. But in 1951 the seller's market for cotton goods began to disappear. Competition increased, especially from Germany, India and Japan, and cost of production became an increasingly serious consideration. The industry suffered a short but serious recession in 1951-52, largely caused by ebbing demand, the Korean war, and credit restrictions, and it never really recovered. In 1956 the labour force had fallen by 85,000 from its 1951 peak. The industry, having done its best in the short-lived favourable post-war conditions, was accused of 'complacency, reluctance to depart from things of the past, and lack of incentives',[1] and such charges no doubt had some truth in them; but the industry's position in the scheme of international comparative advantages was fundamentally weak. The woollen industry fared better. It expanded faster to 1951, doing especially well with sales of high-quality woollens in North America. Total exports fell heavily between 1950 and 1952, but recovered better than in the case of cotton. Italy, however, is now the world's greatest wool exporter. The industry suffers competition from artificial fabrics, and a large proportion of Bradford's output is now a blend of wool with artificial fibres.

Some such story, of ready success in export markets until the economic tide of the world turned about 1951, can be told of many British industries; of paper, shipbuilding, synthetic fabrics, railway vehicles. The real winners were those industries the progress of which was scarcely interrupted by brief recessions in world demand or by the revival of competition; industries such as cars, chemicals, aircraft, iron and steel, and machinery of all kinds.

The success story *par excellence* of the post-war years is that of the car industry. The production figures tell their own tale:

[1] Report of the US Productivity Team on the Cotton Industry.

Year	Cars	Commercial vehicles	Exports
1937	390,000	118,000	116,000
1946	219,000	148,000	121,000
1950	523,000	263,000	542,000
1955	898,000	341,000	629,000
1960	1,353,000	458,000	716,000
1964	1,868,000	465,000	848,000

Even more gratifying, the industry made an enormous contribution to exports, car exports by 1955 being between four and five times what they had been in 1937. This was a changed situation indeed. Britain and Germany now competed for the position of leading car exporter, with France, the United States and then Italy a long way behind. This was the result of a well-organized, determined effort by the industry, made at Government instigation. The home market was deliberately starved of cars until well into the 1950s, while the task abroad was made easier by buoyant demand and, especially in North America, standards of living which enabled many families to run a smaller European as well as a large American car. The dollar shortage, of course, helped Britain in most markets not on the American continent, and the Government did something to help by reforming the ridiculous system of taxation in 1947.

The industry continued to be dominated, as before the war, by the 'Big Five'—the British Motor Corporation (formed by the merger of Austin and Morris in 1952), Ford, Rootes, Standard and Vauxhall. These five firms account for between 80 and 90 per cent of car and commercial vehicle production in the United Kingdom. Two of them are American-controlled; the American Ford Company owns 59 per cent of the ordinary capital of the British Ford Company, and General Motors owns all the ordinary capital of Vauxhall.[1] The Ford works at Dagenham is remarkable for its high degree of integration, possessing its own blast furnace, rolling-mill, and foundry; 'At the largest privately-owned wharf on the Thames,' says the company, '20,000 tons of raw materials arrive every week. The modern new foundry produces 400 tons of castings per day. The Ford power station generates enough electricity to supply a town of

[1] The unit construction body was an innovation which came to the industry via Vauxhall from General Motors in Detroit before the war. Since the war, every other manufacturer of popular cars has adopted unit construction.

227

350,000 inhabitants.' BMC also possesses foundries, and at Longbridge automatic transfer machines have been installed, greatly reducing labour costs and giving BMC almost certainly the most modern assembly line in Europe.[1] All this of course needed money, and the leading manufacturers all began heavy programmes of capital investment in the 'fifties; the Ford scheme alone cost over £65m. Expansion also needed men, and by 1955 the motor industry was one of the two or three largest industrial employers of labour in Britain.

The chemical industry, defined to include petro-chemicals and oil refining, was another prodigious performer in post-war Britain. Some sections of the industry were long-established—explosives, soap, dyes—but it was in the new sections that expansion was most remarkable. Thus there was little oil-refining done in Britain before 1945, and operations were conducted almost entirely overseas; but between 1945 and 1951 imports of crude oil for refining multiplied over ten-fold, and nearly doubled again by 1957. This was a complete change of policy, for 'as late as 1944 the proposal to extend domestic refining was highly controversial'.[2] But building refineries at home was quicker, cheaper and safer. The capital investment was very large, over £30m. per annum in 1950, 1951, 1952 and 1953. Shell began work at Stanlow, in the north-west, in 1947, and in the same year Esso started at Fawley, near Southampton. These plants and others like them virtually created a new industry in Britain. American equipment was used, some of it obtained with Marshall Aid. Fawley, when it went into operation in 1951, was the first catalytic cracking plant completed in Britain, and was the largest refinery in Europe. The volume of employment which the industry offered was not large; the ratio of capital to labour was very high.

Refining oil to produce petrol and other fuels was not the whole of the oil companies' business. There was also the production of chemicals which would serve as the basis of much modern manufacture of plastics and synthetic resins. And there was the

[1] An excellent account of the technical processes of production in the industry can be found in the chapter by A. Silberston in *The Structure of British Industry* vol. II (Cambridge University Press, 1958).

[2] D. Burn in *The Structure of British Industry*, vol. I, p. 183 (Cambridge University Press, 1958).

business of obtaining crude oil overseas, and selling the market-able products throughout the world. By the 1950s the oil companies were among the giants of industry. The Royal-Dutch Shell Group, said its chairman in 1957,

'operates in virtually every country of the free world. It has two parents of different nationalities, and it is therefore by structure as well as by character and extent of its business completely international.'

The gross investment of the Group in the years 1951-55 was as follows:

Exploration and production		£519m.
Oil refineries and chemical plant		£311m.
Marketing facilities		£148m.
Ocean-going fleets		£ 79m.
Miscellaneous		£ 24m.
	Total	£1,081m.

Other companies in what is still broadly defined as the chemical industry operated on a comparable scale: British Petroleum, Distillers, Monsanto, ICI. Chemical exports, especially of petrol, gas oil, diesel oil, fuel oil and plastic materials soared, being about thirteen times their 1938 volume in 1955.

Another industry which suddenly acquired a new importance was aircraft manufacture. In 1951 rearmament brought general prosperity back to the industry. Expenditure by the Ministry of Supply on military aircraft, aero-engines and spares doubled between 1951-52 and 1954-55. Military aircraft predominated in exports in the mid-'fifties, but the world market for civil aircraft is important and is perhaps more likely to go on expanding than the military market. The civil market is a difficult one; each aircraft design must suit a special purpose, must take years to mature, and may in the end prove a disappointment. Yet, despite one spectacular set-back, there is no doubt that the aircraft industry did well. It staked almost everything on the unproven commercial possibilities of the jet engine. As with atomic power, Britain aimed to be first in peacetime if not in military uses. The first, and still the outstanding success, was the Vickers Viscount. This aircraft was a 'turbo-prop'—a gas turbine driving a propellor—a design which, in the late 'forties, 'many engineers, including the United States aircraft industry as a whole, believed impracticable'.[1] The Viscount first flew in July 1948, the first orders were received in 1950, and by 1954 over one hundred Viscounts had been bought or were on order, many of the customers being American. It was, for a short time, unrivalled for short-to-medium-distance services. Similar hopes were entertained of the Comet, a larger, pure-jet airliner for longer distances. This aircraft began test flights in 1949, BOAC having already ordered a fleet of Comets 'off the drawing board'. The first of these aircraft was handed over in 1952, and for a time it seemed as if Britain was five years ahead of her only rival, the United States. But in May 1953 a Comet crashed near Calcutta; in January 1954 a Comet unaccountably broke-up in mid-air and fell into the sea off Elba; and another Comet crashed in April. The aircraft's certificate of airworthiness was withdrawn, and extensive tests began at Farnborough leading to the establishment of the phenomenon now known as metal fatigue. The de Havilland Company paid the unavoidable price of pioneering, and by 1958 the American Boeing Corporation had an airliner comparable to the redesigned Comet in service.

The costs of development are tremendous, and the firms in the industry do not bear them all. The Ministry of Supply spent over £4m. on the development of the Comet, almost £2m. on that of the Viscount, and almost £6m. on developing the Britannia; in 1958 the Government officially 'accepted responsibility for most of the development costs of the new major civil aircraft projects'.[2] Relations between the Government and the industry are extremely close for two other reasons: much aeronautical and aerospace research is carried on in Government establishments; and the Government goes a long way toward determining the size and profitability of the industry through its orders for military aircraft, guided weapons, and so on. A new Ministry of Aviation was created in 1959, and almost its first act was to put pressure on the industry to accelerate the process of concentration which had been going in a leisurely fashion for some years. As a result, a situation rapidly emerged in which there were only five concerns: two for airframes (British Aircraft Corporation

[1] *The Economist*, August 6, 1949, p. 311.
[2] *Hansard*, May 13, 1958.

and the Hawker Siddeley Group); two for engines (Rolls-Royce and Bristol Siddeley); and one for helicopters.[1]

The industry has made substantial contributions to export earnings in the last fifteen years, but competition is intense, especially from the United States. Development costs are enormous, and much depends on being able to deliver an aircraft with the required specification at the right time, and on the terms of sale.

This process of industrial transformation, of the rise of some industries and the decline, or at least the non-expansion, of other usually older industries, continued into the 1960s. Most industrial classifications are too crude to bring out the extent and complexity of the changes which were taking place, changes which entailed extensive alterations in the balance within industries and in the techniques of production. But the following figures give some idea at least of the more conspicuous changes, either in the direction of faster than average or of slower than average growth:

Selected Industries, indices of net output, 1960. (1950 = 100)[2]

Mineral oil refining	456
Motors and cycles	198
Chemicals n.e.s.	180
Aircraft and railway rolling stock	161
Paper, printing and publishing	153
Engineering and electrical goods	150
Iron and steel	138
Shipbuilding and marine engineering	98
Textiles	94
Total, all industries	140

[1] For a most interesting account of this curious episode, see P. D. Henderson in *The British Economy in the Nineteen-Fifties*, pp. 361–9. As Henderson says, two features deserve comment. First, 'the aircraft industry was virtually compelled to concentrate and regroup by a government department . . . the new structure was laid down explicitly and in some detail. There is no parallel for this during the nineteen-fifties in any other industry, whether privately or publicly owned . . .this is a clear exception to the generalization that private industries are less subject to official intervention than nationalized industries. The second feature is the almost total absence of published explanation or justification of what was done.' (loc. cit., pp. 367–8.)

[2] Source: W. Beckerman and associates, *The British Economy in 1975*. Appendix Table 8.7.

This very eclectic account of industrial progress in post-war Britain omits many considerable and important changes. But it brings out the very significant fact that Britain's position in the international pattern of production, and therefore in world trade, has altered very considerably—almost radically. It is not so much that Britain is now responsible for a smaller fraction of world exports of manufactured goods than she used to be— although the difference comparing 1952-53 with 1937 was only one fifth of one per cent; 22·4 per cent in 1937, 22·2 per cent in 1952-53—the difference seems to be rather that her large and growing lines of export are now of different goods of a different character. In 1938 the ten leading British manufactured exports (plus coal) were as follows:

1938

Industry	Percentage of total British exports by value
Machinery other than electric	11
Cotton goods	10
Coal	9
Iron and steel	6
Chemicals	6
Manufactures of metals	5
Vehicles and aircraft	5
Miscellaneous textiles	5
Electric machinery, apparatus, etc.	5
Woollen goods	4

Twenty-five years later coal did not even appear in the 'top ten' (see opposite). Its place was taken by petroleum and petroleum products, and the ranking and importance of the different classes of commodity was quite different.

Machinery other than electric remains at the top of the list; the engineering industry, in other words, ever old but ever new, is as important as before—in terms of its share of the export trade, much more important. Cotton, second in 1938, with 10 per cent, is only a part of 'miscellaneous textiles'. Coal has disappeared, hardly exported at all. On the other hand, vehicles and aircraft, and petroleum, have dramatically increased their share. And what this means is that the old traditional industries have

1963

Industry	Percentage of total British exports by value
Machinery other than electric	21
Vehicles and aircraft	15
Chemicals	9
Electric machinery, apparatus, etc.	8
Miscellaneous textiles	6
Iron and steel	5
Manufactures of metals	3
Non-ferrous metals	3
Petroleum and petroleum products	3
Beverages	2

been replaced at last. Cotton and coal, those giants of the nine-teenth century, still accounted for 19 per cent of visible exports in 1938; in 1963 they accounted for little more than 3 per cent. The products which replaced them were often newer than industrial classification would suggest; chemicals, for example, included the new plastics; machinery other than electric included tractors, a sensational new trade; electric apparatus included radar and navigational equipment, transistors and cathode ray tubes. Britain was making and exporting the complicated capital and consumer goods which, as the steam engine and the power loom had once stood, stood now in the forefront of technical progress.

This was a considerable achievement. But satisfaction with what was done must be tempered by the reflections first that the international circumstances were on the whole extremely favour-able, and secondly that the British performance does not com-pare well with that of several other leading industrial countries.

World trade in manufactures rose very fast in the post-war decades: between 1954 and 1963 its volume almost doubled. Most of this increase in trade took place between industrial countries, but exports from industrial countries to primary producers also increased. Britain, with her exports heavily concentrated on manufactured goods, was therefore in a very favourable position to increase her sales abroad. For a time, when Germany and Japan remained virtually out of the running, all went well; in 1950 Britain had as large a share of the total exports of the five major exporters of manufactured goods as she had had in 1938. But then German and Japanese competition revived, and the British share began to shrink, which principally means that British exports grew less fast than those of her chief competitors. To some extent this was inevitable. But it is disturbing to find that French exports, for example, grew at a faster proportional rate than those of Britain, or that, as the following figures show, the fall in Britain's share of world exports of manufactures continues unabated:

Export of Manufactures
Annual rate of change

	U.K.	11 main exporters	U.K. share in total	Change in per cent share
1953			20·9	
1958	−2·0	− 1·5	17·7	
1959	+4·6	+ 8·0	17·2	−0·5
1960	+6·6	+15·5	15·9	−1·3
1961	+3·9	+ 5·4	15·7	−0·2
1962	+2·4	+ 6·1	15·1	−0·6
1963	+6·7	+ 8·4	14·9	−0·2
1964	+5·0	+14·5	13·7	−1·2

The failure of British exports to grow as fast as those of, say, Germany, Italy, France, Sweden or Japan, has had a serious effect upon the balance of payments, all the more so because net receipts from 'invisibles', upon which at one time Britain heavily depended, fell not only in relative importance but in absolute amount, being only +£181m. in 1962-64 compared with +£338m. in 1950-52.

In a sense, it is easy to make too much of this decline. Britain's share of world trade has been declining for over one hundred years, and she has had a deficit of merchandise trade for a similar length of time. But any change which worsens the balance of payments requires careful examination. There is a widespread feeling that Britain's export performance could be much better than it has been. Some plausible explanations which have been put forward turn out, on close examination, not to hold water. Thus it has been argued that Britain was more heavily committed than her competitors to certain export lines in which demand rose relatively slowly; but it can be shown that Britain has done less well than her competitors in almost every group taken individually. Likewise, there is the argument that British export markets were in the non-industrial world to a greater extent than those of her rivals, and that incomes, and total import demand, rose less rapidly in the non-industrialized countries than elsewhere. This argument is linked with the fact that the protection enjoyed by British manufacturers in most sterling area markets has decreased. There is more force in this argument than in the previous one. But not very much of the comparatively slow increase of British exports can be explained in this way. Much more convincing is the fact that 'the steady reduction of Britain's share of export markets coincided with the steady rise in her export prices as compared with those of three of her main competitors'.[1] This rise was not simply a reflection of the rise in money wages, but of the rise in money wages as related to productivity, that is to say in the relative rise in wage costs per unit of output. For example,

> 'whereas German hourly earnings in manufacturing rose by 55 per cent from 1953/55 to 1959/61 as compared with only 43 per cent in Britain, the much faster rise in German manufacturing productivity meant that German wage costs per unit of output rose by only 11 per cent as against 22 per cent in Britain.'[2]

No simple explanation of the British export performance is adequate. The performance itself has not been simple, for some manufacturers have outstanding records of sustained success; and in any case it is not clear what would constitute, or would have constituted, a 'satisfactory' performance. Analysis and judgment of what was achieved in foreign markets is inseparable from analysis of the whole economy; and for this the reader is referred to a later section.

It remains to examine here the institutional circumstances in which Britain achieved the rapid and far-reaching transformation of her industrial structure previously outlined. The war,

[1] M. F. G. Scott in *The British Economy in the Nineteen-Fifties*, p. 120.
[2] W. Beckerman in *The British Economy in 1975*, p. 58.

certainly, played a very large part. After the war, the attack on monopolistic practices which began with the work of the Monopolies and Restrictive Practices Commission in 1949 and was continued by the work of the Registrar of Restrictive Practices in the later 'fifties no doubt helped to prevent industry from settling down into the old cosy rut of non-progressive non-competition.[1] But the circumstances of world trade played a very important part in stimulating modernization and expansion. There was a world boom from 1945 to 1957, resembling the great boom of the 1860s. Everywhere countries were anxious to create—or at least to acquire—new capital equipment, and at the same time to raise living standards. This was partly because it had been possible to do so little during the war, more because newly independent countries like India and the Sudanese Republic were anxious to show how much they could do in a short time, and because the political division of the world made the richest capitalist countries peculiarly anxious to raise the living standards and promote the autonomy of their poorer neighbours in the free world. In North America and Australia there were boom conditions, due largely to the stimulus of war, technological progress and inflation. In the circumstances, British industry found an eager demand for its products, especially of the more modern types. Inflationary policies made credits easy to obtain, and many countries were able to draw quite freely on their accumulation of sterling balances.

Arrangements had been made towards the end of the war with a view to facilitating international trade. The International Monetary Fund was created in 1946. Each member of this organization paid an initial subscription partly in gold and partly in home currency. The member then had the right to purchase the foreign currency contributed by other members up to a certain proportion of his own contribution. If any currency in the Fund were to become exhausted, and no more were paid in, all

[1] The Registrar of Restrictive Practices had received about 1,200 restrictive agreements for registration by the spring of 1957. By that time the Monopolies Commission had investigated and reported on twenty-two industries where restrictive practices were suspected. It was reckoned in 1957 that about a quarter of Britain's 1,300 trade associations engaged in price-fixing, and that at least 240 kinds of product were covered by price agreements. Many such agreements were said to have been dropped after the Restrictive Trade Practices Bill of 1956.

the other member countries would be at liberty to discriminate against the 'scarce currency' country. The idea of this scheme was simple and sound. Many important countries after the war had totally inadequate international reserves; the Fund made available a certain amount of international liquidity, and in the 'scarce currency' clause provided that pressure could be put upon countries persistently in a creditor position. Also, major alterations in exchange rates could not be made without the consent of the Fund. This ruled out competitive currency devaluation and made for stability in international trade.

These arrangements, which were chiefly of American design, harmonized with the General Agreement on Tariffs and Trade. This was intended as an interim measure of trade liberalization pending agreement to set up a proposed International Trade Organization. This latter project came to nothing, however, and GATT became the framework for new trade agreements. The American approach was to outlaw all forms of discrimination and to limit all quantitative control of trade to emergency periods. This attitude was unacceptable to most other countries, and in the final Havana Charter preferential treatment was permitted for 'development purposes' and discriminatory quantitative import controls were permitted for the correction of 'temporary balance of payments disequilibria'. More important, a series of negotiations for general tariff reductions was begun, and GATT can at least be said to have played a part in fostering a climate favourable to freer trade.

The third and last device thought up for the post-war world was the International Bank for Reconstruction and Development. This was to undertake international investment, and also to help preserve stability by lending in times of depression. The Bank's resources were somewhat limited, partly because the United Kingdom had enough on her hands with repaying the sterling balances and promoting development in the colonies.

These three schemes have encountered diverse fates. GATT did not amount to much more than an expression of American desire that American goods should not be discriminated against, and that the American trade agreements programme of the 1930s should be generalized. Chronic dollar shortage for at least six or seven years, existing even when some countries were trying quite hard to live within their means, made non-discrimination impracticable. Useful reductions of tariffs were achieved at a series of post-war conferences, however, even if what was done by the United States was usually a grudging and belated minimum. The IMF was also a disappointment to its creators. Fundamentally, its fault was that it was a scheme to smooth away temporary difficulties in a world assumed to be already in equilibrium. Keynes had proposed a Clearing Union with assets of $25 billion; the Fund was worth only $8 billion, $3 billion of which came from Canada and the United States. Also, borrowing was not easy; countries could use only a quarter of their quotas each year unless special consent was obtained, and rapidly rising interest rates could be charged for temporary accommodation. In these circumstances, several years were needed for a currency (in practice, the dollar) to be declared scarce. It was assumed, moreover, that within five years the 'normal working of the price mechanism' would be evident throughout the world. Such thinking turned out to have little relation to post-war needs and circumstances. Britain tried sterling convertibility as the price of the dollar loan, and while it might have been done better it is clear that it could never have worked. $20 billion of Marshall Aid and other American help had then to be provided to prevent the economic, and possibly the political, collapse of Europe. The Fund was used and it helped; but its usefulness was marginal. Where it chiefly succeeded was in providing an acknowledged meeting-ground for the discussion and to some extent the co-ordination of national and international financial policy. The large practical scheme which made progress was not the all-round old-style liberalization of international trade (the US Department of Commerce taking over from Mr Gladstone) but the various attempts which were made in several parts of the world at regional integration.

The most important of these was certainly the establishment of the European Economic Community, consisting of the three Benelux countries, France, Germany and Italy. The association of these countries was both political and economic in inspiration as well as intention. A major aim—in many minds the major aim—was to integrate Germany into the European community so that war between France and Germany could never again take place. How far political integration was to be carried was, and is, an open question. But the means were to be partly economic, and these means are themselves an end. The United Kingdom showed no great interest in the Treaty of Rome upon which the EEC is founded, and it seems certain that the Foreign Office under-estimated the importance of the developments which were afoot in Europe in the earlier 1950s. But in 1958 Britain attempted to arrange for the association of a wider Free Trade Area with the Common Market which was now to be set up by the six EEC countries. The British proposal was for something wider, more flexible, and less political than was contemplated by the EEC countries; and it was rejected by France. As an alternative, Britain helped to engineer EFTA in 1959, containing the seven countries (Britain, Norway, Sweden, Denmark, Switzerland, Portugal and Austria) which had been engaged with the EEC in the earlier negotiations. As a result, two trading *blocs* were created, in each case the members progressively lowering their tariffs towards other members. The chief differences between the two *blocs* were that EFTA had no provision for the early creation of supernational politico-economic agencies, upon which the Common Market soon and increasingly depended; left to its members tariff autonomy with respect to the outside world; and had a population about half that of the EEC.

The effect of these arrangements upon the British economy cannot easily be assessed. It became harder for British exporters to sell goods inside the Common Market in competition with members of that market; on the other hand, the valuable Scandinavian market became more accessible. How far the EEC countries will benefit from the trade-creating effects of wide-spread tariff reductions and the (possibly overestimated) industrial benefits of increased specialization and large-scale working remains to be seen. Britain's so-called 'exclusion' from the Continent certainly has economic disadvantages. But the situation is still probably more significant from a political than from an economic point of view—as is suggested by de Gaulle's veto of the British attempt to join the Common Market in 1963.

Taking a still wider view of the world trade situation, mention must be made of the International Bank for Reconstruction and Development. The Bank started slowly. It investigated projects with care, which took time (and infuriated critics who wanted money for what they called 'basic schemes of development which would not yield immediate returns but would be essential for raising the standard of life'[1]). Also, it charged interest at a moderate rate and added a one per cent commission charge to build up a contingency reserve. For some years, inevitably, it made little impact upon the world scene. But by the middle and later 'fifties it was operating on a large scale and was an important factor in world development. Lending was running at between $300m. and $400m. per annum, and by 1957 total loans in thirty-four countries were approaching $3,000m. Most of these loans were to finance transport or power projects. There were loans for improvement and extension of railways in Brazil, France and West Africa; for roads in Columbia, Equador and Nicaragua; for electric power in Brazil, Japan and South Africa, and for the development of natural gas in Pakistan. Elaborate arrangements provided underdeveloped countries with the skilled services and advice which they badly needed in order to make the most of their capital investment, and at the same time achieved for the Bank an enviable record of sound investment.

Great Britain made a similar effort. The first large-scale postwar plan was not a success; the 1947 Plan for the Mechanized Production of Groundnuts in East and Central Africa. To do the Government justice the proposal was hailed even in usually critical quarters with enthusiasm. 'Here at last,' wrote the *Economist*, 'is the sort of economic planning that is needed to change the face of the colonial empire . . . It is difficult to decide which is the more encouraging part of the investigating mission's report . . . the vision with which they look to the future and describe the immense potentialities of the scheme, or the hard-headed practical thinking and costing which have gone into the immediate plan for producing groundnuts.'[2] Never have hopes been more ill-founded. Botanically, mechanically, administratively and financially the scheme was no good. The Ministry

[1] T. Balogh in *The British Economy 1945–1950* (Oxford, 1952), p. 506.
[2] loc. cit., March 1, 1947, p. 365.

of Food, responsible for the scheme, plunged in with little knowledge and without counting the cost, and two years later £23m. had been spent and there was still no margarine. The reputation of Government planning sank; and it was the taxpayer's money. Less spectacular but more sensible efforts by the Colonial Development Corporation, set up in 1948, had more success, and the Colonial Governments were materially helped in their own plans by grants—amounting to £20m.-£30m. a year—and loans from London. Loans were also made to other Commonwealth countries, to other members of the sterling area, and to countries outside the sterling area. The total amount lent was large—not far short of £4,000m. from 1946 through 1957. Most of this was private investment, and an important element in it was the re-investment of retained profits made by UK firms operating abroad.

Money, specialist agencies, expert advice and goodwill were thus all active in providing world development and international trade after the war. Few countries stood to gain more than Britain, always provided that brains, thrift and enterprise could maintain her industrial efficiency.

SOCIAL POLICY, WAGES AND TRADE UNIONS

The basis of all economic policy after the war was the maintenance of full employment. Full employment had implications in all departments of economic life, not least in its social aspects. It meant a high level of consumption—assisted, incidentally, by the rapid spread of hire purchase; it made it easier to leave one job and find another; it greatly increased the power of the trade unions to secure higher money wages. Also, it had some of the character of a new, saving faith. 'The moral fervour which has gathered round the idea of full employment,' said the *Economist*, 'has been due as much as anything to the hope that, with labour acquiring scarcity value, workers would be able to insist on reasonable assurances about their own treatment and the general policy of their industries.'[1] Full employment was maintained. Only in 1946 did the unemployment rate exceed two

[1] *The Economist*, July 13, 1946, p. 43.

per cent; in most years it was nearer one per cent. Workpeople had therefore no difficulty in finding and keeping jobs, and in earning tolerable incomes. The economic system worked, as it had not done for so many people between the wars, so that they could keep themselves and their families.

The difficulty in the '50s and '60s was not the maintenance of full employment over the country as a whole, but the prevention of local unemployment. The traditional policy was to achieve this by persuading industry to locate where men were unemployed. The Government could use the Distribution of Industry Act, 1945, which gave power to designate Development Areas and to use various means to attract new plants to them; and the Town and Country Planning Act of 1947 which gave the Board of Trade power to prevent industrial building where it would not be 'consistent with the proper distribution of industry'. For a time the problem slept; but the recession of 1957-58 caused serious difficulties in some areas, and new measures were promptly evolved and put into operation. The chief of these was the Local Employment Act of 1960. Under this Act, the Development Areas ceased to exist, and a new and extensive list of Development Districts came into being. The criterion for a district to be in the list was that in the view of the Board of Trade, a high rate of unemployment either existed there or was imminent, and was likely to persist. There were powers, similar to those previously existing but more extensive, to give grants or loans to businesses setting up in the area in question; and the system of Industrial Development Certificates, which could be used to prevent industrial building elsewhere, was strengthened. The principal achievements of this general policy were the setting up of new factories in Merseyside by Ford, Vauxhall, and Leyland, and in Scotland by BMC and Rootes. This has marked a major change in the regional distribution of the important motor vehicles industry, previously confined almost exclusively to Coventry and Oxford.

Workpeople thus no longer suffered seriously from unemployment or short-time working. But people's increased ability to be self-sufficient did not lead to any contraction of the social services. On the contrary, the social services expanded in every direction, at a rate indicated by the following table:

242

Government expenditure on social services, at current prices (£m.s)

Year	Education	Health	Social Insurance and Assistance	Housing	Food subsidies	Total
1938	139	99	278	80	nil	596
1950/51	355	484	514	365	162	1964
1965/66	1621	1329	2336	974	145	6627

Supposing prices to have increased by sixty per cent between 1950 and 1965, this table still shows a very considerable expansion to have taken place.

Housing and the food subsidies have already been discussed.[1] Expenditure on education increased both at school and university level. The main legislative change was the Education Act of 1944 which raised the school leaving age to fifteen and proposed to raise it to sixteen as soon as possible. (This latter proposal has yet to be implemented. In 1963 only 45 per cent of those children aged 15 were at school.) This automatically increased the school population, which the 'post-war baby boom' increased still further. This, in time, made necessary larger staffs (which there was great difficulty in recruiting) and more schools, and dissatisfaction with antiquated school buildings still further increased the rate of construction of new schools. The universities shared in the boom in education. As in several previous periods, economic difficulty led the country to question the adequacy of its educational system, especially at the higher levels. By the mid-'fifties, with highly technical developments taking place in chemistry, electronics, metallurgy and atomic work, and assuming a wider and wider importance in the economy, the need for a highly skilled labour force became obvious. The university population increased from 63,000 in 1938-39 to over 100,000 in 1948-49 and was just over 113,000 in 1959-60. The influential Robbins Report of 1963 set a target of 227,000 for 1974-75, and this Report was accepted by the Government. Existing universities expanded, a dozen or so new universities came into being, and numerous institutions for advanced education were upgraded to university status. All this cost money. In 1964-65 educational expenditure by public authorities in the UK rose to £1,485m., almost three times what it had been ten years earlier. This represented an increase

[1] See above, pp. 221–224, and pp. 178 and 180.

in education's share of the gross national product from 3·2 per cent to 5·1 per cent. In the latter half of this period expenditure on further and higher education was rising two and a half times as quickly as school expenditure; on the other hand, the training of teachers was the most rapidly expanding sector within the further and higher educational total.

The National Health Service was proposed in a White Paper of 1944 and the scheme came into operation in 1948. All the population was included (although not all took advantage of the service); the doctors, much to their disgust, became, to some extent, employees of the State; and the Minister of Health became responsible for running the hospitals and for administering most of the scheme. The basic principle of the scheme was that medical attention should be available according to whether people needed it, and not according to the extent to which they could pay for it. This was translated in the Act into the proposition that nobody must pay for anything. When the service began it soon became clear that there had been an immense latent demand for medical attention; doctors' waiting-rooms and hospitals became crowded, and the cost of the service soon rose from £218m. to over £500m. and in 1960 passed the £1,000m. figure. By that date the health services in England and Wales alone employed almost 600,000 people. Capital expenditure was, at first, very small; scarcely any money was made available for hospital building in Great Britain in the twenty years prior to 1957; but in the following years the situation improved. Finance would have been easier had more serious attempts been made to charge the users of the Health Services who could afford to pay. Some such charges were introduced by Gaitskell in 1951; but the idea has always been anathema to the Labour Party, and the very modest charge for prescriptions (brought in by the Tories) was immediately abolished by the Wilson Government when it came to office in 1964.

The most complicated and the most famous social measure of the post-war years was the so-called Beveridge Plan. This was presented as a Report on 'Social Insurance and Allied Services' in 1942. The report put forward a wide-ranging and coherent scheme for social policy after the war. It stressed that the avoidance of undesirable levels of unemployment was a first necessity. Three per cent of unemployment, it was thought, would be a workable and acceptable level. Assuming full employment (in this sense) and assuming the introduction of family allowances and a health service, the plan proposed a comprehensive system of social insurance: tripartite contributions (by the insured person, the employer and the State) to provide retirement pensions; sickness, accident, unemployment, and widows' and guardians' benefits; maternity, marriage and funeral grants. The whole population between sixteen and sixty-five were to become contributors, except that housewives would acquire the right to appropriate benefits through their husbands' contributions. This plan, which was designed to bring into national life in peacetime some of that sense of community and equality of sacrifice and treatment which the war made familiar, was greeted with general enthusiasm. The Government accepted most of the proposals, and embodied them in a series of Acts passed between 1945 and 1948. The Ministry of National Insurance was set up in 1944 and the whole scheme began to operate in 1948. It was expensive. Had the old arrangements stood, the cost in 1948 would have been £351m.; under the Beveridge Plan and the subsequent White Paper it would have been between £400m. and £450m.; under the Bill it was £509m., chiefly because of generosity to pensioners (who had votes) not offset by economies on allowances for children (who had none). Unemployment, of course, presented no problem, and the insurance funds soon acquired substantial reserves. But retirement pensions gave frequent difficulty, partly because inflation continually eroded the value of money benefits and partly because increases in rates of benefit became something in the nature of a bribe for electors. In 1946 it had seemed that the scheme amounted to the virtual abolition of the means test, and so it did; but it did not abolish the need for 'extra' assistance, and in 1955 over a million people, mostly pensioners, were receiving supplementary benefits from the National Assistance Board. Yet the scheme as a whole was a great one. It did not abolish poverty—perhaps no Act of Parliament can ever do that—but it did put a floor of income beneath most people's feet, and it did give to everyone a feeling that they had a right to most or to all of the benefits which they drew. 'Security from the cradle to the grave' was perhaps too high a claim for it, and it was paradoxical, to say the least, that personal economic security was thus built up just at the time when national economic security was at a very low ebb; but in the judgment of most people these measures made Britain a better and a freer society in which to live.

For most people, of course, the merit of post-war Britain lay in secure employment at good wages. To begin with, more vacancies than men to fill them, plus a natural reaction after years of war, produced a certain amount of slackness among workpeople: 'the wage,' said the *Economist* in a gloomy moment, 'is coming to be regarded not as a *quid pro quo* for a contribution to the economy, but as a species of welfare payment'.[1] Government and TUC reluctance to slow down inflation also contributed to inefficiency. Up to 1948 the trade unions were 'able to ignore, and on occasion to procure the withdrawal of official statements on the need to stabilize wages'.[2] But in the 'fifties, after devaluation had compelled all-round adjustments and cleared the air, the atmosphere greatly improved. The need for harder work, or at least more efficient work, became generally accepted. In 1948 the Government, with the co-operation of employers' organizations and trade unions, launched a campaign for higher industrial productivity. A series of productivity teams was sent to the United States; employers were urged to reorganize and to contribute to better industrial relations through joint consultation, improved factory conditions and better-conceived wage structures; trade unions were asked to educate their members in the need for higher productivity and equip them to discuss questions of production. Almost at once it became clear that, assured of full employment, the trade unions were not unwilling to give up old methods and restrictive practices, but they simply did not have the expertise needed to assess time and motion studies or to make useful contributions to the discussion of managerial problems. The issue became one of educating the unions; and the TUC and individual unions took up the challenge. Results were inevitably slow in appearing and were limited; they varied, also, from industry to industry

[1] *The Economist*, September 24, 1949, p. 655.
[2] ibid., February 7, 1948.

and from firm to firm. Nevertheless, considerable progress was made. Workers, shop stewards and local union officials alike became more willing to accept time and motion study (so useless without union co-operation), to relax rules limiting the number of machines to a worker, to allow redeployment of labour, welcome mechanical aids, and agree to the upgrading of unskilled employees to semi-skilled jobs. Employers, for their part, improved amenities, increased their efforts (often far too small in the past) to inform and consult workers about production plans and possible changes in the works, and, especially, introduced information schemes and compensation schemes with regard to redundancy.

Better equipment and better industrial relations increased productivity; but wages rose faster still. In manufacturing industry as a whole, the average annual increase in production from 1948 to 1957 was about 4 per cent; but the average annual increase in incomes was 8 per cent. In mining and quarrying the gap was far greater, the corresponding figures being 1 per cent and 7 per cent. Much the greater part of these increased money incomes was taken by wages and salaries. But of course real incomes could not rise as fast—there was not enough production for that. Consequently, an increase in weekly money earnings per head of over one-third between 1950 and 1957 was translated, through rising prices, into an increase of only one-sixth in terms of real earnings. What was much more serious, labour costs per unit of output rose faster in Britain than in many other countries, as the following figures show:

Unit Labour Costs per hour in Manufacturing
(1960 as per cent of 1953)

	Wage costs per head	Output per man-hour	Unit labour costs per hour
Belgium	138	139	99
France	182	156	117
Germany	158	145	109
Italy	137	(136)	(101)
Netherlands	167	(138)	(121)
UK	155	122	127

Source: A. Lamfalussy, *The United Kingdom and the Six*, Table 13, p. 59.

Appreciation of this point has often been insufficient. It is not that wages, or wages per hour, have increased faster in Britain than elsewhere; but they have increased faster relative to the increase in productivity. And this has seriously weakened ability to compete in foreign markets.

How far and in what way the rise in prices was itself a result of rising wages and salaries is a disputed question. The post-war economy inherited the wartime tendency of prices to rise. Also, from 1946 through 1954 the cost of imports rose by about 10 per cent per annum. It is therefore possible to argue that the main cause of the rise in prices was the rise in import prices, and that the rise in wages and salaries in each year down to 1954 was little more than was necessary to offset previous price changes. It would seem, however, that after 1954 wages and salaries began to increase without stimulus from 'external' forces; that there was, in short, a purely domestic generation of price inflation.[1]

The rise in average weekly earnings shown by the statistics— almost exactly 7 per cent per annum from 1947 to 1957— raised the average figure for all industries from less than £6 to over £10 a week. At least as important, different trades prospered in different degrees. In clothing and textiles, for example, earnings rose from 86s 0d and 94s 0d respectively in 1948 to 140s 0d and 167s 0d in 1957; but in chemicals and metal manufactures the changes were from 120s 0d and 146s 0d to 221s 0d and 268s 0d. Coal mining was a special case: earnings rose from 164s 0d in 1948 to 305s 0d in 1957. There was thus some tendency for the spread of earnings as between different occupations to increase. Against this, the old tendency for the differentials between the pay of skilled and unskilled to narrow continued. In 1914 a skilled man in the building trade received 50 per cent more than his unskilled helper; in 1946 25 per cent more; in 1956 only 14 per cent more. In engineering the story is similar, the skilled man receiving 71 per cent more in 1914, 19 per cent more in 1946, 16 per cent more in 1956; and so on through almost all the trades.[2] This paring down of differentials

---

[1] These views were elaborated by Mr J. C. R. Dow in his article 'Analysis of the Generation of Price Inflation' in *Oxford Economic Papers*, October 1956.

[2] Coal face workers and steel smelters have maintained differentials to an extent far above the average.

was sometimes the result of union policy. Large unions, with many sections of the membership having conflicting aims and interests, were apt to demand all-round wage increases even when the effect was further to increase anomalies and reduce differentials.

For the trade union movement the post-war world was as novel as for anyone. Full employment, pressure to export, cheap money; all this was quite different from what union leaders had been accustomed to between the wars. Now, labour was scarce; employers competed with one another to obtain and secure workers; this was, for trade unionists, the dominant fact. And to begin with, a Socialist Government was in power, the first politically secure Socialist Government trade unionists had ever had to work under in this country. Friendship between the Government and the trade unions, and especially between the Government and Transport House, was often personal. The TUC co-operated with the Government, and its policy statements frequently showed a firmer grasp of economic realities than did the speeches of Cabinet Ministers. But the TUC was not the trade union movement, and its ability to influence the policies of individual unions was decidedly limited. Trade union leaders exercised some restraint upon claims for higher wages down to about 1949, but thereafter there was a general movement to secure such higher wages as could be got. The annual round of wage increases became almost as familiar a phenomenon in Great Britain as in the United States; for a time, the wage awards made early in the year with respect to agricultural workers tended to set the pattern for that year. The nationalized industries, especially the railways, were often the scene of particularly pusillanimous resistance to wage demands. The trouble was that, although the railways lost money, pressure could always be put upon the Government to permit increases in fares. Thus in 1951 the Government sanctioned wage increases which exceeded the limits set both by the Railway Executive and the *ad hoc* Court of Enquiry; in 1953 peace was maintained by exceeding the recommendation of an independent tribunal; in 1955 a new Court of Enquiry found a new reason for giving in to the men's demands:

'The nation has provided by statute that there shall be a nationalized system of railway transport which must therefore be regarded as a public utility of the first importance. Having willed the end, the Nation must will the means.'

This extraordinary dictum did not, however, prevent a strike, which was in effect a quarrel between two unions. The strike lasted for seventeen days, and the volume of freight carried during this period fell by about two-thirds. The terms of settlement were probably such as could have been obtained without a strike. Similar pusillanimous retreats followed in the later 1950s and 1960s in the face of strikes or threatened strikes by engineers, shipbuilders, railwaymen, coal miners and electricity supply workers. Not until 1966 was there anything that could be called serious Government support for an effort by employers (and that includes the Boards of the nationalized industries) to keep wage awards in line with productivity increases.

Contrary to what is sometimes thought, stoppages of work were commoner in the post-war years than before the war; but they were rarely serious. Industry-wide negotiations were the commonest form of negotiation during and after the war. These were usually conducted with skill and responsibility on both sides. Moreover, in the post-war world of full employment and inflation, unions had little difficulty in putting up a good case—rising productivity, a higher cost of living, concessions in comparable occupations; the employers, for their part, finding demand buoyant and credit easy, had little desire to resist wage increases. When negotiation did fail, there was widespread willingness to resort to arbitration; and Ministers of Labour in the 1950s, with elections in the offing and the balance of payments at their back, preferred arbitrators who would stretch a point on wages to avoid a strike. Strikes thus became increasingly local, and were often unofficial—protests against the slowness of the official negotiating machinery or hasty outbursts by a minority against local irregularities, injustices, misfortunes or incompetence. Trade unions, like firms, had become large and sometimes a little unwieldy. With a membership of over 9m. spread among some 700 unions, the trade union movement was dominated by the large unions. The largest, the Transport and General Workers' Union, has over 1¼m. members; it and the five next largest unions[1] contain almost 50 per cent of British trade unionists. The financial strength, voting power and political influence of these unions is very great. Their prestige is less than that of the TUC but their power is greater. In terms of numbers the trade unionist, reasonably well paid, sure of his job, with his union affiliated to the TUC and a personal record of marked disinclination to attend branch meetings of his union, is the representative British citizen of the middle of the twentieth century.

COMMENT AND ANALYSIS

The performance of the British economy over the past fifteen years or thereabouts, and its present situation, can be presented either in a favourable or in a rather unfavourable light, according to the point of view adopted and the aspects of the situation and of its evolution which one chooses to stress. The first of these, which is, or until very recently was, the common and generally accepted point of view, fastens on a number of indubitable and substantial facts which are not difficult to observe and which are of undeniable importance; the second draws attention to less obvious but perhaps more fundamental elements in the situation.

The favourable point of view is supported by three main arguments. First, there is the fact of full employment. One of the major aims of British society, formulated in the early 1940s, was to overcome unemployment and to avoid the kind of situation which prevailed throughout the 1920s and 1930s, when, year after year, more than a million men, and, in the worst years, over two and a half million men were looking for work and were unable to find it. In this laudable aim we have succeeded, and we are perhaps a little inclined to take our success for granted or even to regret that it has been quite so complete. Concerning this achievement, two points should be borne in mind. In the first place, no other country in the world has so consistently kept its

---

[1] These are the National Union of General and Municipal Workers; the Amalgamated Engineering Union; the National Union of Mine Workers; the National Union of Railwaymen; and the Union of Shop, Distributive and Allied Workers.

people very fully employed. Most countries have gone through at least some bad patches; and in the United States the unemployment rate has averaged about 5 per cent since the war. The second point is that the original aim, as put forward by Lord Beveridge and accepted by the Government, was for a 3 per cent average unemployment rate; and this seemed almost unimaginably good compared with the 14 per cent which unemployment had averaged between the wars. But immediately the war ended, pressure of demand reduced unemployment below 3 per cent, and the country has now developed a frame of mind which seems to regard any average unemployment rate above about $1\frac{1}{2}$ per cent as intolerable. Whether this new tacit aim of less than $1\frac{1}{2}$ per cent unemployment is reasonable is not clear. As Beveridge himself put it, 'a margin of unemployment is not simply a business convenience; it is an incident of a free progressive society'.[1] And it should now be asked whether the freedom, progress and social justice which full employment was intended to promote are in fact best served by the very high rates of employment which are now customary. Unfortunately, this whole problem is usually discussed in a fog of emotion, and little is said about one of Beveridge's lines of proposed action, namely 'securing the organized mobility of labour'.[2] Nevertheless, the avoidance of distress due to unemployment has on the whole been very handsomely achieved, and this is a large item on the credit side of the economy's performance.

The second argument in support of the view that the economy has done well over the past fifteen years has already been emphasized in a previous section; namely, that an extensive industrial transformation has taken place, traditional industries having been cut back and new or newer industries developed and expanded to take their place. This was not an easy task. No doubt mistakes were made, and it is probably the case that change could and should have been much faster in certain fields, notably inland transport, the docks, and the shipbuilding industry. But a long-established economy, severely shaken by war and by far-reaching international political developments, might have been expected to show less energy, less imagination and

[1] W. H. Beveridge, *Full Employment in a Free Society*, p. 126.
[2] op. cit., p. 29.

less adaptability than was displayed by Britain after 1945. Here again the record is certainly not a discreditable one.

Thirdly, those who think well of the country's performance can point to the rise in output and in the standard of living which has taken place over the past fifteen years. Between the early 1950s and the mid-1960s gross domestic product at factor cost increased, at 1958 prices, by almost 50 per cent. The obvious way to judge this is by comparing it with what happened before. Reliable comparisons cannot be made for years earlier than 1870. But the figures since that date show that for a growth in GDP of 50 per cent in fifteen years we must go back to the exceptionally favourable period stretching from the early 1880s to the mid-1890s; rates of growth in the '70s, or in the twenty years before 1914, or in the inter-war period were considerably less than these which have been achieved since 1950. By the standards of historical comparison, therefore, no one can deny that Britain has done very well indeed since 1950.

These are the favourable arguments. But what can be said on the other side? One criticism is that Britain's achievement in raising output since 1950 does not look nearly so well if the comparison is made with Continental countries. Figures such as the following support this line of argument:

Output, Employment, and Output per Head, *
1955–64
Annual average per cent changes

Rank by output† growth	Output	Employment	Output per head
Japan	10·4	1·4	8·8
West Germany	6·3	1·3	5·0
Italy‡	5·7	0·1	5·6
Sweden	5·4	1·5	3·9
France	5·2	0·3	4·9
Denmark	5·0	1·2	3·8
Belgium	3·6	0·6	3·0
UK	3·1	0·5	2·6
USA	3·1	1·1	2·0

* *Source: DEA Progress Report 1966.*
† *The definition of output used is gross national product at constant market prices.*
‡ *1960-64 Source: OECD.*

But it is not easy to know what to make of comparisons of this kind. Their validity is not open to question, for, while they may be approximate, the fact remains that after making all possible allowance for the fallibility of the figures the British performance makes a poor showing. On the other hand, do the figures reflect anything more than that the circumstances of the several economies were different? In several (but not in all) cases, rates of growth are to be explained to some extent in terms of special factors. From 1950 to 1955 West Germany was rebuilding her shattered economy, and from 1955 to 1960 she benefited from a large inflow of labour, much of it skilled, from East Germany. Post-war Italy received an important stimulus from Marshall Aid, was helped to an exceptional degree by the growth of tourism and remittances by emigrants, and, like Germany, enjoyed an exceptional growth in labour supply. France was able to transfer a remarkably large proportion of her working population from agriculture to industry (where output per man was higher), and enjoyed the advantages of stable and forceful government—notably absent during the Third Republic. It should also be said that whereas the British growth rate was faster from 1960 to 1964 than it had been from 1953 to 1960, rates of growth in France and Germany slowed down; and that if comparison is made not with European countries at all but with the United States, then the comparison is not wholly to Britain's disadvantage.

In general, it is probably safe to say that unduly tragic conclusions have been drawn by some writers from examination of the Continental figures. The heart of the matter is that there has been on the Continent 'a generally more rapid advance of the productivity of labour'.[1] But that is what one would expect in a post-war period from countries anxious for economic reconstruction and advance, unusually little hampered, because of wartime destruction and dislocation, by old institutions, customs, or capital equipment, and assisted by wealthier neighbours, fairly well able to understand their problems, with capital and technical know-how. On the other hand, there are no grounds for complacency—rather the reverse. The more rapid growth of these countries—and perhaps especially that of Denmark,

[1] A. Lamfalussy, *The United Kingdom and the Six* (1963), p. 33.

Sweden and Switzerland, little touched or untouched by war—encourages one to think that Britain could have done better. Now (always assuming that we wish to keep up) exceptional efforts may be required, for the events of the 'fifties may have put these countries on a steeper growth path than ours, and these paths may continue to diverge. For one thing, the good progress made on the Continent in the past fifteen years has given the Continental countries a stock of capital equipment which will make it more difficult for Britain to compete with them in the future.

The other ground for considering the British performance since 1950 as rather unsatisfactory is, of course, that growth has been so unstable, and has so often been seriously threatened (as well as temporarily interrupted) by balance of payments crises. The story of these has already been told. Their immediate effects were a slowing down in the rate of increase of industrial production, and, as a rule, a modest rise in unemployment. In each case these effects were temporary. But there was always the risk—and in the more serious crises it was a real risk—that whether or not there was a hasty devaluation, sterling would collapse as an international currency, bringing serious losses of overseas earnings and, much worse, widespread dislocation of international trade. Any such train of events would have very adverse and long drawn out effects upon the British economy, and it is a seriously uninformed and shortsighted view which does not regard the possibility as of the greatest consequence. The oftener these crises were repeated, the greater, other things being equal, the risk became. And there is also the point that repeated interruptions to investment programmes are likely to make businessmen more pessimistic and therefore less ambitious in their planning.

In the writer's own view—and it is very much a matter of personal judgment—the economy could and should have done 'better' since 1950. There could have been less social tension, faster growth, more aid for underdeveloped countries, a much more positive approach to the development of international trade—and hence more assurance about the future than we now possess. Britain cannot be described at the moment as a very confident economy or a very confident society.

If one takes that point of view, the question arises, what are the essential difficulties, and why were they not more successfully overcome? This question requires to be divided into two parts. First, what were the fundamental and long-term problems facing the economy? and second, what were the short-term difficulties of management and manipulation?

There seem to have been two major long-term difficulties. The first was the necessity to accept the fact that Britain was no longer one of the greatest world powers, the centre of an empire 'on which the sun never sets'. In the 1930s Britain was still a formidable military and economic power, much as she had been in the nineteenth century, and largely on this basis she wielded enormous and extensive commercial and political influence. But with the rise of Russia and the United States, closely allied to the development of atomic weapons, Britain's importance shrank; while her economic weakness, along with complex forces of nationalism and anti-colonialism all over the world, caused the break-up of the empire. Adjustment to political deflation on the grand scale is no doubt a hugely difficult psychological operation. But costly responsibilities have continued to be borne, and illusions of grandeur have to some extent persisted. There was the war in Malaya, the confrontation with Indonesia, the quarrel with Rhodesia. There was the inept and deplorable Suez adventure, which caused a run on the reserves which the country could ill afford, and exposed the hollowness of her pretensions to be a great world power. There have been and are the nuclear striking forces—the V bombers and now the nuclear submarines; enormously costly and the latter requiring very large dollar outlays. The economist is entitled to ask what the return on all these expenditures is supposed to be, for throughout the 1950s the share of defence expenditure in the gross national product was at least twice as high in Great Britain as in Germany, Italy or Holland, and Government military expenditure overseas has been a perpetual burden on the balance of payments. It can be argued that Britain was thereby doing her duty in the world while others were not; and admittedly, Britain carried over from her more prosperous days many commitments which it was difficult to shrug off. But it is a strange national duty which requires the shouldering of responsibilities in the short run on such a scale as to destroy one's long-run capacity to shoulder any responsibilities at all.

The second long-term difficulty is also a carry-over from the past. Sterling is a key-currency, one of the three forms in which nations can conveniently hold their reserves, the other two being dollars and gold. Prior to the war, sterling was *the* medium in which international transactions took place. The war weakened sterling. But as a result of war-time finance an abnormal situation emerged, in which Britain had sterling liabilities of almost £3,700m. and gold reserves of only about £600m. Britain thus appeared as an international banker with short-term liabilities very much in excess of her reserves of gold and convertible currencies; and sterling continued, whether anyone liked it or not, as an important reserve currency. But it is a reserve currency in which confidence is never very great, partly because of recurrent doubts about its international value, partly —and more fundamentally—because the reserves which support it are so small.[1] In the crises through which sterling has passed, a major factor has usually been liquidation of those sterling balances held by non-sterling area countries.

Carrying short-term liabilities greatly in excess of her short-term assets, Britain has always had to be very careful to check any deterioration in her balance of payments situation. An adverse balance worsens the ratio of assets to liabilities; it also undermines foreign confidence, thereby causing a liquidation of sterling balances; and this further worsens the situation.

Thus having sterling as a reserve currency has sometimes seemed like running races tied to a ball and chain, for every exchange crisis is apt to compel more drastic action than would be desirable, from a domestic point of view, if there were more freedom of manoeuvre. But to let go cannot be contemplated. For one thing, it would be a breach of faith—holders of sterling are relying on the banker maintaining the value of their balances. And there are two straightforward economic arguments. First, reserve countries derive a profit from having their currencies held by other countries or by the nationals of other countries.

---

[1] The ratio of reserves to sterling liabilities improved from 1951 to 1958, but deteriorated 1958–64. The inadequacy of the reserves by 1964 was proved by the necessity to secure emergency support for the pound in the autumn of that year.

Second, international trade cannot be carried on without an adequate supply of international liquidity. It has become increasingly clear in the 1960s that the current supply of international liquidity—gold, dollars, sterling, international credit facilities—is barely adequate, and that another major step will soon have to be taken to create usable monetary reserves through multi-nation action. But in the meantime, and over the past fifteen years, sterling provides and has provided an essential service. The banker has been paid for this service. And besides, were international trade to be hampered, no country would suffer more than Britain. Therefore Britain has had good reasons for maintaining sterling as an international reserve currency. But no one would choose the conditions under which it has had to be operated, and it is now clear that the past fifteen years have seen the prolongation of an international system which is the skilful but imperfect creation of compromise and necessity, and which cannot last.

So much for the long-term difficulties and restraints with which policy has had to contend or which, to some degree, it has had to accept. What can be said, in brief, of the more immediate problems and of the attempts to deal with them?

Considerable progress has been made in the development of techniques for controlling economic activity. Perhaps the most important of these was the resurrection of monetary policy in 1951. The later 1950s saw a tendency to question the effectiveness of monetary policy, a tendency which found full expression in the Radcliffe Report:

'If we look at the actual experience of the 1950s—as far as the evidence has allowed us to trace it—we come to the conclusion that the really quick substantial effects were secured by the hire purchase controls, just those which have the most concentrated directional effects. A considerable, though rather slower, effect probably came in 1956-58 from the "diffused difficulty of borrowing" which resulted from the tighter and dearer money—particularly the squeeze of bank credit—of 1955-56 . . . The monetary instruments employed left untouched the large industrial corporations that control more than half the investment in manufacturing industry; and neither their planning nor that of the public corporations appears to have responded seriously to interest rates.'[1]

But, as Dow has pointed out,[2] variations in building society lending, brought about indirectly by monetary measures, probably also had an appreciable impact on the economy. And the argument seems sometimes to have been little more than the proposition that because monetary policy cannot accomplish everything, it can therefore accomplish nothing. There seems no doubt that academic disenchantment with monetary policy went too far in the 'fifties; and it is significant that monetary policy has continued to play a role in the 1960s.

Fiscal policy, on the other hand, has steadily grown in favour, and has become more flexible. The investment allowances were an important innovation, operating on investment directly. The powers taken in 1961, whereby indirect taxation could be changed substantially at any time, and not merely by the budget, constituted another important and overdue reform, for they gave the Chancellor authority 'to moderate consumption by fiscal measures over a fairly broad field, rather than . . . to fall upon investment . . . or the consumption merely of durables'.[3]

But it is not so clear that the best use has been made of the available instruments of policy. Ministers and their advisers appear to have been obsessed by the desire to maintain an un-employment rate of not more than $1 \cdot 5$ per cent and, partly as a means to this end, to drive the economy as soon as possible on every occasion to full capacity working.[4] Economic theory suggests, and experience confirms, that if the output ceiling is approached too rapidly, an investment boom takes place which cannot possibly be sustained. In the British case, the ill effects of too hasty expansion were reinforced by prompt deterioration in the balance of payments situation, which took place because the increase in home demand for certain items outran domestic supply capacity, and perhaps also because of the constantly

[1] Radcliffe Report, para. 472.

[2] Dow, op. cit., p. 260.

[3] I. M. D. Little in *The British Economy in the Nineteen-Fifties*, p. 273.

[4] The exception to this statement is the leisurely expansion of demand and output which took place in 1955–58. This does not seem to have been entirely deliberate.

increasing competitiveness of foreign manufactures in the British market, due at least in part to the rapid rise in British wages induced by ultra-full employment. Thus each rapid expansion of output was followed, more or less inevitably, by crisis and deceleration.

In the longer run, it was the aim of economic policy to secure rapid economic growth. This objective was pursued by various means calculated to raise the share of investment in the gross national product; and gross investment did in fact rise between 1953 and 1963 from 15·7 per cent to 18·2 per cent of the gross national product. This should certainly have assisted the growth rate of output, for no one doubts that the rate of capital accumulation affects the growth rate. But the relationship between these two variables is far from simple; and the latest investigations suggest that a more important determining factor is the rate of return to investment:

'Faster rates of growth of output per man are associated statistically with higher returns to investment. [This is so] whether the latter result from greater economies of scale, faster technical progress, or a more dynamic management and hence better organization of production in conditions of fast-rising output . . .'[1]

This should not come as a surprise to those who are accustomed to stress the importance of organization or technical progress. Certainly it casts doubt on what seems to have been the major assumption of Government direction of the economy since 1951.

Besides this over-emphasis (as it seems to the present writer) on one particular quantitative relationship (and indeed on quantitative relationships in general; this point is expanded in a later paragraph), the actual handling of investment seems to have left something to be desired. All too often the balance of the economy has been disturbed, and crisis measures have then been taken to discourage investment. A policy of long-term encouragement, punctuated by fairly severe bouts of short-term discouragement, is not calculated to increase business confidence.

[1] Beckerman, op. cit., p. 39.

And it is furthermore true that attempts to influence the level of investment are highly uncertain in their impact.

These difficulties might have been smaller had the authorities been more skilful in foreseeing the future and in calculating correctly the effect of their measures. But on this point another adverse judgment has to be made. After a most careful survey of the problem, Dow sums up as follows:

'The conclusion then is that the rapid expansion of demand and output in the years 1952-55, and that in 1958-60, were both due, directly and indirectly, to the influence of policy. Though this is less certain the same may be true of the slow expansion of demand and output in the years 1955-58: even if due to causes other than policy, policy was certainly not directed to counteract them. The major fluctuations in the rate of growth of demand in the years after 1952 were thus chiefly due to Government policy. This was not the intended effect; in each phase, it must be supposed, policy went further than intended, as in turn did the correction of these effects.

'As far as internal conditions are concerned then, budgetary and monetary policy failed to be stabilizing, and must on the contrary be regarded as having been positively destabilizing.'[1]

Of course it is easy to be wise after the event; but one cannot avoid the impression that a too simple, mechanical, and, in the deepest sense, inexpert view of the workings of the economy was taken by the authorities throughout this period. Especially in more recent years, their feeling for the passage of time, for the making and unmaking of confidence, for the practical problems of business, for the complexity of economic reactions, seems to have been totally inadequate.[2]

It was because of the unsteady growth of the economy throughout the 'fifties that opinion came round to the view that what was needed was

[1] Dow, op. cit., p. 384.
[2] One wonders how many Ministers or advisers had read one of the most perceptive available studies of the scope and limitations of Government action, Professor Erik Lundberg's *Business Cycles and Economic Policy*.

'for the authorities to think in terms of rates of growth, rather than in terms of *ad hoc* short-term adjustments of demand to supply . . . Such a programme requires, in broad outline, a long-term plan. With the experience of the 'fifties it is not too difficult to predict what the economy is capable of, and to produce target rates of growth for the major categories of demand, which will "add-up" in the sense that they will suffice to keep resources reasonably fully employed.'[1]

Such thinking, coupled in some quarters with a perhaps rather uncritical admiration for the achievements of French planning, led to the National Plan of 1964, the brief history of which has already been outlined. It foundered on a combination of over-optimism and the fact, inconvenient for planning but inescapable, that the British economy is anything but a closed system. This is not to say that there is no place for intelligent, flexible long-term planning in Britain.

To sum it all up, the problems of the British economy are exceptionally complex, and many of them are deep-seated. To turn Britain into a fast-growing economy was never going to be an easy task, for growth means change and (at least to begin with) conflict, and British society is in many ways traditional and pacific. This is nowhere better exemplified than in the trade unions, where structure and habits of thought are overwhelmingly conservative and defensive. Unhappily, much history, and also the structure of English society, has bred antagonism between trade unionism and the forces of progress, and episodes such as the attempt to secure full utilization of the liner trains on British Railways have been all too common. It is tempting to say that the trade unions have not responded at all well to the challenge of full employment. But it is almost equally easy to criticize British management. Some firms are among the most efficient in the world. But the best informed observers agree that there is too much amateurism in management, that there are too many family businesses not interested in expansion, too many cosy agreements among businessmen not to compete, or at least not to the point where it hurts.

[1] I. M. D. Little in *The British Economy in the Nineteen-Fifties*, p. 275.

Such criticisms, however, should be subordinated to a more fundamental one. This is, that successive governments have produced an economic environment favourable rather than otherwise to the above-mentioned weaknesses in trade unions and management, and have done so by promoting over-full employment and by concentrating on largely quantitative adjustments effective in the short run, neglecting those more difficult and slower-working measures which, in the long run, would be much more effective. Admittedly, a start has been made. There has been an attempt, although a rather silly one, at indicative planning. Anti-monopoly and anti-restrictive practices legislation has been introduced, and, albeit a little hesitantly and slowly, enforced. Industrial re-training has begun to be taken more seriously than before. Educational opportunities are being extended (and dangerously standardized) and an attempt has been made to promote social and intellectual respect for such despised topics as economics, technology, and the applied sciences. A start has been made on modernizing urban and interurban communications. Tentative moves have been made to reform the world monetary system. None of these lines of policy will yield quick results. But they will make Britain more efficient and therefore more competitive. It is on the competitiveness of British industry (in the widest sense) that everything depends. If that can be secured, faster growth will follow. If it is not secured, no policies for growth will be effective.

The seat of the difficulty has been underestimation of its magnitude. It has too often been supposed that a slightly more skilful manipulation of certain familiar variables—the incidence of taxes, the rate of investment, the number of science graduates from universities—would do the trick. But we are still living out the aftermath of empire and of the easy supremacy which we enjoyed in the nineteenth century. In these very difficult circumstances, strong and long-sighted political leadership has been essential, and it has not often been forthcoming. In its place there has been a fondness for easy solutions. But easy solutions will not bring about the many fundamental changes which have still to be made. Sterling must cease to be an international reserve currency within the existing framework. The vestigial traces of empire, and of imperial responsibilities, will have to go. The half-conscious feeling that 'getting-ahead' is disreputable (especially in the earning of money) and that income can never be too much redistributed will have to be abandoned. Britain may have to become an established borrower, not a lender, on international markets. There will have to be a Tory party not dominated by Eton and a Labour party not dominated by wishful thinking and the trade unions. Above all, the principal aims of policy will have to be competitiveness and efficiency, not growth and minimum unemployment. The new Britain, if it is ever to emerge, will have to be something newer than anyone has yet imagined.

Economic Thought and Policy
between the Wars

T H E most remarkable feature of Government economic activity between the wars was the rate of its extension. In the 1920s the Government subsidized house-building and pursued make-work policies on a modest scale, supporting local authorities in such works from 1921, permitting some money to be steered towards road, bridge and drainage schemes by the Unemployment Grants Committee, and finally, in 1929, devising the Development Act and the Colonial Development Act. In 1931 such policies were abandoned. There were also schemes for industrial training (1926), aided transference (1928), land settlement at home and overseas, and the semi-compulsory cartelization of the coal industry (1930). After 1930 a variety of expedients was tried by the National Government, most of them party nostrums of Tory devising. In this way new and important policies were introduced with respect to tariffs (1931), imperial preference (1932), agriculture (statutory monopolies 1931 and 1933), steel (centralized buying and selling plus international cartelization plus some degree of national planning, 1934 and subsequently), shipbuilding (elimination of surplus capacity, 1935), aid for Special or Depressed Areas (1934 and 1937), and the location of industry (about 1936). Apart from these, there was the enormous and enduring state-enterprise of house building and slum clearance. In the traditional field of monetary policy, where in the 1920s most state activity occurred, policy changes of the most far-reaching importance were introduced in 1925 and 1931, and in 1932 there came one of the most successful innovations of all, 'the Bank of England's secret sponge', alias the Exchange Equalization Account.

This is a formidable list. And yet, looking back on it, it is the tentative, piece-meal nature of this legislation which strikes us almost as forcibly as its extent would have struck a nineteenth century observer. While it may well be true that the 'most significant economic difference between the England of 1950 and the England of 1910' was the control by the State over the volume of investment,[1] and while it may be true that this was the end towards which all things were moving through the inter-war years, it cannot be said that it was an end which had been reached, even perhaps visualized, in 1939. Governments were dealing, as it seemed at the time, with one emergency after another; and it was inevitable that there was no master plan. But at the same time, Governments were also dealing with one perpetual problem—unemployment, existing against a background of rising output and rising national income. Most of what was done was intended to create or to maintain employment. What guidance was given by economic thought in the formulation of policies of this kind? The answer is to be found in what economists wrote about competition and monopoly as well as about employment and the level of activity itself.

The problems of imperfect competition were brought to public notice as soon as the war had ended in the *Report of the Committee on Trusts*. Its recommendations were based on the idea, made explicit in the Minority Report,

'That association and combination in production and distribution are steps in the greater efficiency, the increased economy, and the better organization of industry. We regard this evolution as both inevitable and desirable.'[2]

The recommendations of the Majority Report were for the granting of investigatory and publicizing powers to the Board of Trade, while those of the Minority Report included price control and State ownership. But such checks to monopoly were intended to control it, not to hinder it. The *Economist* did not regard the Report as a very startling document—'a modern postscript to the standard works on the subject'[3]—and, despite

[1] D. H. Robertson, *Utility and All That*, p. 116.
[2] loc. cit., p. 13.
[3] *The Economist*, June 7, 1919.

its belief that the nation was currently submitting to 'a yoke imposed by bureaucratic bunglers',[1] it approved the Majority recommendations. But in Parliament nothing was done. Undoubtedly the nation had been impressed by the powers of organization and production shown to be possessed by big units and combined action during the war,[2] and the great technical economies arising from the operation of the Central Electricity Board from 1927 provided a further impressive demonstration of the possible advantages of large scale organization. The risk of monopolistic pricing in peacetime remained a risk. Free trade was still felt to provide protection from oppressive monopolistic policies. And there were more urgent things to do.

Development through the 'twenties came from the side of theory rather than of empirical research. The first step on the road to *The Economics of Imperfect Competition* and, ultimately, to the Monopolies Commission, was taken when Clapham wrote 'Of Empty Economic Boxes'[3] (deriving from Pigou's discussion in *The Economics of Welfare* of the effects of monopolistic conditions upon the allocation of resources), and the second with the publication in English, in 1926, of Şraffa's celebrated article 'The Laws of Returns under Competitive Conditions'.[4] This led via the symposium, 'Increasing Returns and the Representative Firm', published in 1930, to the work of Shove, who, in two brief articles, outlined a theory of imperfect competition in a very complete state, emphasising the importance of selling costs and of the entry of new firms, and casting doubt upon the idea that imperfect competition must withhold from the consumer remarkable economies. This approach was modified, however, and its emphasis considerably altered, in Mrs Robinson's expanded treatment of the subject, *The Economics of Imperfect Competition*, published in 1933.

The practical significance of the problem was meanwhile being brought to public notice by the rationalization movement.

---

[1] *The Economist*, March 22, 1919.

[2] In its summary of the Final Report of the Committee on Commercial and Industrial Policy after the War, the *Economic Journal* included the remark 'Combination among manufacturers are approved of, and should be legalized'. Op. cit., 1919.

[3] *The Economic Journal*, 1922.

[4] ibid., 1926.

The 1920s and the 1930s were the decades *par excellence* of excess capacity, and rationalization was, as its ablest critic and defender pointed out, 'mainly a question of the scale on which private enterprise should be urged or compelled to reorganize itself by amalgamation'.[1] The purpose of this reorganization by amalgamation was, of course, the maintenance of prices and the restoration of the profitability of working; but, as Macgregor also pointed out, any 'definite policy of urging or enforcing large amalgamations, therefore, requires safeguards against the misuse of economic strength';[2] and he went on

'to endorse the finding of several inquiries, dating from the Committee on Trusts of 1919, that the continuance of private enterprise under the conditions that are coming about will require resort to some tribunal on trade practices which will deal specially with their economic aspects.'[3]

That large scale organization might wear a restrictive as well as a reconstructive air was sometimes officially admitted—*vide* the draft plan of reorganization in the iron and steel trades or the provision of consumers councils in the Agricultural Marketing Act of 1933—but on the whole the makers of policy contined to be more impressed by the virtues than the dangers of amalgamation.[4] Economists who gave most thought to the problem were inclined to argue that restriction was sometimes economically sound and sometimes unsound,[5] but it is not likely that this was regarded as helpful by statesmen in search of general rules or quick solutions.

The rationalization movement was thus industry's (and also part of the Government's) attempt to cope with the problem of excess productive capacity in some sections of the economy, notably with regard to the export trades. It was therefore also, in a way, part of the attempt to cope with the problem of unemployment. Macgregor's view was that recovery from de-

[1] D. H. Macgregor, *Enterprise Purpose and Profit* (Oxford University Press, 1934) p.v.
[2] ibid., p. 57.
[3] ibid., p. 60.
[4] As was the Roosevelt administration up to 1937.
[5] For example J. W. F. Rowe, *Markets and Men* (Cambridge University Press, 1936).

pression would be effected by private enterprise, and that the problem of policy was how 'to encourage enterprise in its own desire for recovery'.[1] Rationalization was thus set within a certain framework, where 'public works, remission of taxation, and inflation of the currency'[2] were also variables. In other words, unemployment—supposing this to be regarded as the major issue—could be tackled either from the side of industrial organization or from the side of monetary and fiscal policy. Both were tried; but the latter raised wider issues and, ultimately, excited far greater attention.

On the purely theoretical level, too, problems of monopoly became submerged in problems of aggregate dynamic employment theory. In retrospect, this is one of the main lessons— perhaps it is the main lesson—of *The Economics of Imperfect Competition*. The aim of this book was to develop the criticism, begun by Pigou, of the idea that the wage always tends to equal the marginal net product of labour, and to explore the relationship between Marshall's notion of a 'representative firm' and his idea that, in the face of a recession of demand, price is maintained through 'fear of spoiling the market'.[3] The resulting ideas are worked out in terms of the classical long-period partial equilibrium analysis. This gave Mrs Robinson the choice of treating normal profits as those just adequate to maintain the size of the firm or industry, or, as Shove later suggested,[4] as those consistent with, in some sense, a 'normal' rate of growth. She took the former course, and this resulted, given the firm by firm and industry by industry approach, in an overall picture which was equivalent to that of a stationary state. Markets, kept separated from one another, show only feeble powers of

---

[1] D. H. Macgregor, op. cit., p. 85.

[2] ibid., p. 85.

[3] Marshall, *Principles*, p. 711. Interest in this idea was intensified by some investigations carried out by Professor Kahn into the working of the Lancashire cotton industry during the depression. These showed that numerous firms, working below capacity and unable to cover total costs, believed that a reduction in price, other things remaining equal, would enable them to expand output, and that this in turn would enable them to reduce their costs. They nevertheless continued to restrict output, not believing that a rise in price, other things remaining equal, was possible.

[4] G. Shove, 'Mrs Robinson on Marxian Economics', in *Economic Journal*, April 1944, pp. 59-60. Shove implies that the 'dynamic' view was Marshall's.

expansion. Time is allowed to enter the analysis only for the purpose of eliminating the rent of factors (this corresponds to Marshall's treatment of quasi-rent). And, therefore, within the time-dimension of the analysis, the dynamic forces making for change and progress—some of which might even be strengthened under monopolization—are made to disappear. This affects, of course, not only the analysis but also the emphasis and the conclusions; for the possibility of oligopolistic expansion, as opposed to oligopolistic restriction, is debarred from consideration, while the problems raised by the entry of new firms, or even those created by major shifts of power between established firms as a result of innovation, are likewise ruled out. This amounted, in effect, to an exposure of the limitations of this type of analysis. But the book tended to be seen as implying that an analysis based on the notions of limited demand and restricted competition—of a sort of dead-enterprise world— was the most appropriate for the contemporary situation; and as an interpretation of the real world this was encouraged or discouraged according to what was considered an acceptable analysis of the economy as a whole. We must therefore now turn to this question.

In the first place it is important to make clear that whereas employment theory was a creation of the 1930s, employment policy was not. This is, in a sense, absurd; for there can be no policy without a theory, if only an implicit one. And this is part of the difficulty; for employment theory was, in those years, implied in current ideas about the flexibility of prices, wages and entrepreneurial expectations, and about the inter-relations of all three. On the other hand, an employment policy recognizable as such had existed in the sixteenth century,[1] and the problem began to come to the forefront with the *Minority Report of the Royal Commission on the Poor Law* in 1909. In the immediate post-war years unemployment became a pressing problem. As early as the spring of 1919 one million men were unemployed, and even after the peculiar difficulties of 1919-22 had been surmounted the unemployment rate continued at over 10 per cent. The clue to the professional analysis of this situ-

[1] See R. H. Tawney, *Religion and the Rise of Capitalism* (London, T. Murray, 1929), chapter III (ii).

ation is supplied by the nature of the action which was taken. This action was monetary. In the early spring of 1919 the further maintenance of a gold standard was seen to require 'a very severe restriction of credit . . . To start peace with a trade depression seemed an appalling prospect'.[1] This resulted in the formal abandonment of the gold standard on March 31, 1919.

To leave the gold standard when in acute difficulties was traditional policy; but not to return to it almost at once appeared revolutionary—and revolutionary in the most alarming sense, for it seemed to substitute chaos for order. As Sir Dennis Robertson has put it,

> 'the case for the old gold standard was not simply that it was a device for keeping step; it was also that it was a rough and ready device (*how* rough and ready the long tale of nine-teenth-century cycles shows) for regulating the volume of home activity. It may have been silly to bother so much about the exchanges; but it was simpler than trying to bother about everything at once, and wiser than bothering about nothing at all.'[2]

The immediate result of leaving the gold standard in 1919 was precisely as traditional analysis would suggest: abandonment 'was responsible for the post-war monetary expansion being extended further, and the price level rising higher . . . than would have happened had the gold standard been retained'.[3] But the gold standard dictated policy through the 1920s as effectively from the grave as from the throne. The influential Cunliffe Committee, of which Pigou was a member, published its final report eight months after the abandonment of the standard, and reiterated its opinion

> 'that the adoption of a currency not convertible at will into gold or other exportable coin is likely in practice to lead to over-issue and so to destroy the measure of exchangeable value and cause a general rise in all prices and an adverse movement in the foreign exchanges'.[4]

[1] Hawtrey, *Currency & Credit* (2nd ed. Longmans, 1923) p. 407.
[2] D. H. Robertson, *Essays in Monetary Theory*, p. 123.
[3] A. C. Pigou, *Aspects of British Economic History*, 1918-1925, p. 148.
[4] loc. cit., para. 2.

Moreover, removal of controls, for which there was such pressure immediately after the war, implied removal of manipulative control over currency, i.e. implied return to the gold standard. Hence restoration of the gold standard became, almost from the moment of its abandonment, the recognized aim of policy; 'endorsed by nearly all persons of authority,' it 'dominated the outlook of the Treasury and the Bank of England . . . until in April 1925, it was finally carried into effect'.[1] The immediate consequence of this ultimate aim was continual concern about American interest rates and the American price level, and its remoter consequences unceasing care by the Bank of England to husband gold reserves, manipulate the money market so as to retain foreign capital, and restrain a recurrent tendency to lend too much abroad.

This does not look like an employment policy. In the short period, obviously, it was not one. It was, first and foremost, a stability policy. Both the Cunliffe Committee and Hawtrey—high priest of the gold standard as well as of the rate of interest—emphasized the, so to speak, negative virtues of a gold standard; 'the only effective remedy for an adverse balance of trade and an undue growth of credit'.[2] After the German experience of 1922-23 these words carried great conviction. But the standard had positive virtues as well. Its restoration, its supporters pointed out, could be the first and the most important step towards international monetary co-operation;[3] it would make more secure the country's international trade position;[4] the financial advantages for the City of London were also borne in mind.[5] To foreigners, the chief virtue of the gold standard was that it acted as a guarantee against internal monetary mismanagement. This suited Great Britain, because runaway inflation destroyed the external purchasing power of currencies and disrupted British foreign trade. As Henderson later put it,

'The runaway inflations which developed in several important European countries entailed, while they were in

[1] Pigou, op. cit., p. 148.
[2] Cunliffe Committee, Interim Report, para. 47. Compare Hawtrey, *Economic Journal*, 1919, p. 434.
[3] Hawtrey, *Economic Journal*, 1919, p. 441.
[4] Cunliffe Committee, Final Report, para. 47.
[5] Hawtrey, *Currency and Credit*, espec. pp. 154 and 156.

progress, a sharp decline in the foreign exchange resources of the countries affected, and consequently in their capacity to pay for imports ... imported commodities became prohibitively expensive to the peoples of, for example, Austria, Poland, Germany, and later France. It was upon finding a remedy for these conditions that contemporary opinion and contemporary constructive effort were rightly concentrated.'[1]

The restoration of the gold standard was thus, at any rate for its clearer-minded advocates, only a means to an end. Nor need anyone have been under any illusions as to the difficulties involved, for they were pointed out by Hawtrey with admirable clarity. Hawtrey was an energetic but by no means a doctrinaire advocate of the gold standard. He pointed out that resumption could be at the old or at a new, lower level. He favoured the former because

'If the real reason for abandoning the standard, under whatever plausible pretext, is believed to be necessity, the national credit will suffer. The nation can only escape condemnation for a breach of faith at the price of a confession of financial impotence.'[2]

But his readers were warned that

'There is a danger that the present war may be followed by a ... period of excessive currency contraction. Financial correctitude, if pressed to the point of pedantry, may lead to a vice of deflationism as bad in its way as inflationism ... Inflation means inflation of the consumers' income, and more especially of profits and wages ... Deflation therefore means a reduction of profits and wages. If wages resist the process and it falls unduly on profits, the result is unemployment ... During the war, wages have everywhere been increased in a very high proportion. It seems not unlikely that the difficulty of reducing them again will be the determining factor in the settlement of the future monetary units.'[3]

[1] H. D. Henderson, *The Inter-War Years and other papers* (Oxford University Press, 1955), pp. 238-39.
[2] Hawtrey, *Currency and Credit*, p. 359.
[3] ibid., p. 362.

These are words of astonishing prescience. Hawtrey in 1919 foretold the difficulties of the 1920s far better than most of his successors in 1945 foretold those of the later 1940s. We may think his insistence on the honouring of obligations and on the dangers for a financial centre of 'loss of confidence in the stability of the currency'[1] overdone and mistaken; we may dispute the separation in his argument[2] of consumers' from producers' demand, especially with respect to the rate of interest; we may concede, with Gregory, that 'whilst it would be unwise to say that the whole of the difficulties of, say, the British coal trade in the last decade [1920s] are due directly to the reimposition of the old parity, undoubtedly the currency situation contributed to the difficulties actually experienced by exporters';[3] but we must acknowledge that the policy of recreating financial stability in the interests of a solidly based national and international economic expansion was well understood by those who made it their duty to advocate it.

Keynes, as is well known, argued against restoration at the old parity. In his *Tract on Monetary Reform*, published in 1923, he wrote a thoughtful and penetrating exposure of the risks of returning to gold. He began by pointing out that fixed exchanges under a gold standard might make unobtainable that desirable possession, a stable price level. It might be necessary to choose one or the other; and Keynes, unlike Norman and all his other opponents, thought the stable price level by far the more important of the two. This fundamental judgment made, he went on to argue that the gold standard was now not an automatic but a managed standard, managed largely by the Federal Reserve Board, which held enormous quantities of the world's gold and whose capacity for wise management Keynes distrusted (rightly, as it turned out in the end). He also questioned the 'pious hope' that international co-operation, needed to make the gold standard work, would actually be forthcoming. And here he was proved abundantly right. What wrecked the gold standard was the self-regarding unwisdom of

---

[1] Hawtrey, *Currency and Credit*, p. 156.

[2] ibid., p. 350.

[3] T. E. Gregory, *Gold, Unemployment and Capitalism* (London, King, 1933), p. 80.

French and occasionally of American monetary policies—or in the last resort, as Norman said, 'the "panic" money which grew to such large proportions in the 'twenties'.[1]

But Keynes's argument in 1923 really came to contrasting the weaknesses of such a gold standard regime as the next few years *might* see with the perfection of a theoretical, ideal, managed system. And when the time came for a final decision, in 1924–25, the arguments which Keynes then put forward were less clear-sighted, less perspicacious and less justified. He condemned a policy which, he said, would raise the external value of sterling by 10 per cent and hence compel a reduction in all salaries and wages of 2s. 0d. in the pound, while at the same time crippling industry by a prolonged course of dear money and credit restriction, needed to retain gold and force down the price level. But, knowing what was known in 1925 and unable to foresee the future, no responsible statesman or banker could possibly have taken the gamble of accepting Keynes's advice. And in 1925 it was not even good advice. To go back at a lower parity, or not to go back at all, carried as much risk of industrial troubles (through inflation instead of deflation) as did the policy actually adopted; not to go back was to do nothing for international stability, and to go back at a lower parity was to do little for the financial position of London. Also, any policy which did nothing for international stability would have reinforced the stagnation of international trade, with consequent ill effects upon British exports and industry. Keynes greatly exaggerated the ill effects upon industry of those measures of credit restriction which a return to gold would probably require— the difficulties of British industry in the later 1920s were not caused by the gold standard[2]—and he seemed sometimes to imply that credit restriction would be unnecessary if only Britain did not go back at $4·86. But this was quite untrue.[3] As

[1] Quoted in Sir Henry Clay, *Lord Norman* (London, 1957) p. 419.

[2] This view, despite the weight of evidence against it, is common. For example, 'His [Keynes's] words [against restoration in 1925] were unheeded. The coal industry was maintained in action by a subsidy during the winter, and the nation *then* [my italics] suffered the great disaster of the Coal Strike and the General Strike'. R. F. Harrod, *Life of Keynes* (London, 1951) p. 362.

[3] For a brilliant exposure of the fallacy that industry would have enjoyed easy credit if only the gold standard had not been restored, see T. E. Gregory, *The First Year of the Gold Standard* (London, 1926) pp. 1–51.

for all the other considerations, he ignored them. He accused his opponents of 'vague optimism' and of treating the gold standard as 'an idol';[1] but those who disagreed with him were not merely the victims of atavistic prejudice.

In 1924 the Dawes Plan appeared to settle the problem of German reparations, and the aftermath of war seemed over. This set the stage for a new beginning, and in 1925 the gold standard, with not altogether unreasonable expectations of success, was restored. Its restoration was later hailed in a responsible quarter as 'one of the turning points in the post-war economic history of the world'.[2] This it was not, although it is no exaggeration to say that restoration was the most momentous financial decision taken by any British Government since 1844. The consequences, as everyone knows, were unfortunate, and there came to be attributed to the gold standard 'both the world depression *and* the peculiar difficulties to which Great Britain was exposed in the period 1925-29'.[3]

Yet the fact remains that none of those responsible for going back to gold in 1925 felt in any way obliged, five years later, to apologize. Before the Macmillan Committee, Pigou, when reminded of his membership of the 1924-25 Bradbury Committee, which had put the final seal of approval on the policy of resumption, retorted, 'Well, I am not particularly inclined to sit in a white sheet over that for several reasons.'[4] These reasons, given and elaborated by several witnesses before the Committee, were as follows:

(i) There was never general support for any policy other than going back and going back at the old parity. 'No politician at the time advocated not going back to the gold system,' said Pigou, although 'since then it has been attacked'. (He added, 'personally I was a stabilizer long before'[5]—i.e. he favoured a policy of stabilizing the price

---

[1] J. M. Keynes, *The Economic Consequences of Mr Churchill* (London, 1925) pp. 23-24.

[2] *Final Report of the Committee on Industry and Trade* (1928-29, Cmd. 3282), p. 6.

[3] T. E. Gregory, *Gold, Unemployment and Capitalism*, p. 79.

[4] *Report of the Committee on Finance and Industry*, Minutes of Evidence, question 6074. Hereafter referred to as the Macmillan Committee.

[5] ibid., question 6075.

level). Therefore the only question which arose was that of the timing of resumption.

(ii) The gold standard, more than any other system, was bound to bring a measure of national and international stability into economic affairs.

Mr Bevin: What would have been the alternative evils if we had not gone on the gold standard?

Sir Robert Kindersley: Nobody else would have gone on the gold standard, and you would have had inflation everywhere, which, in my opinion, is the worst kind of competition that industrialists can have . . . you never know from day to day what the exchange is going to be, and no man can make his plans. I think the industrialists in our country, before these other countries went onto the gold standard, suffered very considerably. They all complained of it . . . The only way of stopping that inflation in foreign countries was for England to set the example . . .

Chairman: You want stability?—Stability is what is necessary.[1]

Mr Keynes: Looking back, after what has happened, would you say it was wise to go back to gold at pre-war parity, or would you have done it at a lower figure?—I think personally it was wise to go back at pre-war parity.

Nothing that has happened since has modified your view?—No. Whether the actual moment we went back was right, I am not a sufficient student of the situation to say, but it was right to go back to pre-war parity, looked at from the broadest point of view.

Mr McKenna: Would you not also say that we had a very great interest in going back to the pre-war parity? We are great creditors of the world?—I cannot imagine that our credit could have survived if we had not.

We have owing us £4,000m.; that £4,000m. is not payable in gold but in sterling; if we could have been paid

---

[1] The reader will note that this means stability of the foreign exchanges, at least in the first instance. It is not primarily that stability of the price level to which Pigou refers.

in depreciated sterling it would have been so much the less?—That was the case.[1]

(iii) When other countries, notably France, Belgium and Germany, subsequently went back to gold, they did so, not like Great Britain at a high level, but at low levels. According to Norman, 'The levels they chose were largely fortuitous',[2] but they certainly put Britain at a comparative disadvantage, one which could not have been foreseen or guarded against. Hence British difficulties were partly due to the way in which other countries after 1925 caused the gold standard to work.

(iv) Pigou conceded that the failure to reduce money wages while other prices fell or were forced down after 1925 led to an increase in real wages which diminished employment; and he conceded that some of the price fall was due to the return to gold in 1925. ('Much more important than that,' he added, 'was what the French did'—i.e. gold sterilization.) But he argued that a mistake was made when it was 'tacitly assumed' that if there had been no return to gold

'money wages would have stood where they were. It seems to me, if we had kept the embargo, the exchange with America would have inevitably slumped, and the result would have been that the prices of a good number of things, wheat and so on, must have gone up. As a result of that, the coal-miners and others would have fought very strenuously for a rise in money wages. If you have got your rise in money wages and prices keep steady, you have just the same embarrassment as you have when money wages are kept up and prices fall.'[3]

(v) It was not necessarily the case, as Keynes and others claimed, that 'overvaluation of the pound' was a serious source of trouble. The source of trouble was the unduly

---

[1] These observations are from the Macmillan Committee, Minutes of Evidence, question 1575 and following.

[2] ibid., question 3363.

[3] ibid., Minutes of Evidence, question 6089.

high level of costs *in some industries*, and what was needed was cost reduction in *these* industries. 'I do not believe,' said Norman, 'in a wholesale scaling down by a direct 10 per cent cut (in wages and salaries) at the present rate of exchange, and I do not believe in an indirect 10 per cent. Neither of these broad general methods of meeting the situation seems to me to be at all satisfactory.'[1]

(vi) As everyone appreciated, new disturbing elements appeared or persisted in international economic affairs in the later 1920s: gold sterilization policies of central banks ('they all made it difficult for each other, and eventually impossible for us'[2]); speculative international investment, latterly encouraged by Stock Exchange activity in New York (call money was at $8\frac{1}{2}$ per cent in New York for most of 1929!); reparations arrangements and uncertainties in Germany. Such forces the gold standard now had to work *against:* and it proved unable to overcome them.

It may thus be said that restoration of the gold standard was an attempt at securing a certain amount of international co-operation and co-ordination. Norman said in 1930 that as Governor of the Bank of England he had devoted the greater part of his time to two international problems: first, 'long, troublesome, and in some ways disappointing . . . stabilization of the Eurpean countries which had lost what they had possessed before the War. That . . . has been for some time in the main achieved'; second, 'to bring about co-operation among the Central Banks of Europe and the world on the sort of lines which were originally sketched at Genoa'.[3] In this latter enterprise, the restoration of the gold standard was the major step. But the achievement was limited, and such as it was, short-lived. As Stamp put it, also in 1930,

'The problem is to get the Central Banks to realize that gold and its use is the controlling factor in the world's prosperity . . . We are at bedrock at the moment; we cannot go lower

[1] Evidence of Rt Hon M. C. Norman, question 9263.
[2] Evidence of Sir Roland Nugent and Mr R. C. Glenday, question 3102.
[3] Macmillan Committee, Minutes of Evidence, question 3317.

in the matter of international grasp—collective grasp—
of the situation.'[1]

The persistence of a large volume of unemployment was already painfully clear by 1928, when there appeared the Liberal
Party's so-called 'Yellow Book',[2] in the writing of which
Keynes, Henderson and Robertson collaborated. This might
be described as the orthodox economists' attempt to improve on
the proposals of political socialism, and to elaborate a policy of
what Robertson has since called 'judicious State intervention'.
But before these proposals could be seriously considered the
slump began, and it soon became evident that the novelty and
gravity of the situation would challenge all traditional beliefs.
Where did political economy stand in this alarming crisis? The
evidence given before the Macmillan Committee, most of it
given in 1930, provides an excellent test of opinion, in which it
is possible to detect three lines of thought. These three lines of
thought, the first two largely traditional, the last largely novel,
may be called: A, the price stability line; B, the structural maladjustment line; C, the gluttability line.

A. The immediate problem and the main problem lying behind the malaise of the 1920s and the disaster of 1929-33 was,
to the great majority of economists before 1936, the problem of
prices. The centre of discussion was what Lundberg has called
'the old and honourable ideas of monetary equilibrium'; adding,
'there is something fundamentally sound in this unrealistic line
of thought'.[3] It is old. It is to be found in Tooke, in Marshall, in
Wicksell; elaborated with the utmost subtlety and skill by
Robertson and Lindahl; equipped with factual information by
Silberling, Jorgen Pedersen and the work of the 'Swedish school'
in the 1920s and early 1930s. It is the basis of that forgotten
classic, Pigou's *Theory of Unemployment*, published in 1933; its
conclusion being that in the absence of friction and imperfections
'there will always be at work a strong tendency for wage rates

[1] Macmillan Committee, Minutes of Evidence, question 3914.
[2] *Britain's Industrial Future, being the Report of the Liberal Industrial Inquiry*
(1928).
[3] E. Lundberg, ed., *The Business Cycle in the Post-War World* (London, Macmillan, 1955), pp. 60-61.

to be so related to demand that everybody is employed. Hence, in stable conditions everyone will actually be employed'; trouble arises because of the inflexibility of money wages and because of 'changes in demand conditions'.[1]

The basis of this line of thought has never been better expressed than by Hawtrey:

> 'Debts . . . are the very foundation of the economic system, and the existence of a network of debts, calculated in a certain unit, is an important and substantial fact.'[2]

The same writer, eleven years later, began his evidence before the Macmillan Committee as follows:

> 'The greatest service that the credit system can render to industry is to maintain the value of the currency unit stable . . . The advantages of a stable currency unit are, in a sense, *negative*. It avoids the evils of instability. Those evils may be summarized as follows:
>
> (a) Injustice between debtor and creditor;
> (b) Disturbance of the due relation between prices and wages, and between prices and fixed costs;
> (c) Fluctuation in business activity.[3]

It was naturally the last of these items which excited most attention at the time. The obverse of the idea, namely that price stabilization might eliminate fluctuations, appeared novel in 1923:

> 'The last few years have seen not, indeed, the birth, but the first serious public discussion of an idea which contains potentialities of far-reaching improvement in social conditions . . . The idea of attempting to diminish, perhaps even to eliminate, general trade fluctuations by means of a monetary policy designed to keep the price level stable.'[4]

[1] op. cit., p. 252.
[2] Hawtrey, *Economic Journal*, 1919, p. 428.
[3] Macmillan Committee, Minutes of Evidence, 'Statement of Evidence submitted by Mr Hawtrey' (April 10, 1930).
[4] From *The Nation*, 1923, reprinted in *The Inter-War Years*, pp. 5-6.

Pigou gave the idea cautious support in 1930:

> 'There is dispute among different schools as to how large an effect you could get through making prices more stable. Some people think, if you made prices almost completely stable, you would do away with industrial fluctuations altogether. My own view rather is that those fluctuations accentuate industrial fluctuations which would take place to some extent anyhow, but I think everybody is agreed that you would certainly greatly lessen the fluctuations if you prevented the general price level from moving about so much;'[1]

and his prime recommendation for policy was that the central banks should 'get together and try . . . to maintain the value of gold more stable than it is now'.

There was thus widespread support for the basic proposition that 'the falling tendency of prices throughout the world is the governing economic fact of the present time'.[2] The question therefore immediately arose, Why is the price fall taking place? Many varieties of explanation could be advanced, but they all had to acknowledge some part to be played by the supply and distribution of gold. Then, whether the link with gold was supposed to be strong and inflexible or weak and flexible, the question was raised, What is the use of the gold standard? Why do we stick to it? The reputation of the gold standard was hopelessly compromised for at least a generation by the price fall which preceded the 1931 crisis.

B. It was a common-sense view that some unemployment was due to the fact that Britain had failed to adapt the structure of her industry to the changed and ever-changing pattern of demand. To many practical men in the 1920s, the post-war economic problem presented itself in the form, 'How soon can we get back to 1914'? Later on it became, 'How completely can we get back to 1914'? Pigou was a shrewd observer of this attitude:

> 'everybody has for all these years kept on thinking that the dislocation of demand, as against coal-mining and against

---

[1] Macmillan Committee, Minutes of Evidence, question 6636.
[2] H. D. Henderson, Memorandum, 1930, reprinted in *The Inter-War Years*, p. 49.

engineering and so on, is temporary. They have all thought that things will come back to what they were before . . . If one thinks that, one naturally hangs on, and that is what has happened in a great number of industries. Mr Keynes used to say during the War, every three months, "The War will end soon." Well, that was bound to come right in the end; but this thing need not come right in the end and it does not seem to show any signs of coming right.'[1]

According to Pigou, who was one of the foremost exponents of the structural maladjustment line, the upward shift in the average volume of unemployment in the inter-war period had occurred chiefly because there had taken place a 'relative shift óf demand unaccompanied by the appropriate shift of people', a misallocation of labour which the wage structure could correct only with great difficulty. No one denies that this was *a* factor in the situation; and in the perspective of history it seems at least plausible to suggest that more than was admitted of the contemporary difficulties was due to political and economic change of an exceptional character forcing upon the British economy adjustments which were far greater that it was used to having to, or could comfortably absorb. At least for a period in his life Keynes himself subscribed to this view, and he stated it with his accustomed vigour:

'The dominating factor in the whole problem is, however, the failure of Britain's industrial system to adapt itself to the post-war world. This lack of adaptability, the outstanding characteristic of British economic life during the whole of the post-war decade, has manifested itself in a hundred ways . . . the failure to carry out thorough-going rationalization . . . rigid wage-rates, immobility between trades and areas, severe Trade Union restrictions and regulations.'[2]

Absence of appropriate structural adaptation, even if it is assumed that this accounted for only one half of the unemployment in coal, cotton and shipbuilding, and for no other unemployment

[1] Macmillan Committee, Minutes of Evidence, question 5989.

[2] *The Nation*, August 30, 1930, p. 666. Compare *The Economic Consequences of Mr Churchill* (London, 1925), p. 25: 'The monetary policy, announced in the Budget, being the real source of our industrial troubles, it is impossible', etc.

whatsoever, was, even in this restricted sense, *directly* responsible for 11·7 per cent of total unemployment in 1931, and was still responsible for 10 per cent as late as 1935. In these circumstances it was, perhaps, premature to reach the conclusion that stagnation, in the sense of a chronic deficiency of investment opportunities in relation to the supply of saving at full employment, had been reached, and that the economic problems of imperfect competition and of unemployment had therefore best be approached from a stagnationist point of view.

The policy conclusions drawn from the structural maladjustment line of thought were:

(a) wages in the expanding home-market industries should be reduced so as to encourage employment in them, and

(b) steps should be taken to reduce costs in all industries. This involved the much-discussed topic of 'rationalization'. Rationalization meant a multitude of things, but it is worth noticing that a lot of tolerance for the cruder, more monopolistic forms of rationalization derived from the 1919 Majority Report of the Committee on Trusts.

Consideration of economic structure did not stop at this point, however. There was also the question of the part played by the City in the nation's economic life. Did the City serve home industry reasonably well? Was it worth making sacrifices in the interests of the City's international position? And this, of course, brings the argument back once more to the gold standard, for the chief sacrifice under discussion was the return to and maintenance of the gold standard.

Over this ground the debate was inevitably vague and inconclusive. Norman, although increasingly concerned with internal industrial problems, took 'the large view':

'In your opinion, I gather, the advantages of maintaining the international position outweigh in the public interest the internal disadvantages which may accrue from the use of the means at your disposal?—Yes, I think that the disadvantages to the internal position are relatively small compared with the advantages to the external position.

'What is the benefit to industry of the maintenance of the international position?—This is a very technical question which is not easy to explain, but the whole international posiion has preserved for us in this country the wonderful position which we have inherited, which was for a while thought perhaps to be in jeopardy, which to a large extent, though not to the full extent, has been re-established. We are still to a large extent international bankers. We have great international trade and commerce out of which I believe considerable profit accrues to the country; we do maintain large international markets, a free gold market, a free exchange market—perhaps the freest almost in the world—and all of those things, and the confidence and credit which go with them are in the long run greatly to the interest of industry as well as to the interest of finance and commerce.'[1]

As regards foreign lending, the familiar point was made 'that the export trade of this country has been built up largely owing to the loans which we have made to foreign countries'.[2] It was even argued, by the Deputy Governor of the Bank of England, that it was investment abroad of the current surplus on the balance of payments 'which produces the markets which . . . are the real cure for industrial depression and unemployment'.[3] Not only City men were in favour of foreign investment; the representatives of the Federation of British Industries took the same line:

'Have you any views upon the effect of capital investment abroad today on British industry?—I should have said that the burden of our Memorandum was that there had not been enough capital invested abroad.'[4]

And there were the wider politico-economic considerations:

'. . . Supposing we lend money to Austria in order to stabilize her currency. That does not involve any industrial orders here or anywhere else, but I believe that stabilizing Austria is an important assistance to the general trade of this country be-

[1] Macmillan Committee, Minutes of Evidence, questions 3332 and 3333.
[2] ibid., evidence of Sir Robert Kindersley, question 1307.
[3] ibid., evidence of Sir Ernest Harvey, question 569.
[4] Macmillan Committee, Minutes of Evidence, question 3166.

cause I believe any kind of stability anywhere helps us as traders. You cannot relate these things to figures.'[1]

Against all this there was the point, made by Norman himself, that the ultimate basis of financial strength was the competitiveness of industry, and therefore there could be no future for any policy which in the long run subordinated the interests of industry to those of the City. And this brought the argument round again to the problems of rationalization. Norman was very active in the 1920s in devising new ways of providing financial assistance for industrial reorganization just because he believed that the country's industrial and financial well-being were inseparably linked. He outlined his ideas on these aspects of the problem in a series of impressive answers before the Macmillan Committee in 1931:

'. . . I think that it is most desirable to make a contrast between the position of the London market in the pre-war period as compared with its position in recent years . . . The essential differences that I see are these. In the pre-war period, London developed as the central money market of the world during the long period when there was an abundant supply of funds saved for investment, part of which was invested in this country and part of which found investment abroad. But, generally speaking, throughout the pre-war period, I think, we may say that there was a preference at any given rate in the mind of the investor for British securities as contrasted with foreign securities . . . a central money market . . . maintains its equipoise in large part because of the preference for domestic issues as contrasted with foreign issues . . . The second difference I see is this. In the pre-war period foreign investments more directly, more immediately, and more largely served to stimulate British exports than is now the case. In the pre-war period, the proceeds of large loans were likely to be expended in large part by the borrower in this country because the sort of constructional material which he needed could in general be purchased more cheaply in this market than elsewhere. I judge the position in the post-war period to be that, to a greater extent than formerly, the bor-

[1] Macmillan Committee, evidence of Sir Otto Niemeyer, question 6834.

rower is disposed to buy his rails, or his electrical equipment, or whatever it may be in some foreign market. That places a direct pressure upon the exchanges which would be in a measure absent if the purchases were made more largely in this country . . . The position is obscured in the case of the London market because by a certain amount of management the short market can be made a bit more attractive and can retain or attract additional foreign funds. But I am disposed to think that the country is in a measure living upon the prestige gained in the past . . . Confidence in the stability of the London market throughout the world . . . must rest in the final analysis, as it would appear to me, upon the ability of this country over the years to develop its industries, and profitably to compete with the rest of the world . . . But the ability to maintain, for a few months, a given rate of 3 per cent or 4 per cent, or the ability to make somewhat more considerable loans, would seem to me, in the absence of plans for the reorganization of industry, or the development of new enterprises and reduction of costs, not to get one anywhere.

Professor Gregory. Could you possibly give us your view of the argument which has been put to us, that the stiffening of money rates here . . . worsens the conditions of the external world from the standpoint of British industry by inducing depression all over the world?—I do not believe that slight differences in the rates charged have a fundamental effect . . . Moreover, I would point out that certainly a part of the explanation of the present world slump is to be found in the over-development of certain countries and the over-development of the production of certain goods. If rates had been lower in the last two or three years, and a somewhat larger amount of foreign lending had occurred, with a somewhat larger outflow of gold, is it to be presumed that the quantity of wheat, cotton and coffee produced would have been appreciably less?

Mr Brand. To return to this country; do I take it that your view is that the fundamental difficulty is that we are out of equilibrium as far as our costs are concerned?—Yes.

Mr Bevin. Then the function that the gold standard was intended to perform in the nineteenth century is now played out?—It is played out in a sense, until the world gets back to equilibrium.

It is rather a useless instrument now for the purpose of regulating or forcing the equilibrium?—I think it is. In the case of extreme departure from equilibrium I do not think that through monetary means alone you can either force an equilibrium by pressure or bring about equilibrium by monetary inflation.

Consistently with this line of thought, Norman defended the return to gold at the old parity in 1925 on the ground that to return at, say, $4·40, would have been to devalue sterling and hence raise the sterling price of imports and thus start an inflationary movement making for an 'equal reduction' in all wages, 'and I do not believe that all wages in 1925 should have been scaled down by an equal percentage, and I do not believe it now'. Norman would not agree that the external value of sterling should be settled simply with a view to trying to minimize the fundamental cost/price difficulties of some of the old export industries. What was wanted was 'an increase in the output of the more highly finished goods and new products'.[1]

C. The gluttability line of thought was to many contemporaries more depressing, more alarming. This was Robertson's approach. The argument may be put as follows. There is irregularity in the flow of investible new ideas. As Robertson put it later, although 'history has always in the end turned out to be keeping another card up her sleeve . . . she has been sometimes rather long in shaking it down'.[2] Also, there are limits to the speed at which costs of production of existing commodities can be reduced. This, coupled with the proposition that the elasticity of demand for known products has its limits, leads naturally to the conclusion that unemployment on a considerable scale at least may—to put it no more strongly—occur. Thus Robertson in 1930 did not so much anticipate the Keynes-Hansen doctrine of chronic stagnation as produce a doctrine of his own of periodic stagnation. As he has said, he got his stagnationism over early,

[1] Macmillan Committee, Minutes of Evidence, question 9246 and following to 9266.

[2] D. H. Robertson, *Money* (4th ed. London, 1947), p. 215.

like the measles; although it wasn't the same brand as other people caught later on. This 'doctrine of temporary gluttability' led to the view—'the merest common sense'—that public and semi-public bodies—governments and local authorities as well as railway companies and electricity commissioners—'should intervene to organize and express a collective need for investment and structures . . . at times when the ordinary commercial demand for investments and structures is in a condition of temporary saturation'.[1] Keynes thought that almost everything could be done by an increase in the volume of credit;[2] but Robertson did not agree:

'. . . from the present point of view the important thing is the demand for commodities, and the demand for labour, and it seems to me that we have reached a situation where that requires organizing in some way . . .'

Mr Bevin: You want a conscious direction of capital investment?—Yes.[3]

Even the emergence of new industries was believed to require 'a good deal of public, or at any rate of semi-public, organizing'.[4]

These proposals, as Robertson himself observed, were

'in direct conflict not only with the so-called Treasury view that such a policy of promoting public works absorbs resources which would otherwise be employed by private enterprise, but also with the doctrine, which has been maintained, for instance, by Mr Hawtrey, that public works "are a mere piece of ritual", achieving nothing which could not equally well be achieved by the banking system acting alone, through a sufficiently great alteration in its terms of lending.'[5]

Robertson's proposals were founded on his own analysis of saving, developed originally in his little book on *Money*, first

[1] Macmillan Committee, Statement of Evidence, para. 13. This idea was not new—at least not to Robertson. It had already been advanced in his *Study of Industrial Fluctuation*, published in 1915.

[2] Minutes of Evidence, questions 4803, 4814 and elsewhere. See below p. 250.

[3] ibid., question 4814.

[4] ibid., question 4875.

[5] Statement of Evidence, para. 13.

published in 1919, and subsequently in *Banking Policy and the Price Level*, published in 1926. The argument was that an increased desire to save (due, in depressed conditions, to a loss of confidence and weakening of enterprise) might merely result in a reduced level of employment and a lowering of the price level unless the banking system were willing to depart from its usual rules and conventions regarding cash ratios and the nature of bank investments. The duty of the banking system was to transform savings into industrial capital. If this was not achieved, increased saving was dissipated in consumption at unexpectedly low prices or checked by the curtailment of production and [consequent] shrinkage of money incomes.[1] It followed that the necessity of state intervention would be minimized if the banks could be persuaded to 'show an increased willingness . . . to find ways and means of financing permanent investment . . . the proper character of banking assets is not [a question] which can be settled *in vacuo* for all time, independently of the state of industry and of the phase which has been reached in what used to be called the trade cycle'.[2]

Robertson was not hopeful, however, that any changes in the banking system could suffice to cure the existing ills. Naturally, he welcomed Norman's efforts to provide improved financial assistance to industry, including the newly-created Bankers' Industrial Development Company. But he thought that State activity was also necessary, and that it would go on being necessary 'for a very long time'.

You would regard this as a temporary expedient, would you; that at some moment when you arrived at some sort of equilibrium this Government enterprise should diminish?—Yes, I would, but I think 'temporary' may mean fairly long, for the reason which I give later, that if you are at the same time rationalizing private industry I do not see how that is to result in anything but a temporary decline in employment, and therefore the need for supplementing private demand by public demand may continue for a very long time.[3]

[1] See Macmillan Committee, Statement of Evidence by D. H. Robertson, para. 3.
[2] ibid., para. 9.
[3] Minutes of Evidence, question 4882.

An interesting exchange took place, in fact, between Keynes and Robertson:

> *Mr Keynes.* . . . in the ordinary course private enterprise would some day revive. What you have to do is to make up the deficiency in the interval?—Yes. But I think one has to face the fact that the interval is longer in the present position than it was in the pre-war period, because of the slower growth of population.[1]

As Robertson pointed out, he was only asking that the Government should do more of certain kinds of things—housebuilding, especially—which it did already and would certainly continue to do. Panic ideas about 'socialism' and 'uneconomic schemes merely to create employment' were out of place. Doubts about Robertson's proposed remedies were expressed, however, not only on the far-sighted ground (by Gregory) that the State-intervention policy would be difficult to implement 'without adding to the degree of dislocation when you stop',[2] but also because there was a decided tendency on the part of very many people to distrust on principle proposals to increase State activity—'is there not the possibility that by the expansion of State enterprise you will still further abridge private enterprise, and that you will not get back to the spirit of private enterprise?'[3]

The gluttability of wants and wasted saving were thus at the heart of Robertson's position—assuming the gold standard. In that connection he recommended 'concerted action among Central Banks to ensure the rational use and distribution of available gold supplies';[4] to this he attached 'the highest importance'. But he pointed out that the difficulties upon which he laid most stress would exist even for a banking system in a closed economy. Much of his evidence, indeed, was taken up in trying to explain to the Committee, including Keynes,[5] the nature of the limitations of monetary policy in conditions of depression.

[1] Minutes of Evidence, question 4908.
[2] ibid., question 4907.
[3] ibid., question 4920.
[4] Statement of Evidence, para. 22.
[5] The reader who doubts that Keynes should be included here is invited to read questions 4762-65, 4803, 4814-15 and 4841, and Robertson's answers.

T *   291

So much for the Macmillan Committee. The arguments to which it listened had scarcely been put forward when, on the heels of the slump, there came the abandonment of the gold standard. After these two events there stood revealed a new world; but also (and this was what mattered more) a new range of policy possíblities. It was upon these that attention became concentrated. Economists in the nineteenth century, as Pigou has put it,

'had grown up, and their whole experience was confined to, a world which, as regards politics and economics alike, was reasonably stable . . . the basic changes were gradual and slow-working . . . How different is the experience of economists to-day! The 1914 War, with its aftermath of ruin; the period of unbalanced budgets and astronomical inflations; the slow readjustment; the terrible relapse of the great depression and the political tensions that accompanied it! This fundamental difference of experience is, I think, largely accountable for the difference in the way in which the old generation of economists and the new approach their problems. Inevitably now the short run presents itself with far greater urgency relatively to the long run than it did then . . . In calm weather it is proper to reckon the course of a ship without much regard for the waves. But in a storm the waves may be everything. The problems of transition are the urgent problems. For, if they are not solved, what happens is not transition, but catastrophe; the long run never comes.'[1]

And the 'urgent problem' of the 1930s was, more than ever, unemployment. As it turned out, the national income, thanks largely to the favourable movement of the terms of trade, could be left to look after itself. The gold standard was discredited. The conquest of unemployment, seeming to imply scarcely less than the maintenance of the existing social fabric, became the supreme end, to which, by now, there existed no agreed means.

It was to a generation baffled by these vital and perplexing problems that the Keynesian revelation came. Other economists stuck on the dilemma that monetary policy appropriate at home

[1] A. C. Pigou, *Essays in Economics* (London, Macmillan, 1952), pp. 3-4.

was inappropriate abroad, or that rationalization, if it reduced costs, was also apt to increase unemployment. Keynes, with the abandonment of gold securely behind him, cut the Gordian knot and plunged for *national* revival by centralized Government action—'a somewhat comprehensive socialization of invest-ment'.[1]

And so it came to pass. But the ideas of Keynes had almost no effect on Government policy in this country before 1939. In that respect they belong to the 'forties, not the 'thirties. But their development in the pre-war years, the extent to which they were shared or anticipated by other economists, formed by con-trast to the views of others or in response to problems of the day is sufficiently interesting and possibly significant to deserve a brief analysis.[2]

In the Macmillan Committee in 1930 Keynes agreed with Robertson that 'the trouble is that investment is deficient', but his attention was mostly directed to the rate of interest. In a discussion, for example, which assumed that world demand was not increasing, he intervened to say, 'all this would cease to be true if one had a world-wide demand for investments throughout the world such as would accompany a very large fall in the rate of interest'.[3] He fell upon the Bank Rate as the prime cause of contemporary troubles, and was able to secure Norman's agree-ment to the following proposition:

'So it is of the essence of the case that the Bank Rate should have an important effect; that when it is raised it should have an effect in the direction of unemployment. That is what you want. Am I right?'[4]

Keynes thus concentrated attention on the fact that a non-stationary capitalist system could, as he put it, 'only work by

[1] *The General Theory*, (London, Macmillan, 1936) p. 378. Compare Robertson in 1915 on the advantages of 'a somewhat saner and more centralized investment policy'. (*Industrial Fluctuation*, p. 246).

[2] The best brief commentaries on modern employment theory and especially on *The General Theory* are 'The Robertsonian Evolution' by W. Fellner (American Economic Review, vol. XLII, No. 3, June 1952), and J. H. Williams, 'An Appraisal of Keynesian Economics' (ibid., Supplement, May 1948).

[3] loc. cit., question 5012. And Robertson replied, 'Would it accompany it?'

[4] ibid., question 3393

creating unemployment from time to time'. He made the point, too, that if there were not enough worth-while propositions at the ruling rate of interest, 'would not the conclusion be that we should cease to save the present amount?'[1] And he returned repeatedly to his favourite proposition that 'each half per cent fall [in the effective bond rate] would bring in still more investment'.[2] His proposals, mostly confined to the monetary sphere, included direction of investment as between home and overseas opportunities, stabilization of prices, the establishment of international monetary co-operation, and sterilization of gold reserves. These proposals were fairly orthodox and were apparently conceived as possibly sufficient, if applied in time and with enough skill, to preserve the existing economic structure. Had not his aim been from the beginning 'the continuance of an individualist society'?

Keynes's unorthodoxy began, not in the Macmillan Committee in 1929, but with the pamphlet which he wrote in collaboration with H. D. Henderson in the same year, *Can Lloyd George Do It?* This was 'unorthodox' not so much in its fundamental analysis as in its advocacy of public works. (The multiplier idea, which it contained, was later developed in an article written by Kahn in 1931, 'The Relation of Home Investment to Unemployment'.) The general attitude was supported by, preceded by and to some extent possibly founded on the ideas advanced by Robertson in 1915 and again before the Macmillan Committee in 1930. The essence of these more modern proposals was that relief could be obtained through public investment—Robertson's 'intervention by the State', Keynes's 'socialization of investment'. Today, this proposal seems merely orthodox; the objections which it raises are administrative and tactical, not fundamental and strategic. But in the early 1930s the opposition to a public works policy was very strong indeed, so strong that what the Government did was the opposite of spending money on public works—it reduced its own expenditure as far as possible and wrote round to local authorities requesting them to do the same. Why was this?

[1] Minutes of Evidence, question 4929.
[2] ibid., question 4832. It is interesting that in his lectures in Cambridge early in 1920, Keynes was advocating a Bank Rate of 10 per cent for at least three years!

Primarily, it was because public opinion was unfamiliar with the idea of increasing certain types of expenditure in a depression, and was hostile, to a large extent, to proposals which would increase the rôle of the Government in economic affairs. But there was also an intellectual opposition. This became known as 'the Treasury View'. What the Treasury View really was is something of a mystery. It first appeared as a 'Memorandum on the Finance of Development Loans prepared by the Treasury', being item six in a set of 'Memoranda on Certain Proposals relating to Unemployment'.[1] These memoranda were the Government's reply to specific public-works proposals put forward by Lloyd George earlier in the year, and supported by the Keynes-Henderson pamphlet *Can Lloyd George Do It?* Then, before the Macmillan Committee, Sir Richard Hopkins, a Treasury witness, set out to amplify the Treasury view, which had been, he said, 'a little misunderstood'. Three points emerge. (1) Treasury criticism was directed, not to all development expenditure, but to the Lloyd George proposals to spend £125m. per annum for two years, followed by further expenditure. 'It was of the essence', said Hopkins, 'that the scheme should be started swiftly and simultaneously . . . but I do not see how it could be carried out on this scale, and swiftly, without a very wide increase in the powers given to the officials who are to carry it out. Those practical considerations seem to me to be very important . . . I should have thought that a scheme of this kind so far from setting up a cycle of prosperity would produce a great cry against bureaucracy.'[2] All this was perfectly true, and experience has borne it out. Extensive public works cannot be organized in a month; and, as Roosevelt found, hasty Government action may produce needless waste, public antipathy, and a curtailment of ordinary business investment. (2) Lloyd George said, and the Treasury agreed, that 'inflation, whilst it would temporarily solve our problems, would mean the departure from the gold standard, a reduction in the real standard of life of those at present employed and the grave risk of economic collapse in the long run. It can be entirely ruled out.'[3] But the

[1] Treasury Memorandum, Cmd. 3331, 1928-29.
[2] ibid., para. 3.
[3] ibid., para. 3.

Treasury argued—in the Memorandum, at least—that money for the development scheme could be borrowed only 'by altering the direction of investment', and that such alteration would require a raising of interest rates to the detriment of normal home and foreign investment. In other words, the Treasury view appeared to be that the amount of capital available for investment is at any time fixed in amount and fully employed. Hopkins denied that this was the Treasury view,[1] but Keynes's comment on his argument was just; 'It bends so much that I find difficulty in getting hold of it.' (3) The Treasury argued that, 'on the long view', a large programme of Government expenditure would not increase the competitive power of British industry and might even, by diverting effort into channels of dubious profitability, diminish it. Members of the Macmillan Committee felt the same way:

> Mr Newbold: How would the building of a road help us to increase our export trade permanently?—(Witness): That is exactly the difficulty I have. (Mr Newbold): It is mine too.

(4) The Treasury view omitted to take account of any multiplier process. This was a culpable omission, for the idea of a multiplier (although not the name) was an old one. The *Economist* made the point at the time:

> '. . . the most important consideration of all is this. The purchasing power of the nation is not to be regarded as a fixed amount, but as something which is constantly changing and, except under unusual circumstances, growing. By getting the whole nation to work we should increase the total of goods and services—some of immediate, others of more remote or prolonged utility—on which the total purchasing power, and incidentally the volume of saving, depends.'[2]

To this idea Kahn, in 1931, concentrating upon 'the final position of equilibrium when everything has settled down',[3] gave a certain timeless precision.

[1] Macmillan Committee, Minutes of Evidence, question 5603.
[2] *The Economist*, May 18, 1929, p. 1095.
[3] R. F. Kahn, *Economic Journal*, 1931, p. 183.

Such were some of the ideas which preceded and led up to the publication in 1936 of *The General Theory of Employment Interest and Money*. In this book Keynes stressed not, like Robertson, the real technical facts of the nature or the periodicity of innovation, but the resistance of the rate of interest against falling to a level low enough to prevent full employment (assuming certain characteristics of the investment function), and/or the rigidity of the consumption function. The important originality of the book lay in its stagnationist emphasis, and in its terminology. The stagnation thesis has never been better stated than by Keynes himself:

> 'The richer the community, the wider will tend to be the gap between its actual and its potential production; and therefore the more devious and outrageous the defects of the economic system . . . Not only is the marginal propensity to consume weaker in a wealthy community, but, owing to its accumulation of capital being already larger, the opportunities for further investment are less attractive.'[1]

This view essentially depended on three assumptions: (1) that consumption is determined by income; (2) that there is a 'normal' relation between consumption and income; (3) that the liquidity function is infinitely elastic at some level of interest rates well above zero. All these assumptions can be, and have been questioned. Also, over many theoretical side-issues raised by *The General Theory*—many of them full of practical importance—protracted battles have been fought; for example, is it the case that 'any level of private investment and Budget deficit will always produce an equal amount of saving to finance these two items'?[2] But the practical message of the book was abundantly clear: interest rates must be kept low; and there must be lots of spending: both these because of the stagnationist character of 'mature' capitalism. At the worst, it would be worth while to dig holes in the ground simply to fill them in again. This, like so much else, had been suggested before the Macmillan Committee.[3]

[1] *The General Theory*, Preface p. VI.

[2] M. Kalecki in *The Economics of Full Employment* (Oxford, 1946), p. 41. Compare Robertson, *Economic Commentaries* (London, 1956), chapter IV, sect. III.

[3] loc. cit., question 4910.

The effect on policy of all these long and deep thoughts of the 1930s was negligible in that decade. Slum clearance, advocated by Robertson, became a policy, but probably as a result of 'social' rather than economic arguments. Otherwise, it was a matter of palliating and propping-up. Markets had collapsed, but some were to revive. The thing was a phase, at least in some respects. Certainly it was wiser than it seemed to many economists at the time to improvise, and to help hard-pressed firms and industries to hold on. Protection, even if bad in the long run, probably helped in the short, because home employment began to be substituted for imports and the fall in primary product prices *plus* confidence in sound money *plus* easier credit gave a background in which new investment in new lines was more willingly undertaken; then gradual recovery of home incomes prevented a reduction in the import bill with unfavourable repercussions on the export industries.

But in the long run *The General Theory* did influence policy; as it was meant to do. 'The philosophers', said Marx, 'have hitherto interpreted the world in various ways; the thing is, however, to change it.'[1] This was Keynes's attitude. Thus the Keynesian analysis is logically acceptable and sufficient in practice as long as one supposes the relationship between the schedules of saving, investment and the rate of interest to be such that intended saving is apt to exceed investment at full employment, and as long as one assigns a minor or zero rôle to such factors as changes in the level or structure of wage rates, in the propensity to consume, in the assessment of the outlook by entrepreneurs, and so on. It is not a fault of this analysis that it is short-run; that, on the contrary, is one of its merits, for it is in the short-run that policy (in which Keynes was so largely interested) is commonly—perhaps too commonly—required to be effective; and this was particularly true in the 1930s. But for *The General Theory* as such, the same defence cannot be made. The fact that one might as well argue that consumption changes determine investment as the other way round, or that the marginal efficiency of capital may be as liable to revival when very low as to continuance at a very low level, or that identical 'constellations' of circumstances will have different outcomes according to the

---

[1] K. Marx, *Notes on Feuerbach*, No. XI.

varying profit-risk-inertia make-up of different groups of entrepreneurs or of the same group at different times—all this is very relevant as soon as one moves out of the short period and adopts a truly general, dispassionate and detached point of view; and then one begins to suspect that Keynes decided which elements to accept as variable and *a fortiori* which policy to recommend *before* he began his analysis.

It is fairly clear that this is in fact what Keynes did. Like Robertson, he knew in 1929 what ought to be done. Like Robertson, he was up against the Treasury view, but he was apparently not satisfied with Robertson's theoretical rebuttal of that view—to the importance of which he himself drew the Macmillan Committee's attention—that 'saving is the one thing that cannot be saved'.[1] Accordingly, Keynes strove to escape from the whole method of thought of his predecessors, to produce something wholly new and thus knock away the entire foundation of popular caution and timidity regarding the public works policy. The result was *The General Theory*. And this is another way of saying that the limitations of *The General Theory* need not be interpreted to Keynes's discredit. Like many of his contemporaries during the years of depression, he regarded the current situation and also the prevailing methods of correcting it or leaving it to correct itself as intolerable. Accordingly, his formulation concentrates attention upon those elements in the situation which can or can be made to produce increased employment in a short space of time. It is true that in a period of unemployment the marginal efficiency of capital *may* revive, the spending habits of consumers *may* become adjusted to changed circumstances; but we may choose not to wait for these things to happen. In *The General Theory* clarity and force are obtained at the expense of generality, but it has become much easier to see how to achieve one of the aims of policy, namely, the reduction of unemployment.[2] Keynes was the successor, not of scholars

---

[1] Macmillan Committee, Minutes of Evidence, question 4922.

[2] That the reduction of unemployment is, especially in the long run, only one of the possible aims of policy was recognized by Keynes but obscured by his presentation of the problem. It is also true that a normative presentation, such as Keynes's, is apt to lead to the conclusion, 'If the world does not behave like the theory, so much the worse for the world', and hence to appear as an argument in favour of some kind of central re-planning.

such as Marshall and Pigou, but of such writers as Mun, Petty, Alexander Hamilton, the Adam Smith of Book Five of *The Wealth of Nations*, and the earlier Ricardo.

In the event, unfortunately, policies of a 'Keynesian' character were put into operation and persisted in just when the capitalist system was showing every sign of vigorous growth and when intended saving was falling grievously short of planned investment in almost every country. A later age, delivered from the immediate difficulties which beset the 1930s, now has the opportunity to combine national policies of full employment with that international co-operation which is their only ultimate secure foundation and which for a time—but only for a time—Keynes was willing to relegate to the limbo of 'those nineteenth century ideals which no longer satisfy us'. The wheel, after a fashion, has come full circle. Having tried, in the 'twenties, for international co-operation while hoping for the best as regards the level of employment, Great Britain tried in the 'thirties for fuller employment while hoping for the best as regards international co-operation. Now, because of the high degree of international co-operation fostered by the war and the cold-war, and because of the acceptance of the idea of full employment in most free societies, there is the real possibility that both can be secured.

Behind this Hegelian synthesis lie forces, therefore, beyond the realms of economic thought. There is the division between Russia and the West—in its origins almost wholly political. More nearly economic, there is the revolution which has taken place in the social ideals of the people and especially in the attitude of the employee towards unemployment. It is hardly an accident, for example that so many policy recommendations in the inter-war years tended to reduce the inequality in the distribution of wealth.[1] And with respect to 'full employment' as an

---

[1] Dislike of inequalities of income is to be found in the works of Marshall, Pigou, Keynes, Robertson and Mrs Robinson. In the writings of Keynes it is extraordinarily ubiquitous, and there is scarcely any train of thought which cannot be made to serve it. For example, a leading proposition in *The Economic Consequences of the Peace* is that capital accumulation in the nineteenth century took place too rapidly for the standard of living of the poor to be raised quickly enough. Towards the end of *The General Theory* the suggestion is made that capital accumulation should go on still faster than before in order that income from the ownership of capital should be wiped out. Two opposite courses are thus suggested but each with the same end in view—the reduction of income inequalities.

end almost in its own right (in the old days it was the gold standard which was in danger of being so regarded) this is a changed social attitude which obtains effective power through a changed political structure. In the early nineteenth century the actual or potential sufferers from industrial unemployment were not strong enough to make this unwelcome novelty a political issue. But in the course of the nineteenth century the poorer members of the British community came gradually to be accepted as the political equals of their 'betters'; and when they succeeded in strengthening their own organization within industry and in enlisting the support of intellectuals of standing and ability and hence of public opinion in their struggle for an improved way of life (as they did first in the Dock Strike of 1889), then they ceased to be willing to accept spells of unemployment as their inevitable lot—to pay this 'price of progress' demanded by the capitalist system. And with this change in political circumstances there came a change in the interests and assumptions of economics.

INDEX

GEORGE ALLEN & UNWIN LTD

Head office:
40 Museum Street, London, W.C.1
Telephone: 01-405 8577

Sales, Distribution and Accounts Departments
Park Lane, Hemel Hempstead, Herts.
Telephone: 0442 3244

Athens: 7 Stadiou Street
Auckland: P.O. Box 36013, Northcote Central, N.4
Barbados: P.O. Box 222, Bridgetown
Beirut: Deeb Building, Jeanne d'Arc Street
Bombay: 103/5 Fort Street, Bombay 1
Calcutta: 285J Bepin Behari Ganguli Street, Calcutta 12
Cape Town: 68 Shortmarket Street
Delhi: 1/18D Asaf Ali Road, New Delhi 1
Hong Kong: 105 Wing on Mansion, 26 Hankow Road, Kowloon
Ibadan: P.O. Box 62
Karachi: Karachi Chambers, McLeod Road
Madras: 2/18 Mount Road, Madras 6
Mexico: Villalongin 32, Mexico 5, D.F.
Nairobi: P.O. Box 30583
Pakistan: Alico Building, 18 Motijheel, Dacca 2
Philippines: P.O. Box 157, Quezon City, D-502
Rio de Janeiro: Caixa Postal 2537-Zc-00
Singapore: 36c Prinsep Street, Singapore 7
Sydney, N.S.W.: Bradbury House, 55 York Street
Tokyo: C.P.O. Box 1728, Tokyo 100-91
Toronto: 81 Curlew Drive, Don Mills

STATISTICS OF THE BRITISH ECONOMY

F. M. M. LEWES

This book has been written as a guide to students and other users of economics, who need to interpret British economic statistics. The author avoids crowding the text with detailed description and seeks rather to point out the economic content of published statistics, showing how these are related to the concepts of economic theory. Stress is laid upon the accounting frameworks used in such main publications as the *National Income and Expenditure* and the *United Kingdom Balance of Payments* and in the way in which other statistics are linked to these.

The ground is covered in nine chapters. 1. INTRODUCTION. 2. LABOUR. 3. PRODUCTION. 4. DISTRIBUTION. 5. TRANSPORT. 6. COMPANIES. 7. FINANCE: includes special notes on 'Calculation of Gross Redemption Yields and Share Indices'. 8. OVERSEAS TRADE AND PAYMENTS. 9. NATIONAL ACCOUNTANCY: includes special notes on 'National Accounts and the Balance of Payments' and 'The Central Government and National Income Accounts'.

Each chapter ends with a valuable annotated bibliography giving under separate heads sources and commentaries.

The author has taught the subject for some years and has had practical experience in Africa of putting together national accounts. At present he is Lecturer in Economic and Social Statistics at the University of Exeter.

INTERNATIONAL TRADE AND ECONOMIC GROWTH

HARRY G. JOHNSON

'. . . by any standards, an important book. In a period when this part of economic theory made some very notable advances in the hands of others also, Professor Johnson was able to push analysis beyond the existing frontiers at a surprising number of points. He has, moreover, in an unusual degree the gift of relating, compressing and frequently simplifying the works of other theorists . . . the high eloquence of his work . . . will probably continue for a long time to impress itself on everyone who wants to be considered a serious student of international theoretical economics'—*Economic Journal*

'Professor Johnson has by this book established himself in the front rank of economic theorists'—*Economica*

GEORGE ALLEN & UNWIN LTD